THE
EXTRA
WOMAN

THE EXTRA WOMAN

HOW MARJORIE HILLIS LED A GENERATION OF WOMEN TO LIVE ALONE AND LIKE IT

JOANNA SCUTTS

LIVERIGHT PUBLISHING CORPORATION

A Division of W. W. Norton & Company

Independent Publishers Since 1923

New York | London

For information about permission to reproduce selections from this book, write to
Permissions, Liveright Publishing Corporation, a division of W. W. Norton & Company, Inc.,
500 Fifth Avenue, New York, NY 10110

For information about special discounts for bulk purchases, please contact
W. W. Norton Special Sales at specialsales@wwnorton.com or 800-233-4830

Manufacturing by LSC Communications, Harrisonburg
Book design by Chris Welch
Production manager: Beth Steidle

Library of Congress Cataloging-in-Publication Data

Names: Scutts, Joanna, author.
Title: The extra woman : how Marjorie Hillis led a generation of
women to live alone and like it / Joanna Scutts.
Description: New York : Liveright Publishing Corporation, [2018] |
Includes bibliographical references and index.
Identifiers: LCCN 2017027416 | ISBN 9781631492730 (hardcover)
Subjects: LCSH: Roulston, Marjorie Hillis. | Roulston, Marjorie Hillis. Live alone and like it. |
Single women—United States—History. | Living alone—United States—
History. | Feminism—United States—History.
Classification: LCC HQ1221.R73 S38 2018 | DDC 305.420973—dc23
LC record available at https://lccn.loc.gov/2017027416

Liveright Publishing Corporation
500 Fifth Avenue, New York, N.Y. 10110
www.wwnorton.com

W. W. Norton & Company Ltd.
15 Carlisle Street, London W1D 3BS

1 2 3 4 5 6 7 8 9 0

For the Live-Aloners, in fact or in spirit.

CONTENTS

THE
EXTRA
WOMAN

INTRODUCTION

A Room of My Own

L ong before I read Virginia Woolf's manifesto, my dreams of the
future were creative and solitary. I had no fantasies about my
wedding day, only about my writing place: a little garret overlooking some scenic rooftops, precise location to be determined,
where nobody, least of all my parents, could come in without
knocking and accidentally banish the muse. I was always, in these
dreams, in the middle of some great creative project, never at the
tentative beginning or the slog-like end, never stuck and procras-
tinating by looking up pictures of bigger, better, prettier garrets
online. I never particularly worried about how I would manage the
other part of the equation that Woolf lays out, the five hundred a
year or whatever that would be today, in London or Paris or New
York or wherever my room happened to be. The important thing
was the room.

I never managed it. I followed my obsession with Woolf and her

Bloomsbury friends to Cambridge, studying and taking my degree alongside the boys as she could not. There, I lived in a succession of semiprivate rooms, overlooking first a market square, then the library's mullioned windows. The rooms always had shared bathrooms up one flight of stairs and shared kitchens down another, friends across the hall, and fascinating semistrangers above and below. I could close my door, but I was never really alone, and it was never really mine. Next year some other student would put her feet up on my desk, doze in my armchair, make out on my squeaky single bed, puke in my sink—and the room would never know the difference. After graduation I kept on sharing and moving through flats and houses that were always just a rehearsal for that real space of my own, the magical room that would turn me into a writer.

When I applied to graduate school, I dreamed of a studio—lovely, loaded word that conjured for me a tiny but magically unfolding place, where an artist might work and an adult might live. It had to be in New York, of course, despite the mathematical impossibility of renting my own place on a student stipend in the middle of an economic bubble. But I made it to the city and spent my twenties there, single, in apartments that were mine, but never mine alone. There were summer rentals in Paris and Berlin, a few weeks of making space among a stranger's belongings, lying awake as strange pipes clanged and neighbors fought in other languages, short breaks playing at living alone, tasting the fear and the dizzying lightness—what can't I do, what can't I get away with, if nobody's watching?

I was neither gloriously independent nor cozily coupled. Friends got married and had babies, but I was stuck with a roommate's cat that peed determinedly on the couch. I was broke, lonely, and nearing the end of my PhD program when the 2008 financial panic canceled just about all the jobs for newly minted English professors. That Christmas, as I was about to graduate, turn thirty, and start my belated independent life, my father died suddenly of a heart attack, a month after his sixty-seventh birthday. I went home to London to my mother and a house full of his books and his unfinished projects, where everything that could be used as a vase was stuffed with dying flowers.

One evening, my best friend Ali, who knew better than to send yet another bouquet, came to visit bearing two bottles of super-market Prosecco and a gift for my mother and me. It was a burnt-orange hardcover book with stiff, lightly foxed pages and a title picked out in navy-blue capital letters: *LIVE ALONE AND LIKE IT.* For a second that title stung like a slap, as lonely and unmoored as I felt. But as the three of us drank the wine we began to turn the pages, taking turns reading snippets aloud, from chapters called things like "A Lady and Her Liquor" and "Pleasures of a Single Bed," and the question-and-answer section "Etiquette for a Lone Female." ("Question: Is it permissible for a youngish un-chaperoned woman living alone to wear pajamas when a gentleman calls?") Despite my proud skepticism toward anything that could be labeled self-help, I found myself devouring the whole book, and taking its lessons quietly to heart.

A forgotten bestseller from 1936, *Live Alone and Like It: A Guide for the Extra Woman* (to give the book its full, even less comforting title) had recently been reissued with a pale pink dust jacket. Not one to buy anything wrapped in such blatant chick-lit clothing, Ali had gone online to find this worn, jacketless original, which bore no more information about the author than her old-fashioned name: Marjorie Hillis. Her book celebrated guts, indulgence, and above all, independence; it was funny, brisk, and endlessly quotable. There were sections on fashion, money, cocktails, travel, and having affairs—all of which played their part in the practical and adventurous life of the woman the author nicknamed the "Live-Aloner." As important and interesting as I found my graduate work, which focused on the literature and commemoration of World War I, it was undeniably grimmer than this lighthearted little book, and I was in no mood to read about mourning. So I started cheating on my dissertation with Marjorie Hillis.

But this turned out to be harder than I expected. She had left only the faintest of Internet traces—not even a Wikipedia page—and I could glean little beyond the fact that she had worked at *Vogue* in New York, and her book had been a surprise international hit. My copy, I eventually worked out, was a British "translation" of the American original, with references to Broadway and the Metropolitan Museum swapped out for the West End and the National Gallery. A few crumbs of information led me to archives in Brooklyn and Indiana, where I pieced together a picture of this plain, pragmatic daughter of a once-famous Brooklyn preacher. Once an aspiring poet, Marjorie became a magazine editor and eventually transformed herself into a self-help guru, who elevated the status of single women from pitiful "extras" into glamorous and self-possessed "Live-Aloners." She followed up *Live Alone* with a series of sequels, mostly out of print, that covered budgeting, entertaining, New York City, and life as a widow and solitary senior citizen. There was even an intriguing little book called *Work Ends at Nightfall* that turned out to be a long poem about the careers and love lives of seven female friends in New York.

Despite the charming retro touches, like the insistence that any self-respecting Live-Aloner ought to own at least four styles of a

mysterious garment called a "bed-jacket," Marjorie Hillis's philosophy struck me as almost painfully relevant to modern single
women like me who were balancing the fantasy of independence
with the fear of being alone. Carrie Bradshaw, Bridget Jones, the
girls of *Girls*, and all their real-life counterparts owed an unspoken
debt to Marjorie Hillis, the original guru of the "extra woman"
whose solitude was nobody's business but her own. And unlike
other stories of single women in which getting a partner is the
end of the story, *Live Alone and Like It* was bracingly realistic about
every eventuality: "The chances are that at some time in your life,
possibly only now and then between husbands, you will find yourself settling down to a solitary existence."

The Live-Aloner in History

In the United States, single people now make up the majority of the
population, and there's little sign of this historic shift reversing.
The balance tipped in 2014, when it was reported that 50.2 percent
of adults over the age of sixteen were now unmarried.[1] Of course,
being unmarried is not the same thing as being single, and this
rough measure doesn't take into account all the permutations of
modern commitment. The tilt of the scale nonetheless felt significant, both to single people tired of their second-class status, and
to those doom-laden pundits who saw it as evidence of the further
decline of the nuclear family and society as we know it. Whether
it's cause for celebration or despair, the shift toward singleness has
profound social consequences. It affects the homes we build, the
cities we design, and the priorities of government—and in more
abstract terms, changes our ideas of happiness, fulfillment, and
the meaning of a good life.

Now that being single is so common—especially in cities, and especially while young—it's easy to overlook the radical potential of the uncoupled state, especially for women. To live alone as a woman used to invite a toxic blend of suspicion, pity, and mockery, and those witchy stereotypes sought to isolate the spinster and turn her into a cautionary tale. But although single women today have probably heard enough cat-lady jokes to last a lifetime, their identity and place in society no longer hinges so strongly, or so negatively, on their uncoupled state. In 2015, when writer Kate Bolick set out to reclaim the label "spinster" in her memoir of the same name, the stakes and the stigma of that word had arguably never been lower. But eighty years ago, when Marjorie Hillis celebrated single women as happy and fulfilled members of society, she was taking aim at the very basis of American women's citizenship.

For most of American history, as for most of human history around the globe, a woman's place in the world was marked out and fiercely guarded by men. Except in a handful of exceptional situations, she could not stand in the full sun of citizenship, but lived in the shadow of her father, husband, or another male relative, "protected" by him from the world—protection for which she paid with all the property she had. Her children belonged to him. If she happened to be a published author, her copyrights belonged to her husband. The legal term for this is "coverture," derived from the French *couvrir*, to cover, evoking both protection and privacy. Coverture deprived women of independent legal identities, effectively conflating the categories of "woman" and "wife." Within this dominant legal framework, "uncovered" women were inconvenient, disruptive, and downright subversive—so much so that their very existence was obscured and denied.

Before the twentieth century, if a single woman needed to bring a case to court, she had to present herself as a wife—in spirit if not in name. Thus a woman who had been abandoned by her lover might sue him for breach of promise and the financial support that would have been due to her as his wife, in what was evocatively known as a "heart-balm" action. A woman who had lived with a man for some time without marrying him could defend herself in court as his common-law wife. A widow, meanwhile, often had to go to court to fight for a more appropriate share of her late husband's estate than the meager one-third that was the traditional "widow's portion" (needless to say, widowers in the same era automatically inherited everything from their wives). In a legal system based on old English common-law principles, single women were forced to open up their intimate relationships for public reckoning if they hoped to survive financially. In each case, the woman had to present herself under "the shadow of marriage" as a wannabe wife, a de facto wife, or a former wife. According to legal historian Ariela R. Dubler, an expert in the entwined history of marriage and the state, "the law compelled single women [. . .] to construct their intimate identities as internal to the general regulatory structure of marriage proper."[2] In 1872, Supreme Court justice Joseph P. Bradley went even further in declaring that women were wives first, citizens second. In a landmark decision, he reframed an American woman's patriotic duty as owing first and foremost to the "constitution of the family," before the Constitution that was the law of the land. Although the judge briefly acknowledged the obvious problem of women who had no family, he waved them away as too rare to challenge the basic rule.

The strenuous nineteenth-century effort to define all women as wives was a deliberate tactic in the long, bitter fight over women's suffrage. To antisuffragists, Justice Bradley's ruling made it clear that there was no need to give women the vote, because marriage would supply all their legal, economic, and political needs, and their husbands could stand in for them in the public sphere—a concept known as "virtual representation"—since it was unthinkable that a man and wife would vote differently from each other. This tenacious argument rested on what Dubler calls a "willful blindness" to the very existence of unmarried women. Even widows, who inspired many pious professions of sympathy from powerful men, were unable to come together and present themselves as a visible social group, and thus a deserving voting bloc.

It's important to note that this brief sketch of the history of marriage, singleness, and citizenship focuses on white American women. Enslaved African Americans were not permitted to marry, so their family structures and intimate relationships were always vulnerable to abuse and rupture. Justice Bradley's equation, marriage = citizenship (and by extension, woman = wife), was a form of white privilege that for generations deliberately excluded black women. Even after emancipation, their access to the rights of citizenship whether through marriage or the vote was relentlessly undermined. The legacy of this racist system lingered into the modern era, in negative stereotypes about the "broken" black family, and in contrasting attitudes to the singleness of black and white women— anxious terms like "spinster" and "old maid" were rarely applied to single black women, whose "safe" incorporation into the regulatory system of marriage was never really the point.

In the early years of the twentieth century, lifestyles and laws changed rapidly for women of all backgrounds. Common-law principles as a basis for American jurisprudence began to fall away— the treatment of widows started to look heartless, while heart-balm actions, by contrast, struck a cynical modern world as an opportunity for bad women to extort good men. These laws were relics of older, preindustrial societies, where kinship ties were paramount. They couldn't serve the needs of the booming, teeming new cities, which were attracting hordes of unattached young men and women eager to make their fortunes. Not for the last time, the dangerous freedom of urban working girls became a national obsession, worried over end-lessly by conservative writers including Marjorie Hillis's own mother.

By 1920, it had become clear that single women were not sim-ply exceptions whose situations had to be distorted or denied to fit them into the marriage-based legal structure. The long-awaited vic-tory of the suffrage movement allowed all women, married or not, to emerge into the full light of citizenship—represented not virtually by their husbands but through their own fully fleshed presence at the ballot box. But it wasn't until the 1930s, when the vogue of the Live-Aloner took hold, that single women of all ages and stages of life truly asserted their political and cultural independence by declaring them-selves happy and fulfilled in their solitary state. Seen in this light, Marjorie Hillis's book becomes much more than a treasure trove of vintage style tips: It was a beacon of social change and a precursor to the feminist revolutions of the 1960s and '70s. *Live Alone and Like It*, along with its many sequels and imitators, helped to make single women visible and their way of life not only viable but enviable, free of the sympathy and scandal it had attracted in the past.

The impact was not restricted only to Live-Aloners. As marriage lost its hold over American women's political and social lives, many people thought it might simply fall away, a relic of an older time—and marriage rates in the 1920s and '30s did fall, while divorce rates rose. But the system was more stubborn than that. Marriage gained a powerful new identity, as a source of emotional support and ful-fillment for both partners. Instead of pretending that single women didn't exist, this new, modern, "companionate" understanding of marriage relied on their cheerful, vocal presence in society in order to underscore that getting hitched was a choice, not an inevitability or a state-mandated necessity. Instead of a threat to the institution that needed to be repressed or ignored, Live-Aloners were proof that modern women who did get married were doing so deliberately and thoughtfully. Even books aimed at helping single women find husbands no longer suggested that just any man and any marriage would do. The veteran advice columnist Dorothy Dix, for instance, in her 1939 book *How to Win and Hold a Husband*, argued that women who were not naturally inclined to homemaking, baby-rearing, and "coddling" a husband might not be cut out for marriage at all. If that were the case, they would do better to throw over Dix, and dive instead into *Live Alone and Like It*.

The Live-Aloner's World

This book uses the subjects of Marjorie Hillis's seven books, published between 1936 and 1967, to tell the wider story of the Live-Aloner, from the depths of the Depression, through the war and the throwback 1950s, to the dawn of second-wave feminism. It explores what made single women happy, and what success meant to them, as modeled by the women in Marjorie's books and by several uncompromising real-life women—single, divorced, and widowed—who helped shape the culture of midcentury America. More than eighty years later, in a world that still judges women for how they live and with whom, the uncompromising Live-Alone philosophy remains an inspiration to many modern readers who have stumbled across *Live Alone and Like It*, as I did, and embraced it. Whether their focus is budgeting, entertaining, work, city life, fashion, or bereavement and growing old alone, Marjorie Hillis's books are inspiring, funny, and clear-eyed about the challenges of singleness. She recognized that solitude was not just the happy, voluntary, temporary state of the young. In fact, her most impassioned and radical message was aimed at older women, divorcées, and widows: that they must guard and fight for their independence throughout their lives.

During the 1920s, while Marjorie Hillis was an editor at *Vogue*, the young and reckless flapper had become an icon of feminine freedom, roaming the city in a sparkly dress and dancing drunk on bootleg booze. She cut a flamboyant figure but presented no real cultural threat—eventually, it was assumed, she would sober up and get hitched (or, like the quintessential flapper Zelda Fitzgerald, get hitched and go right on with the party). But when the Depression hit at the end of the jazz decade, it revealed to all but the luckiest women that depending on a man for economic security was precarious. Marriage rates plunged as couples waited for better times to set up home together, and far more women than in earlier generations got a taste of life as a de facto "extra woman." For some, that taste of a different life was tantalizing. No longer a flighty girl or a doddering widow, the single woman was now a worker and a citizen, mature and independent, and could be perfectly happy, Marjorie Hillis declared, with her lot.

The Depression era that produced *Live Alone and Like It* was a boom period for self-help. Marjorie's peers included success gurus like Dale Carnegie and Napoleon Hill, who did their best to shore up the tottering American dream by arguing that success was a matter of will, coming to those who wanted it most and worked for it hardest. Wealthy industrialists and robber barons were elevated to the status of national sages, just as today, tech entrepreneurs and second-generation billionaires exhort ordinary workers to love what they do, work even harder, roll with the financial punches, and embrace the unpredictability of the market. It's a distinctly American response to economic catastrophe: in place of political revolution, personal renovation. Don't change the system, change yourself.

Marjorie Hillis shared these male gurus' belief in the power of positive thinking and self-reliance, but she recognized that for women, success was more complex: It's harder to scramble up the corporate ladder when half the rungs are missing. Single women in the Depression were among the lowest-paid of all workers, but they had more freedom than their married sisters, who were barred from many professions during the worst of the economic crisis; a 1936 Gallup poll showed that 82 percent of Americans thought wives should not be allowed to work if their husbands had jobs.[3] In their boarding houses, rented rooms, and tiny apartments, self-reliant Live-Aloners could close the door against the world for the first time in their lives, and discovered that perhaps they might like it after all. In her second book, *Orchids on Your Budget*, Marjorie spoke directly to these breadwinning women, advising them on how to manage their money, save, and enjoy a few carefully chosen indulgences—one of which might even be a charming, artistic, but hopelessly unemployable husband. The book echoed a larger cultural theme, voiced by no less a figure than First Lady Eleanor Roosevelt, that women's household budgeting skills were a key part of the battle to help the nation at large balance its books. In President Roosevelt's cabinet, the indomitable Frances Perkins (the sole breadwinner for her own troubled family) was the architect of the New Deal's protections for workers. Her fight to offer material support to families recognized that professional success did not guarantee long-term stability, especially for underpaid women.

Few working women during the Depression had the budget to go out on the town very often, so the home became a site of simple pleasures. Cheap, vicarious entertainments, like radio, magazines, and mass-market paperbacks went from novelties to necessities in this domestic decade. Women were encouraged to make a virtue of this necessity by decorating and entertaining with flair. Marjorie's third outing, *Corned Beef and Caviar: For the Live-Aloner*, included the single woman in those pursuits, with a compendium of advice, menus, and dishes that a single hostess could pull off—whether or not her goal was, as one chapter put it, "Getting the Man with the Meal." If she were bold enough, she might take inspiration from the era's most famous interior designer, the patrician divorcée Dorothy Draper, who urged Americans to flood their homes with acid-bright chintz, bold stripes, and jet-black lacquer. Or, less outlandishly, she could learn to cook with Irma Rombauer, the gutsy St. Louis widow whose cookbook *The Joy of Cooking* appeared from Marjorie Hillis's publisher in 1936, quickly becoming a permanent classic. The repeal of Prohibition, at the end of grim and gloomy 1933, meant that respectable women could stock their own liquor cabinets and throw their own parties.

But when the Live-Aloner did treat herself to a night out, the place to be was still New York, emerging from its scruffy speakeasy past into the height of café-society glamour. Those who could afford to put on their fur and diamonds and take taxis to nightclubs did so in a city that was an uneasy mix of high style and hard times. Poverty was particularly acute in Harlem, where unemployment rates hit almost 50 percent, and the neighborhood's vibrant artistic and political Renaissance staggered under the impact. The architecture, technology, and daily life of the city were documented in a decade-long project by photographer Berenice Abbott, culminating in her 1939 book *Changing New York*. Publicly single, Abbott was a lesbian who lived with her female partner in a quiet arrangement that was common

and becoming increasingly necessary as the era's public morals tightened; her story is a reminder of the variety of intimate arrangements
that could slip under the Live-Alone veil and that cultural visibility
for nonconformist women was still a fraught negotiation.

New York's stuttering recovery culminated in the 1939 World's
Fair, attended by forty million people over eighteen months, and
dubbed "The World of Tomorrow." Marjorie Hillis seized her
opportunity to direct the Live-Aloner to a solo adventure in her
book *New York, Fair or No Fair*, reassuring her out-of-town readers
that the city was perfectly safe, and advising them on reputable
restaurants and hotels. She did warn that if they wanted to visit the
most famous, glamorous nightclubs, they'd have to find a date, as
most were hostile to women alone. Luckily, she was able to point
them to an entrepreneurial service called the Guide Escort Agency,
which would rent out a well-educated, underemployed young man
for the evening. Or so she thought—unfortunately, by the time the
book was published, the city had closed down the service out of
fears of immorality. It was a worrying sign that the Live-Aloner's
brief, devil-may-care heyday was coming to an end.

In the early summer of 1939, with the fair still in full swing,
newspapers reported with gleeful schadenfreude that Marjorie
Hillis, the nation's spinster-in-chief, was getting married after
all. Alongside photographs of the slim, elegant forty-nine-year-old
bride in a figure-skimming satin gown, ran the triumphant story:
the Live-Alone guru had capitulated to the inevitable, betrayed her
readers, and exposed her signature philosophy for a fraud. After
trying for a while to argue her side—that she never said the single
life was *better* than marriage—Marjorie gave up, and contentedly
retreated into life with her husband Thomas Roulston, a dapper,
wealthy widower ten years her senior. At his Long Island country

estate, she maintained a silence that seemed to indicate that she had indeed abandoned her Live-Aloners.

The war that had been a distant threat during the late 1930s would soon overshadow everything else in American Life. As the munitions industry ramped up and soldiers shipped out overseas, women's still-controversial work outside the home was reframed as a patriotic duty, symbolized by Rosie the Riveter, the laborer with the rolled-up sleeves and bandanna who appeared in a Norman Rockwell painting on the cover of the *Saturday Evening Post* in 1943. This fictionalized ideal of the female war worker was patriotic, sturdy but feminine, uncomplaining, young—and above all, temporary. The reality of women's war work was much more complex, and despite postwar pressure to return to the home, the spirit of self-reliance and adventure that working instilled could last a lifetime. One of the real-life models for the symbolic Rosie, for example, a widowed Kentucky factory worker named Rose Will Monroe, who built B-52 bombers during the war, went on to found her own construction company, and finally earned her pilot's license at the age of fifty.[4]

The real shock for white, middle-class American women was not war work but the reaction against it in peacetime. Historians would later argue that the marriage and baby boom of the postwar years, which encouraged girls to find husbands when they were barely out of high school, was not really a return to "normal" life but a cultural and demographic blip. The pressure, nonetheless, was real. Self-help books of the late 1940s painted singleness as an unfortunate state to be hurried through as quickly as possible; one 1949 book, with the Live-Alone-echoing title *How to Be Happy While Single*, turned out to contain quite different advice: "If there is anything around in trousers who is not an absolute jerk, latch onto him now."[5] But there were dissenting voices: 1949 also saw the first publication of Simone de Beauvoir's seismic work of feminist theory, *The Second Sex*, translated into English (poorly, many argued) and made available in the United States four years later. Beginning as a philosophical treatise questioning what, exactly, a woman was—a biological or sociological creation?—it went on to offer a capacious history of womanhood from ancient Greece to the twentieth century, de Beauvoir argued for the importance of reproductive freedom and participation in economic life as necessary conditions for any progress for the "second sex." Her phrase, "One is not born, but rather becomes, a woman," became famous as a way of distinguishing between "sex" and "gender," and revealing the importance of culture in shaping a woman's life.[6]

In defiance of de Beauvoir, however, mainstream self-help writing, advice columns, and marriage counseling throughout the 1950s promoted the idea that getting and staying married were a woman's highest purpose—a message that had formed the backbone of the advice book Marjorie Hillis's own mother had published way back in 1911: *The American Woman and Her Home*. Marjorie herself would feel the full, crushing weight of this marriage-obsessed culture when her husband of just a decade died suddenly in 1949, leaving her alone once more. Her response to personal tragedy and an increasingly suffocating culture for single women was to pack up her country home, move back to the city, and pick up her Live-Alone theme once more. Her 1951 book *You Can Start All Over* was tempered by grief and the awareness that facing life as a middle-aged widow was a much tougher and lonelier proposition than starting out as an eager, eligible twentysomething. But even young Live-Aloners were menaced on all sides in the 1950s. *Life* was one of many magazines to report during the decade on the tragic psychological damage the "career woman" was likely to suffer by placing "masculine" ambition over "feminine" domesticity.[7]

In Hollywood, much had changed since Marjorie Hillis's heyday, when snappy, fast-talking dames like Irene Dunne and Katharine Hepburn went toe-to-toe with leading men in comedies that celebrated independent-minded women. In the late 1940s and '50s, in film noir and in weepy "women's pictures," female characters suffered anguish and violence as they struggled to conform to the rigid rules of gender, race, and class. The ideal starlet was no longer built of angles and sass, but of kittenish softness— Joan Crawford gave way to Marilyn Monroe. It was hard to find a single woman on screen in the 1950s who rejected conventional femininity but was also happy and admirable—with one towering exception. Auntie Mame, heroine of the novel, Broadway play, and movie of the same name, was based on writer Patrick Dennis's own freethinking aunt, and portrayed with unforgettable panache by Rosalind Russell, a mature throwback to the screwball era, who gleefully proclaimed that, "Life's a banquet, and most poor suckers are starving to death!" Though she was embraced and beloved by 1950s audiences, Mame was an old-school Live-Aloner at heart, a holdover from the Roaring Twenties and the independent-minded 1930s. By the time the film was nominated for a Best Picture Oscar in 1959, nostalgia for the Live-Alone era was beginning to take hold. It would become one of a swirl of forces driving the nascent women's-liberation movement.

The 1960s had barely begun before independent women—or rather, "single girls"—were everywhere. Helen Gurley Brown of *Cosmopolitan* magazine was their new guru, and their new bible, her 1962 book *Sex and the Single Girl*. Although she shared an emphasis on financial independence and the importance of a well-decorated home of one's own with Marjorie Hillis, Gurley Brown was far franker about sex and how women could turn it to their advantage (her 1965 sequel was *Sex and the Office*). Having married the film producer David Brown in 1959, Gurley Brown herself wasn't the embodiment of single chic—that role fell to the wide-eyed Marlo Thomas, producer and star of the 1966 sitcom *That Girl*. Sick of the endless wife and daughter roles she was offered, Thomas herself pitched the show to a skeptical NBC executive by asking him, "Ever think about doing a show where the woman is somebody?" and slapping down a copy of Betty Friedan's *The Feminine Mystique*.[8] But although the resulting show focused on the showbiz aspirations of Thomas's Ann and the various jobs she had to take to support herself, it also paired her with a steady, dependable boyfriend for the run of the show.

Newspapers hungrily reported on the adventures of single girls, striking an admiring tone much different from the head-shaking pity of ten years before. Yet their new cultural prominence was shadowed by violence. In 1963, two young roommates were stabbed to death in their Upper East Side apartment in a crime dubbed the "Career Girls Murders," as though the victims' jobs as a teacher and magazine researcher were somehow contributing factors in their gruesome deaths. The following year Queens bartender Kitty Genovese was sexually assaulted and murdered outside her home after a late shift, and the *New York Times* reported that thirty-eight people had witnessed the attack and failed to intervene. What the paper called "The Sickness of Apathy" soon became known as the "bystander effect," and entered the public imagination as evidence that women alone were especially vulnerable in the big, impersonal city—even though the reporting of the actions of Genovese's neighbors was later shown to be wildly inaccurate.[9]

In this fearful and sexualized climate, Marjorie Hillis looked like a refined relic. The closest she had ever come to admitting that single life might be risky was her tongue-in-cheek advice in *Live Alone*, about what to do if a male guest won't leave. "There is little danger that you will have to call the elevator man or open the window and scream. It may happen, but don't get your hopes up. You have to be pretty fascinating." In 1967, her final book, *Keep Going and Like It*, depicted the author on its back cover as a white-haired dowager from a different era, in a flowing silk skirt and with a humorous twinkle in her eye—an elegant figure who had nothing obvious to contribute to the world of Vietnam War protests and civil-rights battles. Her individualistic approach to happiness now looked like a privilege open only to a lucky few. Women across America were beginning to realize that what they needed was radical, collective change.

Yet the Live-Aloner cast a long shadow. Feminist writers and icons like Mary McCarthy and Betty Friedan had come of age during the 1930s and knew that life for single women had once looked both satisfying and thrilling—as it did to the Vassar girls in McCarthy's sexually frank 1963 novel *The Group*, set during the years of Marjorie Hillis's heyday. Friedan, meanwhile, lamented in *The Feminine Mystique*, her landmark account of women's domestic repression, that women's rights and expectations of happiness and independence had rolled back decisively since the Live-Alone era.

The Extra Woman tells the story of a particular type of woman, the glamorous Live-Aloner, during a period of rapid social change. Class and race unavoidably shaped her experiences, as living alone and supporting oneself was, by and large, a privilege of the wealthy and white. Yet the Live-Alone spirit had an impact far beyond the women who could afford to emulate Marjorie Hillis directly. She offered a new vision of happiness and success at a moment in history when Americans were obsessed with finding, and defining, both.

We look back to the midcentury era now for its style, but our connection is stronger than the shape of a sofa or the drape of a dress. In the wake of the 1929 Wall Street crash, as the Depression years stretched out, Americans became increasingly concerned with how to make the best of the new reality. Self-appointed gurus peddled philosophies of positive thinking, self-reliance, and the appreciation of small pleasures in an effort to reassure people that their happiness wasn't pegged to the fluctuating stock market. Others promised to help readers outsmart the market altogether, by focusing so determinedly on their own success that they could will it into being. Today it's possible to detect a similar yearning in the popularity of books, apps, and articles that tell us to purge ourselves of physical and mental baggage, slow down and simplify our lives, and train our minds toward gratitude and optimism. In both eras of economic crisis and slow, uneven recovery, against a drumbeat of terrifying global news, the proliferation of self-help can be linked to the failures of government and the economy to provide ordinary people with material and spiritual security. But such periods of social turmoil can also generate a spirit of creativity and daring, out of the sense that nothing will be the same again.

It may be impossible to read and write about the late 1930s without the crushing awareness that a war was rapidly approaching that would unleash murderous destruction on a still barely comprehensible scale, and would profoundly alter the politics and the social values of the countries that survived it. In the United States, the aftermath of World War II saw a rapid and uncompromising clampdown on women's professional opportunities, and an even more insidious choking-off of possibilities for independence and unconventional living. Although this narrative arc, from war to stultifying peace to social revolution, looks inevitable from our historical distance, it is really anything but. Recovering the spirit of daring that defined the Live-Alone heyday can remind us that a different story is always possible, and might just inspire us anew, to resist and rebel against convention, and to fight to create the life we really want.

1

SOLITARY SPLENDOR

The Bestseller

On Saturday, August 1, 1936, the woman who was poised to become the Depression-era guru of the smart single girl was alone in her midtown Manhattan apartment, preparing to celebrate the release, and the early glowing reviews, of her first book. The following day, the *New York Times* would sound a note that would soon become familiar, calling it "amusing, sensible, worldly wise and very practical"—not gushing words, perhaps, but perfectly suited to both the book and its author, a plain, good-humored magazine editor in her midforties, who would soon be America's most famous "bachelor girl." But this description won't quite do, still less the sour-sounding "spinster." The best word for who and what she was is the one she coined herself: "Live-Aloner." It explains her by the choices she made, not the husband she happened to lack. It was a status that depended on equal parts knowledge, pluck, willpower, and self-indulgence—all of which she would share with readers in her book: the bluntly titled, wildly popular self-help manual, *Live Alone and Like It: A Guide for the Extra Woman*.

For a celebratory occasion like this Saturday night, a single lady needed rituals. First came a long soak in the bathtub, and with it the habitual prayer of thanks that she wasn't at that moment being jostled onto a train at Grand Central Station by commuters bound for the suburbs. After the bath came whatever lotions and perfumes she most loved, whether they were gifts from admirers or treats she'd bought herself. Then, wrapped in a summer-weight negligee (single women ought to own at least two, to be changed with the seasons), she might pour a glass of sherry or shake up a cocktail from the small stash of liquor she kept on a pantry shelf—something her teetotal parents would never have done, but which was now not only acceptable but a marker of a single woman's sophistication. With glass in hand, she could apply her makeup—another formerly scandalous practice, now perfectly commonplace—and choose what to wear for her evening out.

Marjorie Hillis had never been a beauty, especially not in the wide-eyed, china-doll style that was popular when she was growing up in the first decades of the twentieth century. But by the age of forty-five she had grown into her height and strong features, and knew how to command a room. Working for more than twenty years on the staff of *Vogue* magazine, rising from caption writer to associate editor, had taught her how to dress and set her dark hair in flattering and fashionable finger waves. Although she could afford to shop at the best department stores in town, with money she both earned and inherited, she was no spendthrift. Instead, she invested thoughtfully in well-made clothes, making sure they coordinated with what she already owned, and taking care of them diligently so they would last. This philosophy had implications far beyond her wardrobe. Happiness, she believed, lay in making one's own careful choices about everything from what to wear, to where and how to live. And now, in a slim little greenish-gold jewel of a book, she was going to share those lessons of glamorous independence with single women everywhere.

The shiny cover of *Live Alone and Like It* was deliberately enticing and slyly misleading. It depicted a series of bellhops in matching red uniforms marching to the Live-Aloner's door, bearing flowers, gifts, and invitations, suggesting that the ultimate goal of her solitary lifestyle was romantic attention from men—and plenty of it. In his introduction to the book, the irreverent *Vanity Fair* editor Frank Crowninshield played up this idea, suggesting that the truly successful Live-Aloner was just playing hard to get. Like medieval nuns, he wrote, self-reliant single ladies "would soon find suitors playing the guitar under their windows, [. . .] placing ladders against the walls, [and] sending them amulets by the Mother Superior."[1] But Marjorie Hillis's model of the Live-Aloner was far more proactive than this cloistered sister. She made her own choices, mixed her own cocktails, and enjoyed the company of men without feeling any desperation to land one for life. She might spend her evenings in thrall to the adventures of Scarlett O'Hara in *Gone with the Wind*, another brand-new bestseller in 1936, but she had no intention of behaving like the swooning heroine of romantic fiction.

Live Alone and Like It announced in its first sentence that it was "no brief in favor of living alone." Marjorie was not here to argue that a solo state was preferable to any other arrangement, but rather that it was quite likely, "even if only now and then between husbands." A woman could be plunged by death or divorce, as much as by choice, into what the book called "solitary refinement," and in these circumstances the challenge—and the necessity—

of learning to make the best of it was more important than ever. Although marketers and reviewers preferred to focus on the lighter, sexier model of the Live-Aloner, a stylish young woman having too much fun to settle for marriage just yet, the author herself never lost sight of those who were single against their will, nor of how quickly the sands could shift under a person's feet. Conventional wisdom still held that marriage meant security—but then again, people had believed the same thing about the stock market before the crash.

By the mid-1930s, the Depression had dragged on for so long that its conditions had begun to look like the new normal. FDR's government tried everything it could to jump-start the economy, but although the New Deal had plenty of individual success stories, the mood of the country as a whole proved harder to shift. Into this sputtering recovery came a crowd of self-appointed sages and a library of self-help books, which brought their readers psychological comfort, even if their formulas for success were questionable at best. The immediate bestseller among these was Dale Carnegie's *How to Win Friends and Influence People*, published in 1936 and like most of its peers, addressed primarily to white-collar men— aspiring salesmen, struggling clerks, and middle managers—to whom the books promised to divulge the secrets of the conquering corporate heroes, millionaires, executives, and captains of industry. In a relentless fantasia of optimism that refused to acknowledge the power of the economy at large, these books encouraged men to look inward in order to generate success for themselves— and couldn't help but cruelly imply that those who failed had only themselves, not circumstance, to blame. Few addressed themselves directly to a female reader, and fewer still to those who lacked the husband and family that were supposed to make her happy.

Marjorie Hillis, too, believed in the power of positive thinking, but she also demanded that her reader face the reality of her circumstances. The path from "extra woman" to "Live-Aloner" took guts, and it began with throwing off the disparaging nicknames and grudging charity that single women were used to enduring. It meant rejecting the drummed-in lesson of a lifetime, that a woman's true purpose was self-sacrifice to the happiness of others. In this new independent light, Marjorie promised, the Live-Aloner could base the major decisions of her life on her own needs and desires—living where she wanted to, not wherever was most convenient for her relatives. Her book is full of anonymous case studies of women who leave behind suffocating hometowns and husbands for a fresh start, and it's easy to imagine the thrill that these stories of freedom must have offered to readers. It could never be as easy as the book made it sound, to start a life over alone, but Marjorie wrote with such confidence and passion about the value of independence that it was obvious she was speaking from experience. She knew what it was to feel domestically trapped, and she knew what it took to break free.

In *Live Alone and Like It*, a solo apartment-hunter in search of a home goes looking for "A View, Sunshine, Chic, Gaiety" until she lands a place that fulfills those somewhat whimsical and abstract requirements. The unidentified case study sounds suspiciously like the author, whose pied-à-terre in the city overlooked the East River and was in the fashionable urban oasis of Tudor City, a newish apartment complex perched on the edge of midtown Manhattan. She liked it so much that when *Live-Alone*'s success boosted her bank balance, she moved to a different apartment in the same complex. Marjorie did not assume that all of her readers were New Yorkers—her case studies ranged from St. Louis to Los Angeles—

but there was no doubt it was easier to achieve the kind of life she celebrated in a place that allowed for a measure of freedom and economic opportunity, not to mention excitement. Even Brooklyn Heights, where Marjorie had grown up, was sleepy and dull compared with Manhattan. Besides, it was hard for any single woman to create a genuinely independent life if she still lived within walking distance of relatives and neighbors who'd known her all her life, and kept asking when she was going to settle down.

Tudor City was ideally suited to a single woman of means—it was safe and secluded, but still close enough to the theaters, restaurants, stores, and major train stations to supply abundant "gaiety" and "chic." Developed by the real estate tycoon Fred F. French, Tudor City was designed, its early advertisements proclaimed, "not for millionaires but for people of taste and refinement . . . who wish to spend carefully." When it opened in 1927, it set a new standard in modern urban living as the world's first residential skyscraper complex, and the biggest such development New York had ever seen. Made up of fifteen buildings arranged around two central parks and housing nearly five thousand people, it became a beacon for livable, high-density development. The towers were (and still are) topped with a striking TUDOR CITY sign, designed to snag the attention of commuters at Grand Central, a 1920s version of the highway billboards that taunt traffic-snarled drivers with the reminder, "If you lived here, you'd be home by now."

Despite the breathing room that the parks afforded, a Tudor City dweller never forgot she was in Manhattan. Marjorie could see the gleaming turret of the new Chrysler Building from her window and flashes of the East River, which she would later describe as looping the island "like shimmering satin ribbons" and silvering the gap between Brooklyn, where she had grown up, and Manhattan, where she had made her home. She could hear the "friendly, nostalgic river sounds" floating up to her, those "far-off whistles of boats that New Yorkers get to love and miss in inland cities." The view she'd looked for allowed her a glimpse at all the thousands of lives unfolding in the buildings around her, looking at night like "giant illuminated checkerboards." New York was, to her, the most "homelike" and least lonely place she could imagine.[2] One visitor reported that "few dwellings among NYC's famed cliffs so eloquently reflected their mistress' personality."[3]

The success of *Live Alone and Like It* relied heavily on its author's willingness to play the part of the exemplary Live-Aloner, enjoying her privacy and solitude amid the glamour and excitement of New York City. The headline of an interview she gave to the *Washington D.C. News* on November 2, 1936, was typical of the way writer and subject became intertwined: "Author of Best Seller Bases Her Book on Theories She Has Proven for Herself." When a *Boston Daily Globe* reporter paid a visit to the "current expert on the art of bachelor-girling your way to happiness," she found the author living her precepts to the letter. Despite nursing a cold, Marjorie was dressed in "a black velvet lounging robe of the utmost chic," and sipping "a glass of excellent sherry." She was busy with plans for a trip to London to launch the English edition of *Live Alone*, which appeared in December, shorn of its more parochial references to New York personalities and places. The *Live Alone* message was going global.

That fall, Marjorie began to write a regular newspaper column on the single life, tackling subjects like drinking alone, escaping family obligations, and "Christmas for One." Syndicated in more than sixty newspapers, the column also answered letters from readers about the challenges of setting oneself up in solitary splendor.

Often these letters expressed plaintive disbelief that it was possible to live quite so self-indulgently as the author suggested on a truly tight budget. In her book, Marjorie had taken an airy, optimistic approach to the problem of financing the Live-Alone lifestyle, confining money matters to a chapter called "You'd Better Skip This One." But the insistent financial questions gave her the idea for a sequel, which would tackle the unpleasant subject of saving and budgeting head on.

The Live-Alone message was unabashedly materialist, and its success was at least partly due to an ingenious publicity campaign devised by the book's publishers, Bobbs-Merrill of Indianapolis—a mutually beneficial arrangement with department stores, which encouraged them to sell copies of the book alongside carefully selected accouterments for the Live-Alone lifestyle. This was the first time the publishers had undertaken a "tie-up" marketing scheme like this, and their promotional booklet was jubilant at the wide range of potential connections between the book and the department stores' offerings: "Every kind of merchandise is discussed. Gowns, street frocks, negligees, curtains, clocks, china dogs, beds and bedside tables." Reminding the stores that their author was on the staff of *Vogue*, and citing the success of trial campaigns at Bonwit Teller and Wanamaker's in New York, the publicity team included a cheat sheet of quotations from the book that could be turned into posters promoting all kinds of household goods, from furniture to cocktail shakers.[4] They found a receptive audience in stores nationwide: it was a small step from describing the must-have accessories for chic living to displaying them alongside stacks of the shiny little book, on shop floors and in store windows.

The stores didn't pay much attention to context, or the book's more serious message. The Emporium in San Francisco took a moment of tough love for the Live-Aloner—"You will have nobody to make a fuss over you when you are tired"—and turned it into an excuse for self-indulgence, with a display inviting the tired-out single customer to "Make a fuss over yourself, and relax luxuriously in this pink and frothy NEGLIGEE (Negligee Shop, Second Floor)." In New York, Bonwit Teller on Fifth Avenue dedicated four windows to the Live-Aloner, showcasing "negligees, tea gowns, night gowns, cosmetics, etc.—all the little luxuries that Miss Hillis suggest the extra woman should indulge in to pamper herself."

Other marketing schemes were more direct. D. A. Cameron, in charge of publicity at Bobbs-Merrill, devised a word-of-mouth scheme in July, shortly before the book was released, that would get its advice directly into the hands of his target audience. He wrote to a number of businesses, asking bluntly whether their offices contained any female clerks or assistants who lived alone. Insisting that he wasn't being impertinent, but wanted to send Marjorie's book straight to its target audience, he asked the recipients of the letters for these single staffers' names and addresses, and several bosses complied.[5]

Before long, this kind of outreach was no longer necessary—*Live Alone* was selling itself. By the time Marjorie saw the *New York Times* review on August 2, the first edition of her book, published two days earlier, had been "gobbled up." The second printing lasted twenty-four hours. By the time of its "monstrous" sixth printing on August 29, the book was safely in one of the top three slots on every bestseller list in the country. As Cameron gleefully boasted to one newspaper editor, "the book is selling like American Legion poppies on Armistice Day."[6] More than 16,000 copies were sold in August, 19,000 in September, to a peak of 22,366 in October, when the movie rights were sold to Universal Pictures for $4,500—although no film came out of the book. Marjorie had received no advance for the book, which sold for the modest cover price of $1.50, but by December she had accrued almost $10,000 in royalties.

Marjorie found herself swamped with fan letters, which revealed that the book was connecting powerfully with its target audience. There were those who found it a delicious temptation toward selfishness, like the woman who confessed that "Before I know it I will have opened all the perfumes I bought in Paris this summer, for Xmas presents, and be using them myself." Others struck a more earnest note, hinting at how difficult they had found their "extra" status before the book: "Thanks a lot for your grand contribution toward making life a bit saner and more normal for us who walk alone."[7]

Several high-profile women who were already living the Live-Alone principles responded exuberantly to the book. Margaret Fishback, a well-known poet and the highest-paid female advertising copywriter in the 1930s, wrote to congratulate Marjorie "on the gaiety and usefulness" of *Live Alone* and to regret that she hadn't written it herself. "It will do more good than a ton of medicine," she wrote. "The psychiatrists should pin a medal on your boozom."[8] Fishback had gone to work at Macy's as a copywriter in 1926, and had become a well-known single woman-about-town, publishing a hugely successful poetry collection in 1933, *Out of My Head*, which explored the lives of working women in the city. Her breezy, light style found an audience in women's magazines, daily papers, and more highbrow publications, at a time when poetry was a regular feature in their pages. "Maiden's Prayer" was a typical vignette about single life, published in *The New Yorker*:

> It's easy now to get a meal
> From eager gentlemen and sporty;
> But how will they be apt to feel
> And who will feed me when I'm forty?[9]

When Fishback announced her engagement in 1935 to Macy's head rug buyer, her capitulation to matrimony prompted a rash of knowing, crowing articles ("Sneerer at Love Engaged to Wed"). In a few years, Marjorie Hillis would be on the receiving end of a similar outpouring herself.[10]

During the height of the *Live Alone and Like It* boom, the most widely read advice column in the country rarely dealt with the lives of women who lived lives outside the family. But even Dorothy Dix, America's "Mother-Confessor," had to take notice of the new single woman in the fall of 1936. That November, a reader named "Estella" wrote to ask, "Is it a disgrace to be an old maid?" Dix wasted no time telling Estella that she was behind the times, and that her question sounded "like something that you had fished out of the hair-trunk in the attic." Without mentioning Marjorie Hillis directly, Dix made it clear that not marrying is "a matter of personal choice and taste," and that it was no more disgraceful than it would be for a man to remain a bachelor. Perfectly encapsulating the spirit of the Live-Aloner, Dix went on: "No women are more admired or sought after socially than the smartly dressed, intelligent, up-to-date, humorous and philosophical spinsters who would be highly amused at the idea of anyone looking askance at them because they did not wear a wedding ring."[11]

"Estella" went on to ask a related question: "Can an old maid be as great a woman and as much admired as her married sister?" In her reply, Dix cited Florence Nightingale, Clara Barton, and Susan B. Anthony as examples of highly respected "old maids" from history, and added that thousands more "have given their lives to mothering humanity instead of their own children." Yet here she departed from Marjorie Hillis, portraying the "old maid aunt" as a selfless servant of her siblings, parents, and the community—

"the salt of the earth" and a vital support to other people's lives. Such selflessness was admirable, no doubt, but if Estella read *Live Alone and Like It*, she might reconsider her situation—did she really want to devote her life to being the unpaid caregiver for a brood of nieces and nephews? And what did it matter what other people thought of her "greatness" anyway?

Dorothy Dix herself was a keen admirer of *Live Alone and Like It*, even if she might not have shared all its principles. She wrote to Marjorie's publishers that she had read it "with chuckles of enjoyment and deep appreciation of its wisdom as well as its wit." She added that "I get thousands of letters from women on this subject," and vowed to recommend both *Live Alone* and its sequel to them. Dix added that the book would "point the way to a happier living for many a poor femme who doesn't know how lucky she is in being able to live alone."[12] This pointed observation was a personal one. Dorothy Dix (the pseudonym of Elizabeth Meriwether Gilmer) had come to her fifty-year career as an advice columnist by accident, and to her wisdom by bitter experience. At age twenty-four, she married her stepmother's brother: "Having finished school, I tucked up my hair and got married as was the tribal custom among my people," as she later described it.[13] But the experience was miserable—her husband was mentally unstable and unable to work, the couple had no children, and Elizabeth ended up as his nurse and the family breadwinner. A few years into her marriage, she suffered a breakdown, and it was during her recovery that she happened to meet the vacationing owner of the New Orleans *Picayune*, who hired her as a reporter. Before long, the paper reinvented her as Dorothy Dix, columnist, and she caught the eye of William Randolph Hearst, who brought her to New York in 1901 to write for his *New York Journal*.

As a child, Marjorie Hillis would have seen Dix's byline and no doubt read her advice to readers on the relations between men and women. Dix preached what she called "the Gospel of Common Sense" and while she was no feminist, she took aim at many of the lingering Victorian myths about women and family relationships. "It dawned on me that everything in the world had been written about women, for women, except the truth," she later wrote, and she took both sexes to task for marital troubles. Dix believed men and women should marry for love, not out of fear or under pressure, and she always cautioned against couples marrying too young or too hastily. At her peak, during the late 1930s and into World War II, her column appeared in 273 newspapers, with an estimated readership of sixty million. "People tell me things that you would think they wouldn't even tell to God," she said, of the thousands of letters she received every week.[14]

Marjorie Hillis, in the fall of 1936, was getting a taste of what it felt like to be Dorothy Dix. She quickly became used to answering letters from readers seeking advice on everything from loneliness and marriage problems, to what to serve at parties and where to go on a weekend in New York—questions that would soon furnish material for her newspaper column "Says Marjorie Hillis." She also faced a backlash from several readers offended by her morals, and also got used to being misrepresented, misunderstood, or read out of context. "Everyone remembers the chapter on liquor and seems to have skipped what I said about it's being a good idea to go to church on Sunday," she told an audience in St. Louis ruefully. Parents attacked her as a bad influence, and blamed her for persuading their daughters to leave home for the big city, while husbands complained that their wives "had deserted them for a taste of independence."[15]

Most readers, however, got a kick out of the book and its message. "Please permit me to tell you what an uproariously good time
I have had with your book," wrote one fan. "You certainly hit the
nail on the head and have sent many shafts through my old maid
armor!!" This combination of style and substance also appealed to
the majority of reviewers, who responded strongly to the panache
of the prose, calling it "smartly written," "sprightly and not too
motherly" with "plenty of punch," and praising its "joyous flippancy," "refreshing forthright manner," and "fruity suggestions,
good advice and devastating examples." That was not to say that it
was a mere confection—the same reviewers praised the book for
its "sound advice" and "words of wisdom." *The New Yorker*, approvingly, called it "Indirectly a black eye for matrimony."[16]

Male readers were not immune to the charms of the book. May
Cameron of the *New York Post* revealed that "Almost no book I have
read during months of commuting has caused such neck-craning
among the Connecticut commuting gentry."[17] Bobbs-Merrill was
initially convinced that even though men might enjoy it, they
couldn't be expected to buy it. This quickly proved false. One
male reader wrote to ask for Marjorie's assistance in a romantic
scheme, in the hope, perhaps, that his love would ultimately reject
the book's advice: "Will you autograph the copy of your book that I
purchased, so that I may present it to probably the most charming
young lady in the world, to whom, and for whom, you wrote at least
one chapter without knowing her?" By the end of the summer, no
less a male than the president of the United States had jumped on
the bandwagon. "Reporters swarming on to the afterdeck of the
Potomac during President Roosevelt's recent tarpon fishing trip,
found the President reading a copy of *Live Alone and Like It*," the
publisher gloated. "In doing so they uncovered a phenomenon well

known to America's booksellers, namely, that a good share of the buyers of Marjorie Hillis's best-seller has been men."[18]

This combination of high-profile readers, strong reviews, and the innovative department store campaigns helped to establish *Live Alone and Like It* as a cultural phenomenon, with a life that reached well beyond its pages. In newspapers, department stores ran full-page advertisements quoting from the book, targeting the Live-Aloner as a discerning, budget-conscious shopper. The value for the stores was enormous. Those that had survived the worst of the Depression needed to entice frugally minded customers with the notion of "investment" in products that would last, while at the same time encouraging indulgence in inexpensive pleasures—a combination fully in line with Marjorie Hillis's philosophies. Furthermore, by cultivating the loyalty of the young Live-Aloner now, they could keep her coming back after she married and began making larger purchases for her home and family.

The author played an enthusiastic part in these department store promotions wherever she could. In late October, she made an appearance at Halle's department store in St. Louis and directed a fashion show aimed at the Live-Aloner. "In a smart black felt beret with its green quill stuck at a rather mad angle and her black broadcloth dress with green triangular buttons marching down the front, she looked exactly as she wants to look: like a gay and independent person," wrote the local *Star Times* newspaper of the visiting author.[19] Marjorie would later describe herself as "undeniably plain," but she had one essential fashion lesson to share with the ladies of St. Louis, which had led her to that black dress with the green buttons and matching beret: your natural-born looks were nothing without confidence. In *Live Alone*, she didn't tell her readers what to wear, beyond advising that they collect a few smart "street costumes," "at least one nice seductive tea-gown," and "some evening clothes with *swish*." The specifics mattered less than the spirit behind them—the very last thing a Live-Aloner could afford to do was give the impression that she wasn't single by choice. "There is no reason why the woman who lives alone should look any different from the woman who doesn't," Marjorie warned, "and every reason why she shouldn't."[20]

Some reporters expressed surprise that the author of such a witty book could be, in person, so mature and sensible; in St. Louis, Dorothy Coleman ran a large and unflattering photograph of the author under a headline that marveled "Author of *Live Alone and Like It* Human, Even Companionable." Perhaps misled by the pert figure in the book's irreverent illustrations, Coleman reported in surprise that Marjorie was "not especially good-looking," nor as young and petite as she expected. "She must be nearing the 40 mark, and if Schiaparelli dressed her you wouldn't know it." But Marjorie turns out to be much friendlier and more down-to-earth than expected. "She's the sort with whom you could walk through Scotland, antique hunt in New Orleans and actually enjoy a cup of tea anywhere, any afternoon."[21]

Despite all the publicity stunts and energetic peddling of negligees, the Live-Alone message was an earnest one at heart, and Marjorie Hillis took her role of guru seriously. She believed in the transformational power of her message, and like many self-help writers, she saw her own life as irrefutable proof that her theories worked. That meant that she also knew the emotional costs of living alone: having no one to rely on when you were tired, sick, or sad, and having to become exhaustingly self-reliant. "When you live alone," she wrote, "practically nobody arranges practically anything for you."[22] Nevertheless, Marjorie proudly told the *Pittsburgh*

Sun-Telegraph that she considered it "a forward step in civilization" that women no longer needed to marry just to avoid becoming "maiden aunts and barnacles."[23] Behind that quip hovered the awareness of a bullet dodged: just six years before, it looked as though she was headed for just that dependent fate.

Becoming the Live-Aloner

In 1932, the prolific self-help author Walter B. Pitkin published a book whose title would become a bedrock cliché of the decade's cult of optimism and self-reinvention, not to mention an evergreen greeting-card slogan: *Life Begins at Forty*. For Marjorie Hillis, give or take a year or two, the line was perfectly apt. She was past forty when she moved into her Tudor City apartment, finally free to focus on the work of creating a life she could cherish and champion. Up until then, through her teens and twenties and well into her old-maidhood, she lived as the dutiful unmarried daughters of her class always had—at the beck and call of her family.

The Hillis family demanded more of its members than most. As the head of Brooklyn's famous Plymouth Congregational Church, Marjorie's father was a public figure, and his job absorbed the time and energy of his wife and three children. His daughter later described the ministry as "the only business I know in which a whole family is expected to work for one person's salary." But being a part of that family brought abundant rewards. The Hillises were not wealthy, at least not by Gilded Age standards, but they had a secure and respectable place in rather dull Brooklyn society. They traveled a lot, had a house full of books, and family life was full of "variety and interest and fun," Marjorie later wrote, because her father "had great stores of all three." Nostalgically she recalled that her family "laughed more than most people seem to."[24]

The Reverend Dr. Newell Dwight Hillis was dedicated to the intellectual, social, and spiritual improvement of his sizable congregation. Every Sunday he preached a sermon extemporaneously from the church pulpit, then on Monday, working from skeleton notes, preached it again to a stenographer in his study, for publication in the *Brooklyn Daily Eagle*. There were church and social events every day of the week, and Dr. Hillis was a tireless traveling lecturer and the author of more than forty books and pamphlets. He established an educational institute at the church and conceived an ambitious plan for the beautification of his adopted borough. In his zeal for the improvement of his congregation, he was a self-help guru in his own right, preaching self-reliance and drawing inspiration from successful public figures, like his hero and friend Teddy Roosevelt, as well as from religious models and upstanding characters in novels.

Born in 1858 in Magnolia, a small town in western Iowa, Reverend Hillis grew up during a wave of Protestant religious fervor known as the Third Great Awakening, which gripped the country in the second half of the nineteenth century and fueled the abolitionist and temperance movements. Preachers drew huge crowds eager to hear a modern gospel emphasizing education, social welfare, and missionary work, and by the time he was called to the pulpit of Plymouth Church, Hillis was thoroughly steeped in this morally and socially improving ministry. In 1899, just before his fortieth birthday, he moved his wife Annie and his children, eleven-year-old Richard and ten-year-old Marjorie, from Chicago to the east coast. Their new home, the formerly independent city of Brooklyn, had just been swallowed up into the five-borough metropolis of

New York City, in what disgruntled locals called "the Great Mistake of 1898."

Plymouth Church was a prestigious and somewhat notorious appointment. Its first pastor had been the renowned abolitionist and equally renowned adulterer Henry Ward Beecher, brother of Harriet Beecher Stowe, who at the height of his career could fairly be called "the most famous man in America."[25] Beecher invited speakers including Charles Dickens, Mark Twain, and Frederick Douglass to his pulpit, and staged mock slave auctions in front of huge crowds to rally support for the abolitionist cause. Hillis took this media-savvy predecessor as a role model and, like him, preached a politically and socially engaged form of Christianity. When he was appointed to the post at Plymouth, the local Brooklyn newspapers profiled the preacher effusively, drawing attention to his piercing eyes and his boundless energy, and he rapidly became a local legend. "Brooklyn residents are beginning to look upon Dr. Hillis as something of a wonder," wrote one newspaper soon after he arrived. "He can ride a bicycle, write poetry, punch a bag, and preach a series of sermons that sets all the other clergy by the ears."[26] In an unpublished memoir of her early life, Marjorie wryly noted that her father's enthusiasms, like his passion for bicycling, could be short-lived: "When the fad waned, he bought a horse."[27]

When World War I broke out in Europe, Reverend Hillis followed Teddy Roosevelt's lead in advocating for American entry into the war. He traveled to the war zone in France and Belgium and published a pair of lurid pamphlets condemning German atrocities in the war zone, drawing on the widely circulated propaganda accounts of the invading army's treatment of the Belgians. Back in the United States he lectured, traveled, and used his pulpit to urge the government to take up arms in the fight: a position that gained strength after the New York-bound British liner *Lusita-nia* was sunk by a German torpedo in May 1915, numbering 128 Americans among its victims.

There were also powerful forces pushing against the war, not least the fact that many Americans were getting very rich by staying out of it. After the fighting began in late summer 1914, American investors had stepped up to feed the industrial and technological beast, and were making huge profits—the markets rose by more than 50 percent in the first year of the war. Although he was a clergyman, Reverend Hillis saw no objection to reaping some of the profits of that upswing—after all, he was a public fig-ure with a status to maintain, and it was part of his mission to enrich his church, his congregants, and his family. In 1915, how-ever, he went too far.

Marjorie was in her early twenties, still living in Brooklyn and closely entwined with her family, when her father was caught up in a public scandal that would shape her understanding of men and money. Hillis's former business manager and church trustee, Frank L. Ferguson—along with the reverend's nephew—accused his boss of using his powerful position "to draw admirers into speculation." Ferguson claimed that Hillis had begged him not to reveal the full details of his "vast and involved business affairs," out of a concern for the health of his wife and son (perhaps his daughters were more robust or, more likely, they were considered irrelevant to matters of business). After Ferguson ignored Hillis's pleas, refusing to be intimidated, Hillis fired back, accusing his business manager of embezzlement and dismissing his accusa-tions as "a small percentage of facts, mixed with a large percentage of explosive falsehood."[28]

As a financial scandal, even one that involved stock-market

gambling, the affair was much less lurid than the one that had engulfed Reverend Hillis's predecessor Henry Ward Beecher in the early 1870s, when the muckraking feminist publisher and presidential candidate Victoria Woodhull accused him of seducing a married member of his congregation, precipitating a sensational libel trial. Yet Reverend Hillis's scandal, also dragged out in the newspapers, was as much a sign of its times as Beecher's sexual hypocrisy had been in his day, raising questions that would become urgent in the rollercoaster 1920s, about the morality of stock market speculation. Like Beecher's affair, too, the Hillis scandal turned on the relationship of trust between a clergyman and his congregation. The reverend was forced to admit to his flock that he had crossed a line into materialism for its own sake, and to beg their forgiveness. They rallied round with promises of moral and monetary support, and although the legal wrangling continued, the mess at least faded quickly from the newspapers.

For the adult but still dependent Marjorie, her father's financial scandal, with its taint of corruption and humiliating public exposure, only confirmed her suspicion that men could not be trusted to do as they pleased with a family's money. It was one area in which she agreed with her mother. Four years earlier, Annie Hillis had published a generally conservative advice guide, *The American Woman and Her Home*, in which she argued that it was a part of a wife's duty to understand and control the family purse. Any woman who allowed herself to be placed on a pedestal above sordid financial realities, she cautioned, had only herself to blame when her husband cratered the ship. Annie was the devoted manager of her husband's busy working life, which stretched far beyond the pulpit of the church, but it was a role in life that was entirely dependent on her husband's good standing in the community and his continued trustworthiness in the eyes of his congregation.

If the 1915 scandal took its toll on Reverend Hillis's health, he didn't show it by slowing down his exhausting schedule. If anything, when America finally entered World War I, he traveled and lectured even more. Finally, in the fall of 1924, he collapsed in the middle of a church meeting with a cerebral hemorrhage, and his doctors insisted that if he wanted to live, he would have to retire. He and Annie duly left their home in Brooklyn Heights, three blocks from the church, for the bucolic, buttoned-up suburb of Bronxville, just north of the city, where their son Richard had settled with his wife and daughters.

When her father retired, Marjorie, now in her midthirties, was living alone in an apartment building on Columbia Heights, an elegant street running along the Brooklyn waterfront. It was the middle of the reckless 1920s, and a good time to be a single woman about town. A new weekly magazine, *The New Yorker*, was about to launch, showcasing the speakeasy-hopping antics of its pseudonymous female columnist "Lipstick," and the press was full of stories of flappers gone wild. But Marjorie was no flapper, and staid Brooklyn Heights no Manhattan playground. She would later describe the person she was in 1924 as the "minister's daughter"—shorthand for a frump and a prude, who had never had a sip of hooch and had no idea how to run her own life.

Marjorie's status as the old maid of the family was cemented shortly before her father's retirement, when he officiated her younger sister's lavish wedding, at their brother and sister-in-law's summer home in Kennebunkport. Nathalie Hillis was more than a decade younger than Marjorie, born just after her family settled in Brooklyn, making her just as old as the century. She did not have a job like her sister, but was a picture-perfect debutante, who made an even more picture-perfect society bride at her June wedding. The Brooklyn papers gushed over her satin gown, trimmed with lace from her mother's wedding dress, her four bridesmaids in powder-blue chiffon, and the two little flower girls, her brother's daughters, who trotted in front of her in yellow dresses carrying bouquets of pansies. Marjorie, as the maid of honor, wore a dark-blue gown that emphasized her maturity and singleness among all that frothy pastel.[29] After the wedding, Nathalie settled in Albany with her new husband and a year later gave birth to a daughter, Patricia, nicknamed Polly.

With her parents up in Bronxville and traveling often, and her siblings busy with their families, Marjorie was left more alone than she'd ever been, and began to think about what she really wanted to do with her life. She signed up for a course in playwriting at Columbia University and saw her three-act comedy, *Jane's Business*, staged at a local amateur theater. The story took the plot of *Jane Eyre* and dropped it in a modern office, where a philandering boss is temporarily blinded and marries his plain but loyal secretary—at her proposal. When he recovers his sight, the boss sets out to divorce her, before realizing he cannot live without her after all.[30] An arrangement of inequality turns into a marriage based on free choice and companionship, reflecting modern matrimonial ideals and celebrating virtues that would define the Live-Alone philosophy—along with the more personal idea that a woman's physical appearance mattered less than her character.

Elsewhere, Marjorie began to rehearse the theories that would eventually become *Live Alone and Like It*. In November 1924, at the fall luncheon of the Junior League, she gave a talk on "The Independence of the Business Woman to Whom Marriage Is No Longer a

Necessity and Need Not Be Entered into as a Compromise." Years of listening to her father's powerful preaching had clearly paid off, as reports of the event praised Marjorie's poise and ease of delivery. As she climbed the masthead at *Vogue*, she was often invited to lecture on fashion and style. In April 1927, during a speech at the Ritz-Carlton in praise of simple, practical clothes for children, she raised eyebrows by declaring that a fussily dressed infant "is one of the most effective arguments for birth control."[31]

But this public speaking role, which she relished, was soon interrupted. In March 1928, just a month after Marjorie had lectured the Junior League on "Taking Fashion Seriously," her father collapsed again, this time on a train in Florida, where he was spending the winter for his health. A tour of the Holy Land that he'd planned to lead had to be abruptly canceled, and the reverend returned home an invalid. Less than a year later, in February 1929, he died at home in Bronxville, at age seventy. The funeral service at Plymouth Church was packed, and the faithful *Brooklyn Daily Eagle* reported that the mourners, who had regularly heard the minister praise the promise of heaven and "crack the whip of scorn at materialism," were in no doubt that Reverend Hillis had gone to a better place. After the service, his body was cremated and his ashes buried in a cemetery in the aptly named Westchester village of Valhalla. Even in death, he had something to teach. The practice of cremation was still controversial, as it challenged the Christian belief in bodily resurrection—but as Marjorie explained to the *Eagle*, it had been the long-held wish of her father, who saw the practice as practical, hygienic, and modern.[32]

In upstate New York, meanwhile, Marjorie's little sister's marriage was no longer quite so picture-perfect. The young family moved several times, from Albany to Plattsburgh, where her husband's parents lived, and then to the tiny village of Peru. Nathalie came back to the city frequently to attend the weddings of her Brooklyn school friends, and after her father's stroke in the spring of 1928, she had a reason—or an excuse—to make her home in Bronxville for the foreseeable future. By June, when she was matron of honor at a friend's wedding on Long Island, the *Eagle* identified her as "of Bronxville." The following year, she was living at home with her parents and four-year-old daughter, having taken the irrevocable step of divorce.

In early twentieth-century America, divorce was still a shocking step for a married woman to take, and rare by contemporary standards—in the 1920s, rates stood at 1.6 per thousand (versus 3.6 today), or around 170,000 splits per year nationwide. But those rates were rising rapidly, in part because divorce was far less punitive than it had been at the turn of the century, and was slowly shedding its fearsome stigma.[33] Crucially, mothers like Nathalie would no longer lose custody of their children if they left a marriage. "No-fault" divorce was a long way off, however, and couples who agreed to separate could be accused of collusion or even prosecuted for fraud. An accusation of adultery, painful though it was, was usually the easiest path to divorce. Couples could discreetly enlist the services of a professional "co-respondent" like one Dorothy Jarvis, who in a 1934 tell-all confessed to the *New York Sunday Mirror* that she had played the "unknown blonde" in more than one hundred divorce cases.[34]

When Marjorie and Nathalie were growing up, both of their parents had sounded dire public warnings about the evils of divorce. Their mother's 1911 advice book—which she dedicated to her daughters, then ages twenty-one and eleven—railed against the changing social values of the new century and the independent young women it was producing. There was a "new kind of woman very much in evidence in the city," she wrote, who was "self-centered" and held an "exaggerated idea of her own importance."[35] Mrs. Newell Dwight Hillis (as she was credited) was firm in her belief that the roles of wife and mother remained "the career for which every true woman hopes in her inmost heart," and her book was essentially a plea—despairing at times—for the unbroken continuity of nineteenth-century feminine virtues into the modern world.[36]

Several years later, the local newspaper interviewed Marjorie Hillis and contrasted the advice of mother and daughter to single women. Where Annie "warned girls of the danger of moving picture houses" and "suggested that the single woman living alone would best find relaxation at the YWCA," her daughter showed them how to mix cocktails and handle solo male guests. "Mother was an up-and-coming woman in her day," her daughter said, loyally, "but fancy handing out advice like that today. Social standards have marched on."[37]

When it came to divorce, however, Annie Hillis's advice was not just charmingly old-fashioned—it was downright cruel. She reasoned that because the home was the wife's "peculiar province," it was also her particular responsibility to keep it together. Even in cases of desertion, cited at the time in two-thirds of divorces, Annie still blamed the wife: Being abandoned was surely evidence that she was "absolutely incompetent" at housekeeping. She counseled unhappy wives to redouble their devotion to hearth and home, to have more children, and to consider the public consequences of their actions: "For the sake of Society and the State a very great amount of personal suffering should be endured before a woman decides upon the extreme measure of dissolving the marriage tie."[38] Whatever suffering Nathalie endured during her marriage, it was bad enough to drive her to that extreme measure after just five years, Society and State (and Mother) be damned.

By the time of Nathalie's divorce, however, more had changed than the law. The model of marriage that Annie Hillis praised in 1911, of endurance, forbearance, and a commitment to the public good over "selfish" personal happiness, was already looking like a relic, especially now that women had won the right to vote. The new twentieth-century ideal of the companionate marriage saw husbands and wives as equals and friends, sharing interests, aspirations, and emotional support. Happiness was on its way to becoming modern America's defining virtue, and it was easier than ever to end a marriage that didn't supply it. Unhappy people could no longer be shocked or shamed into staying married, so those who wanted to prevent divorce—including moral leaders like Reverend Hillis and his wife—had to look for new ways to help people stay together.

Just as Nathalie's marriage was ending, a new German practice known as marriage counseling was beginning to gain a foothold in the United States. In 1930, Paul Popenoe, a horticulturalist who would later become be a household name for his efforts to preserve the nuclear family, founded the American Institute of Family Relations in Los Angeles. The institute and other, similar programs helped to popularize the notion that unhappiness within marriage could be solved by discussing it with an expert. The principles underlying marriage counseling were closely related to those that would go on to drive the Depression-era self-help boom. Both movements saw happiness as a matter of choice, rather than as a spiritual blessing or simple luck, and preached that with enough sustained effort, it was possible to talk oneself into or out of it.

The people and theories behind early American marriage

counseling overlapped with the eugenics movement, a popular and mainstream movement at the time for general social improvement—and one which Marjorie's father, Reverend Hillis, keenly supported. Along with several prominent senators, professors, and social reformers, including Booker T. Washington, he attended and served on the Executive Committee for the first annual Conference on Race Betterment, convened in Battle Creek, Michigan, in 1914 by Dr. John Harvey Kellogg—populariser of vegetarianism and breakfast cereal, and fiery campaigner against masturbation. At the heart of so-called race betterment lay the belief that the health, strength, and happiness of the population could be improved by encouraging its "fit" members—white, able-bodied, and middle class—to breed. The definition of "fit" and the methods for achieving this goal ranged widely. Some eugenicists advocated improved health care, birth control, sanitation, slum clearance, better diets, and a ban on tobacco—while others in the movement pushed for racial segregation, immigration bans, and forced sterilization of the mentally disabled and members of "unfit," non-white races. At the Race Betterment conference, Reverend Hillis spoke on "Factory Degeneration," but his address had less to do with the working conditions of the urban poor than with the lurid horrors of modern life, the spread of disease, alcoholism, and "the breakdown of character among our wealthy classes, with their debauchery, their divorces and their unending scandals."[39]

Little more than a decade later, his own daughter would be divorced, but Hillis did not live to witness the defining upper-class scandal of the early twentieth century. On the heels of the release of *Live Alone and Like It*, in the fall of 1936, that scandal forced Americans to reckon anew with the morality of divorce and the meaning of marriage, in a story that brought modern attitudes into conflict with ancient tradition. In the middle of Marjorie's nationwide tour promoting her paean to the single life, Baltimore-born socialite Wallis Simpson filed for divorce in England from her husband Ernest, on the only grounds that were permissible in that country: adultery. But not hers, although her affair with the recently crowned king of England was an open secret. Mrs. Simpson, called "Wally" or "Wallie" in the press, had already been married and divorced once, and her second husband didn't contest the split. Over the next few months, through her divorce, public romance with the king, and his subsequent abdication of the throne, Simpson received intense scrutiny that threw into question what it meant to be a modern woman, a moral woman, and a queen.

During this battle, the British press and political establishment, representing everything that was retrograde, stuffy, and absurd, refused to cover or comment on Mrs. Simpson's divorce. By contrast, it received daily coverage in American newspapers, which printed verbatim transcripts at the end of October of the seventeen-minute divorce trial. "He kept me alone and often went away for weekends," Simpson revealed, before her lawyers produced evidence of Ernest's assignation with another woman in a hotel in Bray, a village on the Thames outside London. The hotel's waiter was called as a witness, and testified that he had served Ernest breakfast in bed with another woman, and that the bed was indeed a double.[40] These intimate details raised larger questions about how husbands and wives ought to treat each other, and what were acceptable grounds for separation (not to mention the limits of what the newspapers ought to print). Marjorie's readers were eager to know what she thought, but whether she was sick of the press's prurience, or old-fashioned enough to believe it was none of her business, she told an interviewer in October that she would discuss anything—

her grandmother, her home life, her love life or lack of it—"But I won't open my mouth about Mrs. Simpson." Adding that she was soon to go to England to publish the British edition of *Live Alone*, and that "maybe if I'm lucky I'll get a glimpse of her," she nonetheless didn't want to get drawn into the debate. "I'm not getting into any story arguments about whether or not King Edward would or should marry Mrs. Simpson," she declared firmly, just a few weeks before he announced his intention to do just that, whether it cost him his throne or not.[41]

Even though she refused to discuss this particular scandal, Marjorie Hillis was much more sympathetic to divorce than either of her parents, with her beliefs no doubt shaped closer to home, in her sister's unhappy experiences. Whatever gossip and judgment Nathalie endured in her small town when she returned there a single mother, she had a staunch ally in her older sister, in whose books divorce appeared as an unpleasant but practical solution to domestic unhappiness, with no hint that women who left their husbands deserved to be punished or pilloried. In later years Marjorie would often hold up the Duchess of Windsor, the erstwhile Wallis Simpson, as a glamorous role model. The "case studies" who suffered the most in her books were always women who valued social status over personal happiness and stuck with a brute of a husband simply because he was rich, or out of fear of what the neighbors would say.

After her father's death in early 1929, Marjorie sacrificed some of her tentative independence and moved to Bronxville to live with her mother, sister, and niece in a mock-Tudor mansion on Ellison Avenue, near her brother Richard's home. The suburb was quiet and affluent; among the Hillises' neighbors were Joseph P. Kennedy and his nine children. Every morning, the husbands and fathers of the town assembled at the train station for the thirty-minute ride into Manhattan, with Marjorie a rare woman among them. Despite the family turmoil, she refused to give up her job at *Vogue*, which she had held for twenty years, thus staking her claim to independence and a continued connection to the city. Heels clicking on the marble floor, she would march every day along the passageway connecting Grand Central Station to the hulking Graybar Building on Lexington Avenue, which housed the Condé Nast offices, and her particular version of freedom.

Nathalie also began to stretch her wings and rebuild her life after divorce and her father's death. A talented amateur singer, she enrolled in the fall of 1929 at the prestigious American Conservatory in Fontainebleau, outside Paris, for a course of voice training, apparently with the goal of performing professionally. But that charming dream quickly evaporated. On the morning of Tuesday, October 24, the *Brooklyn Daily Eagle* blared a headline that would herald the end of an era: "WALL ST. IN PANIC AS STOCKS CRASH." In their wealthy suburb, among bankers and lawyers whose fortunes were suddenly wiped out, the Hillis women joined the rest of the country watching the news unfold in horror. In the ensuing days, banks failed in their hundreds as desperate citizens demanded access to suddenly valueless savings. Some years later, F. Scott Fitzgerald would remember the collapse as though it were actually audible, a crash reverberating as far as Africa and echoing in the "farthest wastes of the desert." [42]

The turn of the year brought no improvement. Spring gave way to a brutally hot summer as dust storms swept the Great Plains, lending the crisis an apocalyptic shade. In Bronxville, the Hillis women weathered the financial turbulence as best they could, adjusting to a straitened reality, but Annie was unmoored without her forceful husband by her side. In the end, she outlived him by less than two years. On an unseasonably warm morning in mid-November 1930, mourners gathered once again at the house on Ellison Avenue. Annie Louise Hillis had died at age sixty-eight, and would be buried (though not cremated) in the same cemetery where her husband's ashes were scattered. This staunch advocate of marriage and motherhood left behind two single daughters, a spinster and a divorcée, to shift for themselves in a household without a man.

Even years later, Marjorie still felt how hard it was to absorb the series of personal and national shocks that upended those years and opened a chasm between her old life and the unknown future. "It ended," she later wrote, "not all in a moment, but with sufficient rapidity to leave me shaken and to make a new start difficult."[43] The Hillis sisters didn't embrace their all-female enclave for long—in fact, it didn't last the winter. Just three months after Annie's funeral, Nathalie married again. Her new husband was a local banker fourteen years her senior, twice widowed and raising two teenage daughters alone. The wedding was small and efficient, taking place at the Bronxville house on a Saturday morning, and unlike at Nathalie's first wedding, there were no bridesmaids or flower girls, and no guests except close family. Soon afterward, the newlyweds and their blended family moved to Valley Forge, Pennsylvania—more than a hundred miles away from Bronxville. Marjorie suddenly found herself alone in the big, empty house.

But she was not a Live-Aloner yet. Around the corner from her brother's growing family, she saw what lay ahead: the dismal life of a maiden aunt, with nothing to do but "moon around as a spare part that could easily be spared." She wanted no part of it, and promptly booked a trip to Venezuela, the newly oil-rich nation that was welcoming American tourists to grand hotels along its Caribbean coastline. Travel, as much as possible and as far afield as you could afford, was something she considered a necessity. At some point during her vacation, Marjorie came to a decision: She was never going to fit in "with the bridge-players of the suburbs," so after she sailed home in April 1931, she packed up the Bronxville house and made her escape to Manhattan. Her period of exile had shown her the value of city society, and she offered a daily prayer of gratitude as she bathed and dressed for dinner: "the train for Bronxville is just pulling out now and thanks be to all there is, I'm not on it."[44] Instead of joining the commuting crowds, she could fill her evenings with cocktail parties, concerts, dinners, movies, and the theater—everything she wanted, and nothing she didn't. After a tumultuous three years, she found herself unexpectedly liberated from family obligations, rising high in a job she loved, and living exactly where and how she liked.

The city, however, was still bruised from the impact of the crash. Its newest skyscraper, the Empire State Building, was completed in 1931, rising "lonely and inexplicable as the sphinx" out of the "echoing tomb" that was once-roaring Manhattan, as F. Scott Fitzgerald described it in his 1932 essay "My Lost City," around the time he decamped for Hollywood, and Marjorie Hillis settled into Tudor City. From the top of the city's newest, tallest building, the urban romantic could suddenly see all the way to the outer limit of New York, which is to say, to the end of the world. Fitzgerald set the nostalgic tone for a story that would be repeated over and over until it crystallized into myth: the Wall Street crash marking the sudden end to the long party of the 1920s, and the beginning of a decade-long hangover. Yet for single, working women like Marjorie Hillis, the 1930s were a time of possibility and promise. New ideas about happiness, and new ways of finding it, were opening up in the space left by the collapse of old certainties. Who, after all, had anything left to lose?

2

"SOMETHING TO GET YOUR TEETH INTO"

Going out to work was not a new experience for Marjorie Hillis, which made her something of a rarity among women of her class once the Depression hit. Since 1907, when she first took a job as a caption writer at the biweekly *Vogue* magazine, work had been a defining part of her life. Perhaps in the early years she still expected to leave when she got married, but as a husband proved elusive and the years passed, her career became more and more central to her identity.

Marjorie did not grow up in a world of fashion—far from it. Her family had "all the right books, but wore all the wrong clothes," and as a minister's daughter she dressed, as she put it, "TERRIBLY."[1] At *Vogue* she gradually learned to respect an industry she'd been raised to think was worse than frivolous, and she saw her colleagues as offering a public service. In her books, she firmly laid down the rule that there was no sense or virtue in thinking oneself "above" fashion for moral or intellectual reasons.

There was also no reason for women to feel that dressing well was a mystery—it took only a little study, and it was an obstinate and self-defeating woman who ignored the lessons of the magazine editors whose job it was to unravel that mystery.

By the time she began to write *Live Alone and Like It*, Marjorie had worked her way up from fashion reporter to features editor and was a trusted deputy to the editor in chief, Edna Woolman Chase. Edna and Marjorie were cut from the same cloth: outwardly conservative women who harbored progressive sentiments for their time and milieu, and, most importantly, thoroughly loved and lived their work. Edna Chase had been with *Vogue* since 1895 and was the person responsible for establishing it as the world's preeminent fashion bible. When she joined the magazine, it was an illustrated weekly paper filled with high-society gossip, fashion notes, and weak jokes, aimed at those who frequented the balls and parties of New York's elite, or wanted to pretend they did. Its most popular column, "As Seen by Him," was written by an anonymous snob who instructed readers—men as well as women—in etiquette and social distinctions. In 1905, a young publishing impresario from St. Louis named Condé Montrose Nast bought *Vogue* and reconceived it as a fashion magazine for women. At first, it was essentially a catalogue, showcasing a mind-numbing parade of anonymously captioned illustrations of gowns, frills, and furs, but it gradually developed a distinctive editorial identity. In 1914, Nast appointed the loyal, hardworking Chase, then thirty-seven, as the magazine's editor in chief, a role she would fill for an astonishing thirty-four years.

Unlike most of the magazine's staff, Chase didn't come from money. She was born in Asbury Park, New Jersey, and after her father "drifted out" of their lives, her mother settled in New York with her second husband—leaving Edna to be raised by Quaker grandparents who addressed each other with "thee" and "thou," and whose rural lives couldn't have been further removed, cultutrally speaking, from Gilded Age Manhattan. As soon as she was old enough, Edna followed her mother to the city where, as a young, single woman, she lived in a boarding house and lucked into a job at the fledgling *Vogue* after a friend working there left to get married. She began by addressing envelopes in the mailroom, and soon found that her work ethic far outpaced that of her upper-class colleagues. "As we were staffed by ladies and gentlemen no one worked very hard and anyone who wanted extra duties was welcome to them," she noted drily in her 1954 autobiography.[2] Young Edna fell immediately and lastingly in love with the hard work, long hours, and camaraderie that went into editorial production. Even after she married her first husband in 1899, she kept her job—an unusual arrangement that divided her from most of her female friends, whose lives and conversations were dominated by "the beaux and the babies, the servant troubles, and the social aspirations" that bored her intensely. "I was professional," she recalled, palpably proud even after half a century. "I could earn my own money, or I could be fired if I were inefficient. It was something to get your teeth into. It was living."[3]

Over her years as editor in chief, Edna Chase not only reinvented *Vogue* but was at the forefront of the creation of the modern American fashion industry. The first runway show was an event that she dreamed up after the outbreak of World War I, in order to support the struggling French design houses. She oversaw the founding of the British edition of *Vogue* in 1916 and its Italian and French counterparts in 1920, and spent her time traveling between London, Paris, Milan, and New York to monitor the progress of her European fledglings. Through two world wars and a slow revolution in women's lives, the indefatigable Chase and her staff, including Marjorie Hillis, made *Vogue* an international authority on style and society.

During the early years of Edna Chase's leadership, however, the magazine was a stuffy, spinsterly place. Dorothy Parker, while she was still unmarried Dorothy Rothschild, worked briefly at *Vogue* until Frank Crowninshield poached her in 1917 to write acerbic theater reviews for *Vanity Fair*. "They were plain women working at *Vogue*, not chic," Parker later recalled. "They were decent, nice women—the nicest women I ever met—but they had no business on such a magazine."[4] Edna Chase, for her part, remembered Parker as "a small, dark-haired pixie, treacle-sweet of tongue, but vinegar-witted."[5] While there, she wrote mostly anonymous fashion captions, including her famous (unpublished) quip, "Brevity is the soul of lingerie." It benefited her rebellious image to look back on *Vogue* as a bastion of "niceness" that could not contain her.

But those nice, plain women in their "funny little bonnets" might not in fact have been so different from Parker—especially Marjorie Hillis, who had been Dorothy's classmate at the refined and exclusive Miss Dana's School in New Jersey. Indeed, Marjorie was frequently compared with Parker, directly or indirectly, when reviewers praised her witty writing style, which they said might have leaped from the pages of *The New Yorker* or *Vanity Fair*. One effusive male writer in the *Philadelphia Record* wrote that her second book placed her in the ranks with "the great and kindly satirists of your sex, with Dorothy Parker, with Colette, with Jane Austen, with E. M. Delafield."[6] Early in her career, Marjorie had contributed to Condé Nast's other title, *Vanity Fair*, whose editor Frank Crowninshield, a mentor to Parker, provided the introduction to *Live Alone and Like It*. But *Vogue* itself did not set out to satirize, and took its subjects and its audience more seriously than perhaps they deserved—or than its writers might have wanted.

Vogue's formality in print did not mean that there wasn't fun to be found behind the scenes—especially in the vanity of the men who graced its pages. Early on in her *Vogue* career, in 1910, Marjorie supervised a photo session with Mikhail Mordkin, lead dancer with the Bolshoi Ballet and a bona fide international celebrity, who had decided at the last minute that "his personality would be more dynamic if he wore only a cotton fig leaf." Twenty-one-year-old Marjorie didn't bat an eyelash at this change of plan and "breezed through the sitting without a qualm." But when her current beau arrived to pick her up "and spied all that Mordkin," he was shocked. " 'I think you should remember, Marjorie,' he said coldly, 'that you are a minister's daughter.' "[7] Edna Chase's telling of this anecdote shows Marjorie to be unflappably professional and pragmatic, as she deals in quick succession with a prima donna and a prig.

Live Alone and Like It was further proof that an education at Edna Chase's white-gloved *Vogue* did not turn a girl into a buttoned-up old maid. The book frankly addresses the question of "affairs," taking an approach that was more pragmatic than moralizing. Marjorie advised against taking a lover before the age of thirty, believing that a woman needed time to discover who she was and what she wanted. After that it was a question of cost-benefit analysis—Was the man worth the risk? "A Woman's Honor is no longer mentioned with bated breath and protected by her father, her brother and the community," she wrote boldly. "It is now her own affair."[8]

Edna Chase was no modernist trailblazer, but during her tenure at *Vogue* the magazine evolved with the times, and by the 1920s was holding up a racy, jet-setting ideal of "chic." Slender models were sketched or posed in motor cars, waving cigarettes in long holders, dressed in outfits tailored for adventure: "streamlined" was the adjective of the moment, applied to everything from cars to coats to undergarments. A new generation of "smart" magazines—

including Condé Nast's own *Vanity Fair* and the new *New Yorker*—
was nudging *Vogue* to become a sharper, snappier product. Like
"cool" a few decades later, "smart" was the watchword of the 1920s
and '30s, meaning bright and quick, stylish and fresh. It was everything that *New Yorker* editor Harold Ross meant when he declared
that his magazine was for "a metropolitan audience," and not "the
old lady in Dubuque." The smart reader, male or female, urban
and urbane, prized the clever quip over the close embrace.[9]

If the 1920s saw magazines setting the cultural standard for
what was chic and modern, during the 1930s they moved into
a golden age of popularity, as printing costs fell and readers
embraced cheap, entertaining escapism. A crowd of new or revived
publications jostled *Vogue* on the newsstands: celebrity magazines
(*Hollywood, Modern Screen, Silver Screen*), general-interest weeklies
(*Newsweek, Life,* and photo-heavy *Look*), fashion and lifestyle titles
for young women (*Glamour, Mademoiselle*), and for men (*Esquire*).
Woman's Day and *Family Circle* appealed to the older, married
sisters of *Mademoiselle* readers and flew off supermarket shelves.
Vogue's response to the competition was to set itself apart. Its version of high fashion reached ever higher, far beyond the budgets
and lifestyles of any but the wealthiest readers, to become the stuff
of pure fantasy. The celebrated photographer Edward Steichen,
hired by Condé Nast in 1923, filled the magazine's pages with
arresting photographs that spelled the end of the era of fashion
illustration. He played with light, shadow, and scale to dramatic
effect, displaying the lines of a woman's back against the curva-
ture of a grand piano or the railings of a cruise liner, and drap-
ing the slender bodies of models and movie stars in shimmering
gowns by Madeleine Vionnet and Paul Poiret. Through Steichen's
lens, in the pages of *Vogue*, fashion photography became fine art.

Elegance and style, in this era, did not belong exclusively to the young. During her season of notoriety in the late 1930s, forty-year-old divorcée Wallis Simpson was among the most famous and photographed women in the world, setting the fashion for hairstyles and clothes on both sides of the Atlantic. In December, a week before King Edward announced his abdication, one newspaper printed his paramour's portrait above a caption comparing her to Helen of Troy—a connection that highlighted both her beauty and the political tumult it had unleashed.[10] Simpson was a fixture in women's pages, gossip columns, and magazines—and later, as the Duchess of Windsor, she and the former king exploited their glamorous image for fame and money, when the generosity of the royal family faltered. Although some commentators painted her as young and flighty, "the sparkling-mooded American girl," bored by her husband and seduced by the glitz of royalty, many were fascinated with the prospect of a mature, independent woman as a style icon.[11] The gossip columnist Sheilah Graham argued that thanks to Simpson, who was "over forty but youthful and soignée," the reigning queens of Hollywood felt free to reveal the shocking fact that some of them were out of their twenties. Joan Crawford, "thirtyish," was "def[ying] Father Time" by adopting the era's solipsistic self-help mood, and refusing to worry about anything "except herself and how to improve, mentally and physically," Graham wrote. Kay Francis, thirty-seven, could thank her studio for paying as much attention to her hair, hands, and nails as would be given an "expensive race horse." Other stars claimed that they stayed young by avoiding nightclubs and going to bed early. All but the reliable rebel Mae West, then forty-three, who continued to keep her age a secret: "I'll stay just as long as the men want to come up and see my pictures."[12]

Although her professional life followed the fluctuations of high fashion, Marjorie Hillis herself swore by the importance of style, a more timeless and individualistic quality. She believed that the confidence necessary to forge an independent life began with a well-cut dress. In *Live Alone and Like It*, an ageless line-drawn figure flits through the pages in a variety of elegant outfits—whether mixing up cocktails, smoking in bed, or raking leaves in dungarees and a wide-brimmed hat. She was the visual embodiment of the Live-Aloner's self-reliant, can-do spirit. The illustrations were the creation of another trailblazer, Marjorie's friend and *Vogue* colleague Cipe Pineles, an Austrian-born graphic designer who in 1942 became the first female art director of an American magazine, at *Glamour*.[13]

The era that gave birth to the Live-Aloner is remarkable for the paradoxes it contained. In the pages of *Vogue*, the lavish stage sets of Hollywood musicals, and the polished dance floors of Manhattan nightclubs, it was a period of unmatched glamour. The sparkle was all the brighter for the darkness around it: For most Americans, economic misery dragged on throughout the 1930s. At Condé Nast, Marjorie Hillis learned the power of fantasy and aspiration to conquer or soften grim reality, and she never forgot that lesson. She urged her readers to study fashion magazines and never to discount the importance of keeping up appearances. But the pleasures of fantasy were not to be confused with self-delusion, whether in matters of money or romance. A single woman needed to see the world, and her place in it, with clear eyes.

Give Yourself a Chance!

The Depression taxed the resources of ordinary people to the utmost, even if they were not entirely desperate or destitute. An atmosphere of uncertainty and fear dominated the decade's public discourse, memorably articulated in President Roosevelt's March 1933 inaugural address, in which he told citizens that they had nothing to fear but "fear itself." In this famous speech, which argued that the national crisis was as much in people's heads as in their pocketbooks, the president echoed the message of many contemporary self-help writers who tried to convince readers that success was a question of attitude. FDR's pep talk went on to claim that true happiness lay "in the joy of achievement, in the thrill of creative effort," rather than "in the mere possession of money." Although the New Deal policies that FDR's administration championed throughout the 1930s rested on a spirit of "we're all in this together," the self-help writers of the time encouraged readers to see their own individual, indomitable will as the essence of their identity as Americans, and key to their success.

In her book *Bright-Sided*, a skeptical history of the positive-psychology movement, Barbara Ehrenreich traces the American love of self-help back to the beliefs of the early Puritan settlers, whose precarious new lives reinforced the stern theology they brought with them from the old world. At the mercy of their inhospitable surroundings, the settlers sought to control what they could: their own minds. They kept a vigilant watch on their motivations and desires, and punished themselves and one another for transgressions of thought as much as for sins of behavior, believing that God could witness their inner battles as clearly as their outward actions. Before Freud's influential stratification of the mind into the id, ego, and superego, it was common to believe that the mind could be divided against itself, a site of warring good and evil impulses.

But over time, the Puritans' paranoid self-policing gave way to a more positive view of the self as something malleable and improvable. If a person could learn to guard her mind against sinful thoughts, why could she not also train it toward virtue and goodness? Couldn't vigilance be a path toward self-improvement as well as a means of self-flagellation? In the twentieth century, as people began to move farther from their families and from the tight-knit communities that helped bolster religious faith, the social obligation to adhere to strict moral codes began to fade. Urban living and corporate labor demanded different skills and rewarded different behaviors, leading to a shift that is sometimes characterized in broad terms as a move from "character" to "personality." The importance of a person's internal, largely invisible, moral character lost ground to social skills, popularity, and adaptability. In response, a new kind of self-help emerged that claimed to teach readers how to make themselves more personable—to seem better rather than be better.[14]

Reverend Newell Dwight Hillis was fully immersed in the self-improvement theories of the new century, and did not believe that personal happiness on earth was incompatible with spiritual rewards. When they weren't trying to drum up support for World War I, his books and pamphlets—with titles like *The Quest of Happiness*, *Right Living as Fine Art*, and *A Man's Value to Society*—were intended to help his congregation embrace worldly success. In *Great Books as Life Teachers*, for instance, he held up works by George Eliot, Nathaniel Hawthorne, and Alfred, Lord Tennyson as sources of practical inspiration for living well. In other books he celebrated the example of historical figures, like nineteenth-century British prime minister William Gladstone, as offering up a template for ordinary people's lives. His own journey from rural Iowa to boomtown Brooklyn, and his position of leadership and power, was an aspirational model for none other than Dale Carnegie, author of the enduring bestseller *How to Win Friends and Influence People*, who as a young man devoured Reverend Hillis's educational pamphlets.[15] (The minister might, however, have raised an eyebrow at his acolyte's most audacious act of "self-improvement": changing the spelling of his given name from "Carnagey" to Carnegie, in order to imply a family connection to Andrew, the country's leading industrialist.)

By the time Dale Carnegie (re)made his name, in the midst of the Depression, readers were willing to entertain pretty much any path to a better life. Popularity was the means and the message of *How to Win Friends and Influence People*, published the same year as *Live Alone and Like It*, which set out to help readers develop a "personality" suited to the corporate world: flexible, upbeat, friendly, shallow, and always with an eye out for opportunity. Optimism and self-belief were the twin pillars of 1930s self-help. In the wake of economic disaster and political uncertainty, the culture was receptive to gurus who preached that it was possible to transcend financial insecurity and unemployment simply by tackling one's mental attitude. With the period trappings stripped away, these theories still resonate today, for instance, in the dazzling claims made for the power of "mindfulness" to focus the attention and generate clear visions of a better self. Dale Carnegie's book, meanwhile, continues to sell some three hundred thousand copies a year.[16]

Marjorie Hillis's instinctive faith in optimism was elevated to a spiritual dogma by the writer and preacher Norman Vincent Peale. Peale originally wanted to be a journalist, before he attended seminary and was ordained into the Methodist Episcopal Church, but his true calling was as a salesman. After his 1924 ordination he was assigned to the moribund Flatlands Church, Brooklyn, and

immediately set about rebuilding his congregation with a successful direct-marketing campaign of "doorbell ringing and postcard
mailing." After a move to Syracuse where he deployed similar tactics, Peale landed a radio show, and shortly afterward arrived at
Marble Collegiate Church in Manhattan, where he would be based
for the rest of his career. According to Steven Starker, one of the
few historians to look critically at modern self-help, Peale's early
books, called *The Art of Living* (1938) and *You Can Win* (1939), were
too vague and theoretical to stand out from the flood of similar
titles at the end of the Depression decade.[17] Peale refocused his
efforts on his radio show, and after World War II rose to the fame
that would last through the 1950s and beyond, thanks to his 1952
bestseller *The Power of Positive Thinking*, which promised the world
to people feeling scared and uncertain within it. To the horror of
many of his religious peers, Peale reduced the complex and mysterious bond between man and God into a straightforward transac-
tional relationship, reducing prayer to the first part of a three-part
formula for happiness: *prayerize, picturize, actualize*. Telling
his devotees that their unhappiness was self-manufactured, he
encouraged them to deploy mantras and visualizations to achieve
a life of joy, happiness, and material success, despite the looming
fears of the Cold War. With appealing anecdotes, simple formulas,
and practical-sounding to-do lists and techniques, Peale's blend-
ing of the spiritual and self-help genres proved especially popular
with middle-class women.

Taken to its logical extreme, positive thinking could be presented as a quasi-magical shortcut to wealth and power. Napoleon
Hill, author of 1937's *Think and Grow Rich*, expounded a particularly shaky philosophy that depended heavily on the repetition
of affirming mantras and other mind-control techniques such

as visualization and autosuggestion. The author claimed to have analyzed over a hundred American millionaires, who were quite happy to expound on how their personal fortitude and self-belief (rather than privilege or luck) had made them successful. *Think and Grow Rich* mystified their road to success in a way that both intrigued and frustrated its readers, promising a "secret" that it never really explained, beyond urging them to cultivate a "burning desire" for success. More than fifteen million people bought it anyway—almost as many as have bought into its twenty-first-century heir, Rhonda Byrne's *The Secret*, since 2006. Byrne's secret is as vague as Hill's: she claims that a "law of attraction" governs the universe and shapes our lives, and that by banishing negative thinking and visualizing our desires, we can "attract" whatever we want.[18]

Byrne and her 1930s predecessors were indebted to the teachings of New Thought, a multifaceted spiritual movement that traced its origins back to a nineteenth-century Maine clock maker with the gloriously hucksterish name of Phineas P. Quimby. Quimby was fascinated by the power of the mind and how it might be controlled by hypnosis and harnessed to heal the body—Mary Baker Eddy, the founder of Christian Science, was his patient and student. New Thought, as its name suggests, was a broad and adaptable movement, able to incorporate ideas derived from Ralph Waldo Emerson and the Transcendentalists, as well as various European and Asian mystical traditions, all of which, in their different ways, rejected the dominant lessons of scientific empiricism. The theoretical basis of many success manuals, that mind control was possible and achievable through visualization, autosuggestion, and the repetition of mantras and slogans, was derived from New Thought, and given authority by examples from life that supposedly demonstrated the success of the book's methods. Historian Stephen L. Recken observes that "words such as power, mastery, and control dominated the literature of the movement," helping to explain its powerful appeal to readers whose lives lacked those very things.[19] Nothing in mainstream 1930s self-help suggested that there might be a way to improve your own situation by working with other people—on the contrary, the route to success usually depended on leaving those other poor suckers in the dust.

Although the business of selling success in the 1930s—like the business of selling anything—was dominated by men, several women found a receptive audience for their particular brand of life advice, paving the way for Marjorie Hillis, but usually putting forth a less independent-minded, and much less entertaining philosophy. The most successful of these was Margery Wilson, who built a career selling women on the power of "charm." Born Sara Barker Strayer in Tennessee, Wilson got her start in the movie business, where she learned early on the power of smoke and mirrors. After stints as a touring entertainer, she wound up at director D. W. Griffith's Reliance-Majestic Studios aged just fourteen, and landed a job on camera, according to *Photoplay* magazine, by strapping padding to her undeveloped body, "until she presented a rotund and mature appearance."[20] The doe-eyed, ringleted Wilson racked up an impressive number of screen credits, most prominently as "Brown Eyes" in Griffith's 1916 picture *Intolerance*.[21] By the early 1920s, Wilson was not only an actress but also a screenwriter, producer, and director. In its freewheeling early phase, before roles and hierarchies became strictly defined, the movie business—like many fledgling industries—had plenty of space for talented women who knew how to seize an opportunity.[22] When the talkie era dawned in the late 1920s, Wilson saw a chance to reinvent herself as a speech coach for those actors and actresses caught unprepared, with thick accents and squeaky pitches, for the advent of sound.

After her marriage, Wilson began to write scripts for a radio show on "charm," and in 1928 published the first version of *The Woman You Want to Be: Margery Wilson's Complete Book of Charm*, which was revised and reprinted in 1933, 1935, 1938, and 1942. In the book, Wilson stressed that the program was a response to a need on the part of her readers, not rooted in her own experiences, as Marjorie's books would be. "The three courses in this book grew from the questions, the problems, and the needs of actual women," she wrote. "This is a living book, not a compilation of static ideas. It is a pulse of the modern woman's progress in personal achievement."[23] "Charm" was a feminine version of what Dale Carnegie called "personality," the basis of his formula for corporate success. But charm, Wilson claimed, was more reliable. Noting that "fashions in personalities change as surely as do hair-arrangements," she declared that charm, by contrast, was "classical and enduring."[24] Charm could work equally well for a woman whether she was trying to land a husband and run a pleasing home, or whether she was looking to make her mark in a career outside the home. Success, as both Carnegie and Wilson imagined it, sprang from the impression one made on others— clearly something the Hollywood veteran could well understand.

Wilson's "charm" was an elastic quality, encompassing a large and often contradictory set of behaviors and beliefs. Although it now carries the ring of the superficial and untrustworthy, and is often associated with men, for Wilson it was exclusively female, and had enormous potential to change a woman's life. She even elevated it to a nationalistic virtue. At the beginning of *The Woman You Want to Be*, Wilson makes the case that "the hope of any nation lies in the personal qualities of its individual members," and in the 1942 update she added that now, "as our way of life is challenged" by war, it was more important than ever to help readers achieve "personal strength and healthy minds." The notion that charm was a rock-solid base under the mistiness of changing fashions is an odd idea, made stranger by its elasticity. Charm is self-confidence, Wilson tells us, but it's also unself-consciousness. It can be faked until it becomes real, although how you tell the difference is never explained. Charm lies in being your best self, but only if that self is also attractive to others and free of cynicism. A list of methods to make other people like you includes a vicious formula for positive thinking ("pour a strong mental germicide on any lurking self-pity") alongside submissiveness to implicitly male judgment ("keep your voice soft, lilting and uncomplaining").[25] Whatever its potential, cultivating charm was at heart a project where the power lay in the hands of other people.

Unlike Marjorie Hillis, Margery Wilson did not base her lessons on her own experiences or those of her friends, and she spoke only briefly and in general terms about the importance of tangible details like work, money, and life at home. The few specific people she cited to illustrate her theories tended to be famous—one report of Eleanor Roosevelt's "charming" behavior at a White House tea serves both to support the principle and burnish the author's reputation. Meanwhile, who could argue with a flourish of authority like, "Elizabeth Arden once told me her theory of breath"?[26] Wilson relied heavily on bold, vague declarations and where the sentence alone didn't do it, italics or all caps drove home the point: "*You must have a goal.*" "PRETEND POISE, THEN GET IT."[27]

In common with many contemporary self-help books, Wilson combined her bracing rules with practical exercises and lists for study, and provided space in the back of the book to write out one's own personal program. These tasks spanned the practical and the emotional, including writing out an hour-by-hour daily routine, with time for grooming, answering mail, "a little daily informative reading," and exercise. A version of the popular modern practice of keeping a "gratitude journal" appears in the instruction to make a list of "100 people and things you like," with a view to cultivating a more positive outlook on life. A reader of *Live Alone and Like It* inadvertently demonstrated how popular these kinds of techniques were, when she wrote to Marjorie Hillis to thank her for *not* including them: "I am so glad that you didn't give us any breathing excercizes [*sic*] or ridiculous diets," she wrote. "As it is now the book reads just like a fairy tale of possibilities within the reach of anyone."[28]

Wilson's 1940 sequel, *Make Up Your Mind*, displayed the uncompromising and even violent individualism of some late-1930s self-help, nurtured in a world of encroaching fascism. In this book, decision making begins as a thrill, like "swimming off the Maine coast the first time," but quickly expands to promise far more: "If a man uses his individual power of thought he is almost a god." Other people, it assumes, are mere sheep, who lack the inner fortitude to train their own minds, or get pointlessly distracted by external events—in 1940, a fairly reasonable excuse, but not to Wilson, who shrugs, "Conditions have always been upset. There have always been wars."[29] Even the tiniest lapse was evidence of a lack of commitment to one's personal goals. A woman who appears in public with dirty fingernails, for instance, has made a deliberate choice, not a forgivable lapse: "She chose to stay in bed an extra five minutes instead of getting up to clean them." As distractions from the project of self-mastery, neither the threat of global war nor five minutes' laziness was acceptable. Did you want to watch somebody else make himself into a god, while you worried and slept?

Unlike Wilson, Hill, and others, Marjorie Hillis did not believe that self-improvement was a zero-sum game that depended on defeating weaker rivals. Although she believed that attitude was important, she did not pretend that a person could rise above her circumstances and responsibilities by sheer force of will. From her own experience, she knew that independence was a matter of balance, and that even the most determined Live-Aloner had to take the interests of her family and community into account—this was simply a woman's reality. She also did not suggest that she held any secret formula for overcoming the economic disaster of the Depression, and she was explicit that her books were not written for those in really dire straits. But she did believe that it was possible to stretch a modest income to accommodate an independent life—as long as you had a plan, a budget, and a clear sense of what you did and didn't want. "The basis of successful living alone is determination to make it successful," she wrote by way of introduction to her book. "Whether you belong to the conservative school that calls it will-power, or the modern school that calls it guts, the necessity is there."

Marjorie's lively, nuanced, and realistic approach to self-improvement, met an unexpected challenge in late 1936, when a similar-sounding book, *Wake Up and Live!*, began to chase *Live Alone and Like It* up the bestseller lists. The book, by Chicago-born journalist Dorothea Brande, was adapted loosely into a musical and a movie the following year and went on to sell more than a million copies. The similarity between the titles of the books, and the gender of the authors, meant they were often mistaken for each other. The confusion was compounded when a racy anonymous satire, *Wake Up Alone and Like It*, appeared at the end of the year—a sign, at least, that the two books had captured the cultural zeitgeist.

But Dorothea Brande's book had much more in common with Margery Wilson's bracing bromides than with Marjorie Hillis's gospel of good living. It was a manifesto aimed at men and women alike, advancing a Nietzschean theory, in which individuals are governed by a "Will to Power" and a competing "Will to Fail." Brande advocates a ruthlessly individualistic form of success, and relentlessly categorizes the various forms of "failure" that the reader must identify and cast out of his or her life—including the seemingly innocuous "embroiderers and knitters," "aimless conversationalists," and "takers of eternal post-graduate courses." The simple yet elusive formula that made *Wake Up and Live!* a bestseller—"Act as if it were impossible to fail"—held great attraction for those who felt powerless. It is not entirely coincidental that in the same year *Wake Up and Live!* was published, its author married the socialite, publisher, and fascist sympathizer Seward Collins, joining him as an editor on his right-wing *American Review*. Brande and Collins met after the end of his affair with Dorothy Parker, back when he was still a liberal. Collins was born into money and used it to shortcut Dale Carnegie, buying friends and influencing people through the acquisition of the respected literary magazine *The Bookman*. (He also used his fortune for less literary purposes, including to amass a vast collection of rare erotica that was his pride and obsession.)[30]

In the spoof *Wake Up Alone and Like It!*, a young female narrator follows Brande's precepts for success and races through four husbands by the age of thirty—the subtitle is *A Handbook for Those with Cold Feet*. The gleefully violent satire is distinctly gendered, with a note purportedly about the author describing her as both superficial and sadistic, "a mean little brat even when she was three years old, when she was found by her mother trying to give the cat a fashionable, stream-lined tail by pulling out all the tail hairs one by one." Its main target, however, was the self-help trade in general, a vast confidence game in which the only people really profiting are the likes of Brande, Carnegie, and Hill. "Use the book in every way you can think of," the author instructs the reader, with tongue in cheek. "Wear it out as soon as you can and buy another. If you buy enough of them, I shall feel that I have Not Failed."[31]

It was undeniably true that the public's yearning for a formula for happiness translated into huge sales for self-help books, which always promised to be the last one the reader ever need buy (unless, of course, the author produced a sequel). How far these books changed anyone's life is impossible to measure, but even the most gullible of readers must have realized that not all the millions who bought Hill's *Think and Grow Rich* actually, well, grew rich. Did that mean they were all failures? Or might there be a way to reassure those who weren't at the top that they could still be happy, and learn to appreciate what they had, finding satisfaction in daily living, cheap everyday pleasures, and, especially, life at home. At times of economic strain and political uncertainty, in the 1930s and today, some savvy self-help authors found a way to recast belt-tightening and penny-pinching as opportunities to clear the clutter and focus on what's truly important.

These contentment writers often looked overseas for inspiration. To this day, a popular corner of the self-help section is stocked with books that promise to share the wisdom of another place as a counterweight to American consumerist excess. The appeal of Japanese decluttering guru Marie Kondo's bestseller *The Life-Changing Magic of Tidying Up*, and its sequel, *Spark Joy*, relied heavily on quirky, distinctly non-Western precepts like thanking rejected objects for services rendered before tossing them into the garbage. Such books romanticize older and more seemingly "traditional" cultures, usually European or Asian, in order to teach readers how to eat better (without getting fat), raise better-behaved children, have better sex, and take more time for themselves.

The foremost contentment guru of the late 1930s was the prolific Lin Yutang, a Chinese author, translator, and inventor who emigrated to America in the middle of the decade. He fed readers' desires for wisdom from a far-off place with roughly a book a year, including *The Wisdom of Confucius*, *The Wisdom of China and India*, *The Wisdom of Laotse*—and eventually, *Lin Yutang on the Wisdom of America*. But it was his 1937 bestseller *The Importance of Living* that established his winning formula of mythologizing Chinese village life and translating its lessons for Western readers. The book conjured up a world of slow, settled, supportive communities that contrasted favorably with thrusting, urban, dog-eat-dog America. Lin turned the pillars of the success gurus' gospel—efficiency, tireless dedication to work, and the drive for achievement—into his core vices.

At a time when documentary photographers funded by the WPA were traveling the country to record the desperate poverty of migrant farmworkers, any idealization of rural life during the Depression depended heavily on fantasy. Contentment writers like Lin Yutang have been called "apologists for unemployment," who by praising the blessings of leisure, reinvented forced idleness as soul-enriching free time, and overlooked the severe psychological strain of being poor and out of work.[32] But the contentment books did not simply encourage their readers to drift through the day, smelling the roses and savoring the sunset. Instead—as suggested by the rather aggressive title of Edmund Jacobson's 1934 self-help guide *You Must Relax*—they often turned leisure time into an extension of productive work, a time when readers could develop skills and positive mindsets that might in turn make them more competitive in the job market. The benefits of rest and relaxation were usually touted with one eye on the corporate workplace: a well-rested worker, after all, could redouble her efforts in the office, and a happy, optimistic demeanor (as Dale Carnegie emphasized) could help secure her promotion.

Marjorie Hillis blended the positive-thinking approach of the success manuals with the contentment writers' emphasis on satisfaction, tempered with a dose of Dorothy Dix's common sense, in order to create her decidedly modern, funny, and nascently feminist version of self-help. She firmly believed that living alone did not exempt a woman from creating a stylish and comfortable home, and that objects could be sources of genuine pleasure. Her philosophy was a deliberate assault on the Puritan tradition that denounced worldly pleasures as sinful and shallow. Indeed, in the newspaper column she began to write shortly after the publication of *Live Alone and Like It*, Marjorie went so far as to suggest that carefully chosen "glamorous things" for the home could make up for missing human company. "I do believe that those who lack just the personal relationships they'd like can fill their lives so full of charming things that they scarcely miss the other," she wrote—a daringly materialistic claim to make at any time, but especially in the midst of a Depression. She insisted, however, that a beloved lamp or scarf or armchair was not just a consumer good, but also, and more importantly, an expression of an individual's taste and personality, which could bring lasting joy. "A great many people are much too noble about what they call the material things of life," she added, with a dismissive scoff. "They are usually rather drab people."[33]

In Live Alone and Like It, Marjorie's message, that single women could work, play, and live exactly as they chose, was nothing short of revolutionary, although its trappings were lighter than air. The pleasures of eating, drinking, decorating, and entertaining for nobody else but yourself were the kinds of things that could be called brazenly selfish, especially when women of Marjorie's generation had been raised to expect that they would devote themselves to others: parents, husband, children, and then anyone else who asked. The Live-Aloner refused all that, and poured her energy instead into stylish living quarters, well-mixed cocktails, and the company of charming guests—no chaperone required. Her independence came at a practical cost, however, unless she truly was an heiress. How realistic was it, for an ordinary single woman during the Depression, to reject family ties and make a life of her own?

3

(NOT) A QUESTION OF MONEY

"A Slight Financial Pressure Sharpens the Wits"[1]

The success of *Live Alone and Like It* made the fall and winter of 1936 a whirlwind for its author. By year's end the book had sold more than one hundred thousand copies, and was the eighth most popular nonfiction book of the year, according to the tally compiled from booksellers by *Publishers Weekly* magazine, which was touted by the publishers in its promotional efforts. Marjorie's syndicated column "Says Marjorie Hillis" could be found in sixty-five daily newspapers across the country, and it was becoming impossible to devote her full attention to her duties at *Vogue*. In January 1937 she hung up her editor's hat, said her goodbyes, and applied herself full time to her new position as America's guru for the single girl. By February, having moved to a new, larger apartment in a neighboring Tudor City building, Marjorie Hillis was hard at work on her new book, still untitled, which she promised to her publishers by April 1.[2]

In the course of her promotional tours, visiting department stores and women's clubs, giving lectures and interviews on the radio and to the women's pages of newspapers, Marjorie had heard over and over again the same worry from interviewers and readers alike: money. How could an ordinary woman, who was not a best-selling author, magazine editor, and the daughter of a famous clergyman, possibly hope to replicate the Live-Alone lifestyle? What was the hope of happiness for a single woman who was merely scraping by?

Marjorie and her publisher agreed early on that her second book ought to dive more deeply into this question of personal finance, but it was a tricky subject to make appealing, even in a climate of cautious recovery. The very notion of budgeting relied on a steady and predictable income, healthy enough to be parceled out with something left over—but steadiness and predictability were the very economic pillars that had crumbled since the crash. In such circumstances it was difficult to convince people that their money was in their control. So in order to repeat the success of *Live Alone*, Marjorie's budgeting book had to give the impression that it was actually about something else: pleasure, indulgence, and shameless fun—a cocktail that had done the trick before.

Live Alone and Like It had taken a breezily optimistic approach to money. Its chapter on budgeting was called "You'd Better Skip This One," suggesting that the sparkling Live-Alone fantasy would be muddied by too much economic reality. It didn't help that writing about budgets was no more fun than sticking to them. A month after the deadline for her budgeting book had passed, Marjorie confessed she'd hit a major snag: "The fact is that I HATE budgets." Until that point, she had been able to convince herself that she wasn't really writing about them, but it was pretty hard to keep up the pretense once she hit the chapter called "Almost Balancing the Budget."[3]

In the end, the budgeting system Marjorie would advocate in her new book was basic enough to be followed even by those who shared her dislike, with only one ironclad rule: "Don't follow anyone else's figures."[4] As with everything else in the book, the binding principle was the same one she had established in *Live Alone*: for the reader to know herself. From there, she could cut back on whatever didn't matter—to her, not to the world at large. If she lived to travel, then she ought to take a smaller apartment. If going to the theater mattered more than clothes, so be it—just the same as if fashion was more important than fine food. Marjorie wasn't going to judge anyone's priorities—she simply advised making sure the "miscellaneous" envelope was sufficiently padded in order to cover "the fun and the flavor and the trimming in your life."[5]

Wherever her passions lay, there was one arena in which a Live-Aloner could not afford to skimp: her savings. Here Marjorie whipped off the gloves. "You might as well face the fact early in the game that if, at forty, you are living alone, you will probably still be living alone, or wishing you could, at fifty, sixty, seventy, and even eighty," she wrote. "Some of that time, at least, you will not be able to go out and earn your own Martinis."[6] It was far better to economize while you were young, in order to look forward to an independent and comfortable, even glamorous old age.

In telegrams back and forth, Marjorie and her editor, Laurance Chambers, hashed out the title of the book that would entice her original readers back, while also playing down the "live alone" language in order to appeal to a wider audience. Chambers favored a bold bait and switch: *The Art of Being Smart: It's Not a Matter of Money*. That was a little too strong for Marjorie—of course, it *was* a matter of money, or at least what you did with it. She pushed blithely for a different subtitle, distinctly of its time: *A Guide for Gay Economists.* Eventually they settled on the phrase *Live Smartly on What Have You*, implying that the book's lessons could be freely adapted for whatever happened to be lying around.

That left only the main headline. Chambers and his team favored the blander, broader *Art of Being Smart*, but Marjorie wanted a phrase that promised a specific luxury to balance the ugly word "budget." She toyed with champagne, but didn't want to risk offending the temperance types who had reacted so violently to her earlier praise of drinking. Orchids represented a purely decorative, slightly exotic, and entirely frivolous pleasure. But how much of that pleasure could she promise? Even as Bobbs-Merrill was hyping the new book to newspapers for reviews and syndication deals under the working title *An Orchid on Your Budget*, Marjorie wasn't satisfied. "I tried it on some of the *Vogue* Staff," she wrote to the New York office in April, "and they all thought AN ORCHID was stingy!" *Orchids* it was—as many as you could afford.[7]

When the manuscript came back from its anonymous readers, however, it became clear that stinginess was hardly Marjorie's problem. Rather, her assessment of "what have you" was wildly out of touch. In her chapter "Almost Balancing the Budget" she throws out a sample annual income of $4,000, because the figure was easy to divide and "we may as well be optimistic." But for most Live-Aloners, $4,000 a year—equivalent to around $150,000 today—was more daydream than reality. It was more than Marjorie's own *Vogue* salary, even in her most senior editorial role. Indeed, it was a number she could arrive at herself only through a combination of her salary, inheritance, and the royalties for her books—she made almost twice this amount in the first three months of the release of

Live Alone. Almost all the book's advance readers raised the alarm at the figure, calling it "much too high to be of vital interest to the average budgeter." Cutting it in half would still be "fairly optimistic," one said, at a time when $2,000 was enough to place a family comfortably beyond the worst effects of the Depression.[8]

Marjorie won the battle. Her instinct was that her readers would prefer to imagine that she was, or could become, a "successful business woman" on four thousand a year, than to base her budget on a more pinched reality. Optimism was everything. Even skeptical readers seemed to understand that fantasy was more powerful than practicality. "I hope she took care of the great multitudes who cannot swish along beside big bouquets of pale pink roses in a perfumed room after a perfumed bath, having the maid bring in a tray of mosquito's wings on toast," wrote Leola Allard, the women's columnist at the *Chicago Daily News*, privately to the Bobbs-Merrill publicity department before the release of *Orchids*. "It sounds grand, but how to do it!"[9]

Different worries began to plague the author once the manuscript was finally turned in—chiefly over the new book's case studies. In late May, Marjorie wrote her editor in a panic to ask if she could make some last-minute edits, worried that two of the cases in particular were too revealing of their real-life inspiration. On learning that it was too late to change anything, she wrote back apologizing for her anxiety. "Do all inexperienced authors take on so about a second book?" she asked. The pressure of expectation after her first success was "distinctly nerve racking," she explained, adding that she "would love to hibernate or take dope till a month after publication."[10]

As it turned out, no drug-induced oblivion was necessary. The "case studies" were flattered, rather than offended, by their inclusion.

"Mr. L"—described in *Orchids* as a smart young man-about-town with an "almost embarrassing" reputation as an excellent chef and host—came to the book's release party at the Gladstone Hotel "as pleased as Punch," Marjorie reported, adding that he was the only guest who got drunk. Her worries about the originals of her other case studies proved baseless: "You'll be entertained to know that the friends I thought might be insulted were among the first and most cordial to write me," she told Chambers the day after the party.[11]

The buoyant mood that accompanied the release of *Orchids* was borne out by the reviews, many of which proclaimed the book to be even better than *Live Alone*. The *Philadelphia Inquirer* called it "more pungent, equally sane, and broader in view," and other reviewers agreed that this second outing would appeal still more widely than *Live Alone* had. "There are 132 pages of succinct and lively wisdom in this slim and sapient little volume," the *New York Times* wrote, alliteratively, while the *Herald Tribune* praised its "chipper common sense."[12] By August, three months after its release, *Orchids* had sold more than forty-four thousand copies and was vying with *How to Win Friends and Influence People* for the top spot on the *Herald Tribune*'s bestseller list.

The cover of *Orchids* jettisoned the quartet of bellhops bringing gifts and flowers to the Live-Aloner's door. Instead, it presented a quartet of women who could clearly pay for and enjoy their own flowers. Lithe and smart in their outfits of navy blue and raspberry pink, the women swing briefcases and baskets of flowers. The shiny cover proclaimed that this was an object to treasure, and would not contain dreary admonishments of self-denial. *Orchids* encouraged readers to take pleasure in money: in amassing it, allocating it, and spending it. Even savings, Marjorie made clear, were a source of pleasure, not just duty: "we have observed that most people seem to get as much fun out of buying a bond as out of buying a bracelet, once they've tried it." The nudge in the ribs to the female reader is deliberate—she goes on: "That money-in-the-bank strut appears to be very satisfying, and it's nice to observe that it's no longer a purely masculine goose-step."[13]

The last in the line of elegant budgeters gracing the cover of *Orchids* holds a small child by the hand, making it clear that the audience was no longer just the self-supporting Live-Aloner. It might even be for the single mother, though there wasn't much in the book that addressed her situation directly. Marjorie recognized that the elegant simplicity of budgeting for oneself was no longer much use when the needs and desires of husbands, children, and relatives were thrown onto the balance sheet. Nevertheless, she urged women to take care of themselves, perhaps haunted by the memory of her mother's vulnerable position, back when her husband's reckless investing had threatened to shame and sink the family. Faced with husbands who refuse to confront reality, or who treat their wives as useless objects, or who become depressed and bitter when they don't achieve the success they think they deserve, the married "case studies" in *Orchids* either get out or go under. Divorce, as in *Live Alone*, carries no obvious stigma. During the Depression, married women were encouraged to see supporting their husbands as their most important job, but Marjorie made it clear that he had to be worth supporting. In the burned and sober years after the crash, no woman could afford to let a man hold the purse strings and remain in the dark about the waxing and waning of her family's wealth.

A husband might also be a kind of orchid—a delightful splurge for a self-supporting woman. Why not marry that penniless artist, if he's charming and willing? In chapter four, "Can You Afford a Husband?" Marjorie presents men as allowable indulgences for successful women. "It may be an extravagance, but even the periods of strict economy should include some extravagances if possible," she begins, tongue firmly in cheek, putting men in the same category as lace underwear and scented bath oil.[14] The joke of the chapter lies in treating an "unprofitable" man as an expense roughly comparable to a bigger apartment or a trip to Europe, but Marjorie's serious point was that this approach to marriage was no less reckless than marrying a charmless man simply because he would be a good provider. Far better for a woman to take care of her own finances, and take the man on his merits. As long as prospective husbands and wives knew what they were getting into, and had actually discussed what marriage meant to them, then Marjorie thought they ought to "take the Leap" as soon as possible, rather than waiting for the economy to pick up. Modern marriage was about "affection and companionship," rather than hope chests and "linen enough to last a lifetime." The benefits of a husband are portrayed as social, decorative, and occasionally practical—but not so as to intrude upon the pleasant, self-determined independence celebrated in *Live Alone*: "It is perfectly understandable that any woman should like to have a man to sit at the head of her table when she entertains, and make a fourth at bridge, and go to the theatre with her, and open the ginger-ale bottles, and get out the ice cubes."[15]

Even if she was largely spinning a fantasy for her female readers of financial security and autonomy in marriage, it was a sign of how profoundly the Depression had shaken up gender expectations that Marjorie could blithely imagine women in the masculine role, choosing a partner based on looks and personality rather than earning power. She describes a happy marriage between one such "delightful" man and the self-sufficient woman who chooses him, as though it is a form of artistic patronage, giving no hint that the man in question feels emasculated by the arrangement. The wealthy patroness-wife in this case study seeks out her unworldly husband because she knows how dull the rich are, having devoted themselves to the twenty-four-hour-a-day pursuit of wealth, which is wholly antithetical to the "arts and graces."[16]

This playful rethinking of marital roles served to underscore one of Marjorie's more earnest points, directed at her upper-class or upwardly mobile readers: It was absurd to try to maintain an arbitrary social position when the Depression had shaken up old hierarchies and "remoulded current opinion" around social status. The turmoil of the period had allowed for the emergence of a new class, the "Smart Poor," who were not interested in faking their way into elite society, while even the stuffiest gatekeepers had to admit that "Nice People were often poor." Society would only be enriched, Marjorie insisted, by welcoming in those who had deeper personalities than pockets.[17]

Majorie's breezy review of the way that the Depression had readjusted both social class and the marriage market perhaps overstated the extent to which "arts and graces" were now valued—the smart poor, after all, were still poor. In George Cukor's hit 1940 film *The Philadelphia Story*, the broke writer played by Jimmy Stewart protests to Katharine Hepburn's heiress that the idea of artists being supported by "a patron Lady Bountiful" has rather "gone out." Even with the romantic twist of marriage, a generous patron still reduced the artist to a position of dependence—something that Marjorie counseled women to avoid at all costs.

An exception who proved the rule could be found in the case study of "Miss C." A pretty Southern girl who arrives in Chicago for work during the summer, Miss C. walks home past a string of tempting boutiques, and ends up wasting her entire small salary on the temptations she can't avoid. When winter comes, she can't afford the warm coat she truly needs, and ends up in a hospital with pneumonia. There, she's lucky enough to catch the eye of a handsome and eligible doctor, so her story leaps from cautionary tale to fairy tale, putting her firmly out of the book. It's clear, however, that this lucky escape is a rarity. The lesson of her story, like the fable of the ant and the grasshopper, is to save prudently for a big purchase before you need it, and not to rely on the slim chance of rescue by a white knight—who might not turn out to be reliable in the long term. Throughout the book Marjorie warns that dependence on others—whether friends, family, or a husband— will corrode affection and poison pleasure. As tough as it might be to resist the treats in the shop window, managing money and exercising independence were one and the same thing.

Don't Keep Up with the Joneses . . .

The central moral lesson of *Orchids* was one that the Reverend Hillis might have preached from his pulpit: Envy is a deadly sin. Not, for Marjorie, because the Bible says so, or because it will send you to hell—she has no obvious opinion about that. The problem with envy is simply that it's futile. "A house like the Smiths'" will not make you happy, and to pine for it is a waste of the energy that is a Live-Aloner's most precious resource.

A book-length call to resist envy might seem like a surprising move from a writer who built a career selling rich women on the latest style of hat, and whose self-help philosophies were anything but self-denying. Envy was, after all, the engine of the economy in which Marjorie Hillis was raised, the driving emotion of the industrial boom of late nineteenth- and early twentieth-century America, which soon became a consumption boom. During this Gilded Age, according to historian Susan J. Matt, what had once been a Victorian sin became a simple fact of life in the new consumer society.[18] Quality of life became an arms race, as wealthy families jostled elbows to build grander houses on better avenues, make better marriages, and throw ever more lavish parties at which ever more elaborate gowns could be displayed.

"Keeping up with the Joneses" is a phrase from this era, and the name of a comic strip in the *New York World* that debuted in 1913. It's been suggested that it derives from an actual family of Joneses, one of the wealthiest in New York, into which a daughter named Edith was born in 1862, who would grow up to become Edith Wharton, chief chronicler and critic of her social-climbing era. Keeping up with the Joneses was an impulse born of proximity—the desire to be better than your closest neighbors—and it held sway especially during a period when cities were growing but high society was small and exclusive, limited to the four hundred who, legend had it, could fit in Mrs. Astor's ballroom.[19] During the wild stock exchange ride of the 1920s, however, more and more people from more and more places found themselves able to compete, to build their own palaces with even bigger ballrooms. They could come from nowhere, like Fitzgerald's Jay Gatsby, and status was no longer determined by birth and breeding, but by cash and conspicious consumption.

The arrival of the Depression shook things up once again. Early on in *Orchids*, Marjorie sets the scene for the new economic order that prevailed even among the privileged classes: "If you take out your address-book and read through from A to Z, you'll be startled to find that a fair proportion of the people listed have changed their scale of living during the last few years, some of them moving up and more of them moving down."[20] In this shunted-around society, envy and competition had been replaced with a combination of sympathy, schadenfreude, and the obligation *not* to flaunt one's wealth. Everyone had to budget now, even the Joneses; the first chapter of *Orchids* is called "Well, Who Isn't Poor?" Thrift was no longer a rare, old-fashioned virtue but the most modern of morals. It could be satisfying and even fun ("up to a point," Marjorie admitted)—because everyone else was doing it, too.

Poor, of course, was relative. The chapter "The Old Homestead" gives a taste of the class of reader Marjorie imagined herself speaking to, who had to weigh the expense of keeping up a large, inherited home against the practical gain of moving to a smaller house, and who had the luxury of worrying whether her address adequately reflected her social status. For those who didn't have a sprawling mansion to pack up, the advice Marjorie gave about where and how to live was still rooted in the principle of knowing yourself. Messy people would be miserable if they tried to cram into a too-small space, and ought to sacrifice a better neighborhood in the interest of bigger rooms. A neat freak, on the other hand, would be safe in a stylishly located studio.

. . . But Do Keep Up

With the publication of *Orchids on Your Budget* in June 1937, the nationwide department store "tie-up" campaign that had been such a success the previous fall cranked again into high gear. This time the publishers' traveling salesmen were equipped with a more polished, three-color prospectus and the reassurance of the successful earlier campaign. The stores that had taken the gamble on the untapped market of the "Live-Aloner" were now eager for a repeat performance with Marjorie Hillis's new book—and a promised audience that would extend beyond the single woman to any shopper who was interested in chic and economical goods.

Fashion remained central to the marketing campaign, even though Marjorie was no longer with *Vogue*. Stores in New Haven and Hartford planned fashion displays and presentations themed for *Orchids*, while in Milwaukee, to coincide with Fashion Week in September, the store took the theme literally, furnishing models with "live orchids in cellophane boxes," which they threw into the audience at the end of a fashion show.[21] The Emporium in San Francisco, meanwhile, demonstrated how the lessons of *Orchids* could profitably be spread throughout the store. In addition to clothing displays, it devoted several windows to other chapters, showcasing "slacks and plants from the roof garden" for the chapter on the home, and "gingham house dress and table settings" for the chapter called "You Have to Eat."

Even the best-laid promotional plans, however, could go awry. In Baltimore, a woman in the store's advertising department reported privately to Marjorie a comic mishap with its display, which featured mannequins paired with signs quoting the book, such as "Miss D. got the job." After the display had been up for two days, the designer, a Miss Spicer, was checking on some missing items and asked the decorator where he had put them. "All was explained except a pair of white panties," wrote the advertising whistleblower. "Oh, he said, I put them in her hand. And to Miss Spicer's horrified delight—there stood the mannequin—Miss D. . . . got the job—with the panties nonchalantly dangling from her fingers!" She concluded that "I hope we have not cast aspersions on your Miss D.—but are afraid ours is not a Nice Girl, at all."

As an experienced fashion editor, Marjorie was well used to the inherent cognitive dissonance of advertising new goods for sale while preaching a message of thrift and sensible spending. During the Depression, even a magazine as upscale as *Vogue* was forced to acknowledge the prevailing economic mood and to repackage extravagant purchases as "investments," or as classics that wouldn't date, no matter how cuts and hemlines changed. In *Orchids*, Marjorie's rules for putting together an economical wardrobe likewise assumed that the reader had at least some money to spend, but needed help to spend it wisely and to resist the "semi-annual crop of temptations" that stores and magazines offered up.

Her advice did not begin with specific styles but with the command, once again, to know oneself. Before a woman could safely step inside Lord & Taylor she needed a detailed list of what she needed, "based on age, size, type, locality, what you do all day, and with whom you do it."[22] And before she could budget for the "orchids" that might be more fun to buy, she needed a solid wardrobe of clothes for the places she actually went, not the nightclubs she wanted to visit—which meant a hat, gloves, purse, shoes, and furs that all matched, or at least coordinated. As magazine editors would continue to do for the rest of the century, Marjorie recommended a little black evening dress as a versatile base for any kind of embellishment, and advised that a cheap evening wrap was a much smarter buy than a cheap pair of shoes. Cheapness was not just a question of price. It carried the risk of signaling something worse: a lack, or looseness, of morals. Especially in this era of shifting and uncertain class boundaries, it was acceptable to buy cheap items only as long as they could pass for something more expensive—economizing ought not to advertise itself. Anything that looked "extreme" or "too-too"—something with too much trimming, or a rhinestone buckle, or anything too skimpy or tight—ran the risk of upsetting the fragile balance of clothing and class.[23]

Another sign of the dreaded cheapness, just as obvious as extreme taste or flashy fabrics, was a wardrobe that was dirty, shabby, or threadbare. The ever-reliable French, the epitome of everything both sensible and chic, "would no more loll in a broadcloth suit than they would wear it to do the family washing."[24] French modes of fashion, food, and furnishings—not to mention sex—had been a source of inspiration for modern American self-help writers since Edith Wharton had extolled the virtues of what she saw as their more mature and sophisticated culture in her 1919 book *French Ways and Their Meaning*.[25] For the American fashion industry in the 1930s, in thrall to the dictates of Paris, the superiority of the French way of doing things was still mostly taken for granted. The most notorious recent iteration of this idea was Mireille Guiliano's 2006 bestseller proclaiming that French women don't get fat—a goal that Marjorie also advocated, but not because it was stylish, or French, but because it was "an excellent economy."[26] Maintaining one's figure and maintaining one's wardrobe, just like sticking to a budget, were admittedly less fun than eating chocolate and shopping. Marjorie's challenge, in *Orchids*, was to make this kind of self-restraint sound like a treat.

Marjorie was not alone in trying to convince her readers that taking care of their clothes, figures, and homes was satisfying and valuable—that it would "pay and pay and pay." The message was widely broadcast during the Depression, especially to those women who didn't work for wages but took care of a home, and for whom economizing was necessary but not a matter of life and death. Women's magazines, which proliferated in the 1930s, built their empires on money-saving tips and ingenious ways to be both elegant and economical. The relentless challenge to cut down expenses without seeming to cut back on quality of life was presented as a prolonged exercise in ingenuity and triumph over circumstance. The gnawing anxiety that might accompany economic uncertainty was downplayed, and no doubt some readers found such an upbeat message patronizing and unrealistic. For thousands of others, however, books like *Orchids* offered an important shot of hope and solidarity in the grinding daily battle to stay within a stringent budget.

Just as there was a fine line between looking stylish and looking cheap, so it was perilously easy to tip from thrifty to mean. "A hair-line separates sensible economy from the first suspicion of closeness, one of the most unlovely qualities known to humankind," Marjorie warned—and included a quiz ("This Will Tell You the Worst") to help readers judge whether they had crossed it.[27] But although her rules sounded arbitrary, there was a logic to them that measured up to the values put forward elsewhere in the book. The budgeter had gone too far when her penny-pinching made others pay, or went against the rule to take care of herself and her belongings. It was fine to save the string on a parcel or double check a restaurant bill—but whoever avoided paying her share, stiffed the help, or ruined her shoes in the rain to save on cab fare ought to know the bitter truth.

Although Marjorie was still writing mainly with independent women in mind, many of her case studies, like many of her readers, were married. For those women, it was part of the job to remain attractive during "lean periods," even if it seemed frivolous to spend money on cosmetics and grooming. Letting yourself go was one of the "Things You Can't Afford," and was a graver sin even than gaining a reputation for meanness. Reflecting the prevailing wisdom of the time, and informed by her own somewhat cynical view of men, Marjorie implied that a husband who was out of work, or had seen his status reduced by the Depression, was going to look for someone to blame—"and a slovenly wife is as good an excuse as any other, if not a little better than most."[28] It might not be fair, but the wife should be prepared—and devote time and energy to keeping herself attractive and her husband's spirits up. If for no better reason than that if she didn't, it was all too likely that another woman would. Even this gloomy scenario, however, was dispensed with briskly. Marjorie presented it as the unfortunate consequence of a "lean period" that could easily be remedied if the wife in question made more effort—an uncanny echo of how Marjorie's own mother might have counseled the woman in question to behave.

Orchids on Your Budget did not presume to tackle the problem of serious, prolonged poverty. It spoke to readers who had a choice between options that were not too bad, rather than those who had no choice at all—as Marjorie put it, the difference between being able to choose whether or not to butter your bread, and being forced to forgo bread entirely. The latter case was not hard times but "destitution," and she couldn't tackle that in a shiny gold-wrapped book. But in her final chapter, Marjorie returned again to the problem of genuine poverty. She likened the frightening sensation of having no money and no job to "crossing a raging river on a plank without a railing," evoking the metaphors of falling, drowning, and natural disaster that were commonplace in the language of the Depression economy. Marjorie's advice on how to weather a financial storm reflected her class status, in her conviction that poverty was a temporary condition that could be alleviated with a little help from one's better-off friends. The worst approach to financial disaster was misplaced pride: "Most people, and especially most men, would rather admit ignorance, dissipation, being jilted and a collection of physical disabilities than having no bank account," she went on.[29] Her advice, therefore, hinged on overcoming this pride, and confessing the situation to friends.

Self-help readers desperately wanted reassurance that it was possible to ride the Depression's raging waves. The success manuals competing with Marjorie Hillis for shelf space rarely concerned themselves with anything as mundane as budgets, but promised instead that a reader could vault over the raging river with the help of mantras and magical thinking. During 1937, the wild ups and downs of the economy seemed to prove once again that fiscal prudence was no more advisable than crossing one's fingers and hoping for the best. At the beginning of the year, the economy had bounced back to pre-1929 heights, and despite lagging unemployment, the most fortunate Americans were confident that the worst was over. But by the time *Orchids* was published in June, everything had tumbled again—industrial production fell by 32 percent, unemployment hit 20 percent, and a yearlong recession within the Depression began. The downturn was severe and lasting, and a sign that security was still elusive.[30]

In this climate of sudden advances and reversals, it was no wonder that people were willing to believe that any economic situation, wealth or poverty, was temporary and wholly unpredictable. The runaway Hollywood hit of the previous fall was a screwball comedy based on the idea that class and economic status could turn on a dime. *My Man Godfrey* stars William Powell as a suicidal millionaire, who escapes his former life by disguising himself as a homeless "forgotten man." He's living in an encampment on the banks of the East River when he's picked up as a prize in a scavenger hunt by a ditsy heiress, played by Powell's ex-wife Carole Lombard. She then hires him as her butler and of course, falls in love with him, unaware of his true identity. When her wealthy father confesses he's about to lose everything in a bad stock trade, the butler reveals that a clever trade of his own has made him rich and will save the family. He quits his job to open a nightclub called "The Dump," which will employ his old down-and-out comrades from the East River camp as waiters. At the very last minute, the restored heiress and the restored millionaire get married, but this ending doesn't feel like a return to order, so much as just another spin on the merry-go-round. The madcap plot of the film was ideally suited to its moment, when no reversal of fortune was too absurd to contemplate, and the difference between a butler, a bum, and a millionaire was just an outfit.

Hollywood in the 1930s was obsessed with portraying the antics of unruly heiresses, who were given license in a string of comedies to misbehave with a freedom no ordinary woman could enjoy. The middle-class audiences who flocked to those pictures also ate up stories about the actresses who played the heiresses, whose riches and glamour seemed no less a fairy tale. Movie magazines were full of highly manufactured stories of starlets who'd been plucked out of their ordinary lives and given a new look, a new name, and a shiny studio contract. To be an heiress or a movie star seemed like just the same kind of magic.

At the other extreme of portrayals of women in the middle years of the Depression sits Dorothea Lange's iconic photograph of Florence Owens Thompson, known as *Migrant Mother*, of a prematurely aged woman unable to break out of her own despair to comfort the children who cling to her. This photograph, taken in Nipomo, California, in February of 1936, 160 miles up the coast from Hollywood, makes it hard to believe that optimism could be part of the story of the era. Yet for women on their own, especially in cities where there were more opportunities to scrape together a living, there was the promise that they could finally exert control over their money.

Between those extremes of wealth and poverty, Hollywood and Nipomo, lay millions of women who adjusted to their new circumstances by going out to work, often for the first time. The mass unemployment after the Wall Street crash began in heavy industry, where very few women were employed, and affected men to a far greater degree. The country still needed teachers, nurses, and garment workers; it still needed maids and cooks and nannies, albeit in smaller numbers than before; and it needed the cheapest possible office workers. Women with families, who could get by without working outside the home, saw their domestic roles changed and expanded. A housewife became a household manager, economist in chief, and family morale booster. Her contributions to the economy, as a careful consumer, were valued as never before. And in contrast to the men who suffered the psychological blow of losing the ability to provide for a family, plenty of women found pride in their new responsibilities.

Marjorie Hillis's contribution to this new reality was to suggest that a "household" did not have to contain a husband in order to require smart management, and offer insight into economics. Indeed, unmarried women, divorced women, wealthy widows, and single mothers could understand the relationship between what was earned and what was spent all the more acutely because they had no one to whom they could cede that responsibility. Quietly and determinedly they held their households together, took low-paying jobs, and bought cheap cuts of meat. They learned that they could survive, and that pleasure was not out of reach. For more

women than ever before, the Depression offered the thrill of independence, of work outside the home and the satisfaction of a paycheck with their name on it. Having never been treated as fully
equal or respected members of the labor force, women did not
attach the same level of self-worth or status anxiety to their jobs as
men, and were therefore able to think more flexibly about the ways
that the Depression's upheavals might be worked to their own, and
the nation's, advantage. Many of them never looked back.

4

SETTING FOR A
SOLO ACT

I n November of 1936, in one of the last issues of *Vogue* to which
she'd contribute as a regular member of staff, Marjorie Hillis
wrote a feature that reads like an extended, illustrated version of
one of her *Live Alone* case histories. Titled "Bandbox by the River," it
brought to life one of her own surest principles for Live-Alone success: trading a large, labor-intensive house for a small, convenient
city apartment. Although she admitted that such a move was often
not a choice, even for *Vogue*'s well-heeled audience, she nevertheless invited the reader to enter into the fantasy by imagining that
the change was "purely a matter of preference" on your part, and a
temporary change that one just might get used to. The woman in
the profile has packed her old furniture in storage, rented out her
summer home, and now lives in a Manhattan pied-à-terre. "It is a
far more modern way to live, she thinks."

The new apartment-dweller, like a case study in *Live Alone
and Like It*, wanted "a view—and open fire—sunshine—gaiety—

luxury—comfort—and chic," and has found all of her requirements on the edge of the East River in a small enclave called
Sutton Place. The apartment is on the ground floor of a building with a living room that opens onto private gardens, "with the
Fifty-Ninth Street bridge hung like a back-drop across the river."
In parentheses, Marjorie added her own defiant note about the
beauty of this particular view, which she shared from her apartment a few blocks south in Tudor City. "Some day, when just one
more person gets lyrical to us about the romance of the Seine or
the beauty of the Thames," she wrote, "we are going to get up and
make a speech about the East River, with its bridges and its boats
and its border of fantastic flowers."

Inside the one-bedroom apartment, small by *Vogue*'s standards
if not by regular New Yorkers', there is plenty of ingenuity on display. The "infinitesimal foyer" serves as coatroom, powder room,
and even—in an above-board revival of a popular Prohibition-era
apartment feature—a hidden bar: "One of the innocent-looking
doors opens, and there is a bar with bottles and glasses and shakers in racks, and a shelf lifts up to hold them." The living room is
set up for entertaining, with nests of tables that can be "set with
doily and glass and china and silver, as correctly as in the most
formal dining-room" and placed in front of guests around the fire.
In the bedroom, there is an extreme space-saving setup: two beds
stacked to create a "double-decker four-poster" with curtains going
up to the ceiling, a ladder, and integrated reading lights. In the
corner, there's a basket for the resident Dalmation. "The result is
a small apartment that has everything," Marjorie enthused. "We
mean really small, and we mean EVERYTHING."

The most striking feature of this apartment is the décor. Everything is painted a "pale sky-blue," from walls and ceiling to wood-

work, furniture, and picture frames—even "a lovely mahogany secretary" gets a coat of the same shade, so that it "melts into the wall." There are mirrors everywhere, taking up one entire wall and reflecting the garden by day, and at night, candlelight and "the necklace of lights that outlines the bridge." Even from the black-and-white photographs it's possible to get a sense of the impact of the wall of decorative plates above the fireplace, the sofa and matching armchair upholstered in a brightly contrasting chintz, pale deep-pile rug on the white floor, tall thin candelabras, and oversized lamp with its two-tone pleated shade. The exposed bricks around the fireplace are painted mauve, while the brass andirons and fender "have been finished in shining chromium." Even the terrace outside is shaded by a striped pale blue awning.[1]

The owner of the bandbox apartment was one of the most famous interior decorators of her day, and a divorcée identified in the article as "Mrs. Tuckerman Draper." Readers would have known her better by the name she used for her business: Dorothy Draper, or simply "DD." Like Marjorie Hillis, Draper was a child of the Victorian era in home decorating—a period of clutter and shrouded lamps, brocade and velvet and gloom—and equally eager to cast off its weight. Marjorie recalled with particular distaste the parlor of her childhood home in Brooklyn Heights, with its enormous chandelier, "a large sepia print of Sir Galahad resting on an elaborate brass easel" and "an enormous fern drooping from a tall brass plant-stand."[2] In the early twentieth century, she was far from alone in her desire to tear down the heavy velvet curtains and let in some daylight. No less a luminary than Edith Wharton (a Live-Aloner from her divorce in 1913 to her death in 1937) had begun her career as a writer with a book championing lighter, brighter living spaces. She brought her principles to life in the creation of the Mount, in Lenox, Massachusetts, her home from the turn of the century until the breakdown of her marriage, where she wrote many of the stories, essays, and novels that made her famous. In *The Decoration of Houses*, which she cowrote in 1897 with her friend, the architect Ogden Codman Jr., Wharton pushed back against the competitive opulence that marked America's Gilded Age, when millionaires vied with one another to build and furnish more and more garish palaces. Instead, the book took inspiration from eighteenth-century France and Italy, celebrating the balance and symmetry, light and space, to be found in elegant châteaus and palazzos. The authors' aesthetic preferences—for "sincerity," "harmony," and "simplicity"—handily doubled as moral judgments on the inauthentic excesses of the superrich.

When Marjorie visited Mrs. Draper's chic modern pad, interior decorating was still mostly an amateur pursuit, and decidedly an upper-class one. In contrast to the male-dominated profession of architecture, the early luminaries of interior design were women of independent means and ideas who shared Wharton's taste for light and symmetry if not for restraint. Dorothy Draper's professional trail was blazed by a handful of idiosyncratic forebears, including Elsie de Wolfe, a former actress and socialite who lived for many years with her female partner (and was a keen yogi, renowned for standing on her head at parties). But DD surpassed them all, and by the mid-1930s was on her way to being not only the most famous decorator, but one of the most famous businesswomen in America, guided by her inarguable dictum, "If it looks right, it is right." She transformed down-at-heel apartment buildings into the most desirable addresses in town, and she established the resort hotel as the quintessential midcentury space of glamorous, see-and-be-seen leisure. Moreover, she did it alone, after her husband made off with another woman (also, as it happened, an interior decorator) in the same week as the Wall Street crash.

Despite this double disaster, Dorothy Draper was a firm believer in looking on the bright side. When her husband left her, she started to see a psychiatrist, who recommended the teachings of positive-thinking guru Norman Vincent Peale. DD became so convinced of the power of optimism that she sold her brownstone and sank fifty thousand dollars (about three-quarters of a million today) into creating her own self-help correspondence course. The twelve lessons, which she advertised widely, made up a program of self-improvement called "Learn to Live." Her venture was unusual among such publications and programs for actually fulfilling its promises, and therefore proved to be a financial disaster—nobody saw the need to subscribe beyond the first issue or two, since by then, they reported, Mrs. Draper had solved all their problems.[3]

Tall, beautiful, and unflaggingly self-assured, DD's signature self-confidence was born, not built. Before she married a Draper, Dorothy was a Tuckerman, and the branches of her family tree were entangled with Roosevelts and Astors all the way back to the Mayflower. She grew up in the late nineteenth century in Tuxedo Park, New York, a rustic old-money utopia where staff wore uniforms topped with Tyrolean hats, and children like Dorothy believed they roamed free, until they banged up against the high, hidden fence ringing their kingdom. For the first nine years of her life she was an only child, nicknamed "Star" by her family, and educated only so far as was absolutely necessary. Although later in life she would sometimes regret her lack of schooling, in her chosen profession it hardly mattered—schools could not instill the vision and chutzpah necessary to saw the legs off an antique dining table, slap black lacquer on a mahogany dresser, or line a blue velvet curtain with lime-green silk and edge it with crimson piping.

Dorothy was a debutante before she was a decorator. In September 1912, she did the expected thing and married George Draper, known as Dan, who was as well born as Dorothy but bored by high society. A doctor from a family of doctors, Draper devoted himself to research instead of chasing the wealthy patients who might cement his social position. He became a specialist in the treatment of polio, at the time a mysterious and crippling disease, which remained a mostly theoretical interest until the mid-1920s, when his childhood friend Franklin D. Roosevelt was struck with its symptoms. Draper became FDR's personal physician, treating him in secrecy so as not to damage his political ambitions. The Drapers, who had three children, lived near Franklin and Eleanor Roosevelt in New York, in an Upper East Side enclave almost as exclusive as Tuxedo Park. Both Mrs. Draper and her neighbor Mrs. Roosevelt chafed against the conventions and restrictions of their environments, and both wanted to make the world a better place. For Dorothy that was a tangible, physical task: a matter of walls and furniture rather than laws and rights.

DD began her decorating career with her own home, a typically gloomy brownstone at the eastern end of Sixty-Fourth Street, tall and narrow and overshadowed by trees and other buildings. She decided to turn the house upside down by pushing the ground floor out to the back of the property line, swallowing up the dank backyard with a vast living space that could accommodate some two hundred party guests. The garden was simply lifted up to the roof of the extension, into the light. Her friends and neighbors clamored for her help, and being who they were, their interest and their influence counted. DD saw her opportunity to make the sort of money her husband was reluctant to chase. In 1925 she set up a business called the Architectural Clearing House, a kind of match-making agency between architects and society women who wanted to renovate their homes. Her social circle included real estate mag-nates like Douglas Elliman and the partners of the McKim, Mead & White architectural firm, who needed her "feminine intelli-gence" to shape their visions to female consumers. At first, they understood this intelligence in narrowly practical terms—Mrs. Draper reminded them that lady clients liked their dressing rooms and closets to be deep enough for coat hangers. But DD would not be patronized. She quickly proved that her understanding of what made a home pleasurable—plenty of light, a sense of drama, and above all, color—was not a matter of measuring tape but of soul. Soon, everybody wanted a piece of it.

In their private homes, however, few people wanted to bring in quite so much color, and quite such color, as Dorothy Draper. She quickly grew impatient with the restrictions imposed by cau-tious clients who preferred cream to crimson and began to pursue the public spaces that would make her a lasting legacy. In 1928 she took on the lobby of the Carlyle Hotel on Seventy-Sixth Street through her friend Douglas Elliman, and laid a bold black-and-white marble floor, a look that would become one of her signatures. Oversized mirrors, chandeliers, and marble columns heightened the drama of the small, transient space, and, softened with satin and velvet curtains and sofas, it became somewhere to linger. Even though the hotel went bust in the crash before it opened (it was sold and reopened later in the 1930s, when DD was hired to dec-orate the whole interior), the Carlyle was the first step toward her real life's work—reconceiving the public spaces of hotels as eye-catching social spaces, rather than bland pass-throughs. Today, chains like the Ace Hotel have revived DD's concept of the hotel-as-lifestyle, creating lobbies and lounges that look like fantasy versions of the guests' own homes, where they can hang out halfway between the public and private worlds.

Soon after she tackled the Carlyle, DD proved she had a knack for big results at low prices when she took on the renovation of a block of tenements at the southern edge of Sutton Place, on the far east side of Manhattan. The owners of the apartments had struggled to rent them, but had little money to spare for a serious overhaul. DD's renovation was purely cosmetic, and like a good Hollywood makeup artist, she focused on dramatic effects that would photograph well. She painted the grubby brick exteriors a uniform black and set them off with contrasting white windowsills and doors in primary colors. The dingy hallways were brought to life with flowered carpets and wallpaper, and the block was renamed Cannon Point Row. Before long, apartments that the owners had struggled to rent at fifteen dollars a month were fully occupied at more than four times that. After her divorce, the decorator ensured the new stylishness of the address by becoming a tenant herself, in the pale blue "bandbox" apartment Marjorie Hillis had so admired in the pages of *Vogue*. She shared the apartment and its double-decker bed with her youngest daughter, Penelope, then aged thirteen, and her Dalmation.

Dorothy Draper instinctively understood the power of rebranding, of a literal or metaphorical fresh coat of paint. After the dual shocks of the crash and her divorce, she ditched the dull-sounding "Architectural Clearing House" and put her central asset out in front, launching Dorothy Draper Incorporated with a distinctive logo of intertwined *D*s. In its heyday, her business made and lost eye-popping amounts of money, many times over. In the mid-

1930s, DD became the first female decorator to be entrusted with an entire apartment building renovation, signing a contract for just shy of four hundred thousand dollars to renovate Hampshire House, a thirty-seven-story white elephant on Central Park South. Her transformation gave the building an instantly recognizable identity, with a design scheme that pulled together everything from bedspreads to staff livery to matchbook covers. It was a legacy of Tuxedo Park, where the look was equally distinctive and seamless—you always knew exactly where you were, which was exactly where you, and everyone else, wanted to be.

As the upper echelons of the economy rebounded in the late 1930s, DD's style found more and more elaborate expression, and more and more devotees. Its apotheosis was the resort hotel, where the superrich would spend weeks or months at a time. These rambling, secluded palaces offered a prestigious but cheaper alternative to maintaining one's own country home or traveling to an insecure Europe on the brink of war. Instead, one might take the dedicated train to White Sulphur Springs, West Virginia, to the Greenbrier, owned by the Chesapeake and Ohio Railway—and carry on a life of luxury at the southern estate quite unselfconsciously nicknamed "Old White." The Greenbrier today is the most complete surviving example of Dorothy Draper's style, a riot of greens and pinks, wide stripes, and giant rhododendron chintz, a look that's been aptly described as "Scarlett O'Hara drops acid."[4]

In Southern California, meanwhile, a comfortable distance from Hollywood, the Draper-designed Arrowhead Springs resort became a retreat and a playground for movie stars—its gala opening in December 1939, featuring Rudy Vallee and Judy Garland, was broadcast around the country. During the war, as American belts tightened, a Brazilian gambling magnate came to the rescue of Draper's company with a project for a lavish casino resort in Petrópolis, outside Rio de Janeiro. By then, DD was over fifty and left most of the details and the stress of actually executing her projects to a loyal staff, although she remained the face of the brand and the wellspring of its vision. Her untrained instincts and her brash colors horrified more intellectual designers like Frank Lloyd Wright, who called her an "inferior desecrator" at a dinner at the Waldorf Astoria in 1952. Draper herself was in the audience, and didn't turn a hair.

Dorothy Draper was as successful as she was in part because she was that rare member of the truly wealthy who understood just how aspiration worked. It was not the same as envy. She knew that when people hired her firm or saved up to visit the Greenbrier, they were not just buying the trappings of a lifestyle, but the feeling that came with it—that this life was theirs, by divine right. In her Tuckerman youth, you had to have come over on the *Mayflower* to get into that exclusive club (or, as one matron of Boston high society famously claimed, to have sent your servants over on it). Now, you just had to have the money, and the confidence to stride across the polished black-and-white floor.

Hopeful Hostesses

Despite the fame of her resorts, DD never lost her interest in teaching ordinary people to live their best lives. More and more of those people, especially women, were taking an interest in the way their homes looked—whether or not they were married. Isabel Smart was one such woman. Like thousands of her peers in the mid-1930s, Isabel moved to the big city to make her fortune and found herself a Live-Aloner, by choice and circumstance. In a previous generation, she might have lodged in a boarding house with a motley collection of strangers, in an arrangement of shared meals, strict landladies, and close quarters. (*Vogue* editor Edna Woolman Chase looked back with nostalgia on her boarding-house days, remembering the setup as more protective and sociable than the "makeshift kitchenette-Hamburg Heaven kind of existence" that was the lot of the midcentury working girl.)[6] But although it could be lonely, a studio apartment like Isabel's spelled freedom: from a landlady's or a roommate's surveillance, from house rules and set mealtimes, and not least, from somebody else's taste in furniture. The living space that's tiny but all your own has long been part of the romance of the city transplant. For generations, ambitious, domestically minded Live-Aloners have deployed ingenuity and creativity, bolts of cloth and cans of paint, to turn unprepossessing, out-of-the-way apartments into jewel-box hideaways.

For Isabel Smart, transforming her "tiny, dreary little room," was not just an aesthetic choice but a social necessity. If she wanted to invite a male friend for dinner, things were apt to get uncomfortable, in more ways than one, with nowhere to sit but on the bed. Her inconvenient room was giving her an inconvenient reputation, as "the sort of girl who must always be taken somewhere and not brought home until it's time to say good night." But Miss Smart was aptly named. She decided to tackle the limitations of her room, using pillows to transform her bed into a respectable divan, and squeezing a table and chairs into a corner. Before long, her ingenuity was rewarded with more guests and invitations than she had days free in the week.

As it happens, Isabel Smart was not a real person, but a "case history of a young lady who was lonely."[6] She could have sprung from the pages of *Live Alone and Like It*, but in fact she was Dorothy

Draper's creation, and a character in her bestselling 1939 book *Decorating Is Fun!* On the hot pink striped cover of the book, a slim figure in high heels and a chic day-dress, who also might have flitted over from *Live Alone*, was poised halfway up a stepladder to adjust a curtain. Despite the book's lighthearted title, its author believed passionately that decorating was not a frivolous matter. The home was a stage set for the life you wanted to live, and decorating it with panache and personality was essential to domestic happiness.

Decorating Is Fun! was as much self-help guide as design manual. As bluntly as it set down rules of scale and symmetry, it also took the nervous housewife by the shoulders and gave her a good shake: Don't be a slave to tradition or to your mother-in-law's taste. Paint the ceiling, hang your own curtains, and fill the space with what you love. "Your home is the backdrop of your life, whether it is a palace or a one-room apartment," DD decreed. "It should honestly be your own—an expression of your personality." If her reader was a single woman, she might have no one to help her hang her curtains, but she'd also have to answer to no one's taste but her own. If that sounded daunting, the book could help, by teaching the fundamental principles of successful interior design (and successful living). At the top of the list was "courage."[7]

The high-society pedigree of interior design was showcased in the preface to *Decorating Is Fun!*, written by Mrs. Theodore Roosevelt Jr., daughter-in-law of the former president and cousin by marriage of the current one. Mrs. Roosevelt invited readers from all walks of life to participate. "Every woman in her secret heart believes herself to be a potential interior decorator," she wrote. To cater to this apparently universal feminine trait, a slew of dedicated interiors titles were launched in the magazine-mad 1930s, including *Country Life in America, House & Garden,* and *House Beautiful,* while decorating tips and advice columns became regular features in general-interest women's magazines. Dorothy Draper played her part, contributing an advice column to *Good Housekeeping*—although according to her biographer and professional heir, Carleton Varney, she tended to think of her column as something that happened by magic, and it was usually up to her loyal staff to get the thing written.[8] Even the rash of new movie-star magazines, like *Hollywood* and *Silver Screen,* showcased the stylish home interiors and spectacular hotel hangouts of the new celebrity elite.

At all levels of the magazine market, consumers were encouraged to imagine themselves into spaces and lives that were more elegant, coordinated, and luxurious than their own. Advertisers and retailers quickly responded to the aspirational spirit of the times. Instead of lining up wardrobes or dining chairs in uninspiring rows, department stores began to arrange their products on shop floors like miniature stage sets. As they browsed among couches and armchairs clustered around coffee tables, glowing lamps, and sparkling glassware, customers could mentally cast themselves in the role of happy housewife or chic hostess. Well before the era of design blogs and Pinterest, department stores and magazine culture suggested that a beautiful home ought to be displayed to the world as an extension of its inhabitants' personalities, and that keeping up appearances was as important inside the home as out.

Dorothy Draper's love of chintz may not now strike us as particularly "modern," but the ethos underlying all that bright flowered fabric was part of a larger revolution in what a home was supposed to look like and how it ought to function—as well as how it could be achieved. The style on display in department store advertisements aimed at Marjorie Hillis's readers was selfconsciously modern and suited to city living. Furniture was compact, efficient, and convertible, made of lightweight wood, glass, and the ultimate modern material, shiny "chromium." It was an Americanized version of the severe and spectacular European modernism of the 1920s, made "livable" during the Depression by a fusion of the forward-thinking ideas of Le Corbusier and the Bauhaus with reassuring domestic comfort. In 1934 the Metropolitan Museum of Art's exhibition of modernist American design featured creations by leading homegrown designers like Russel Wright and Gilbert Rohde, the latter praised by Lewis Mumford in *The New Yorker* as "one of the few designers who realize that 'modern' is something that you are, not a theatrical effect you try to achieve."[9]

Modern homes both reflected and shaped the modernity of their inhabitants. In contrast to older styles that divided space by gender, separating the masculine library from the feminine parlor, the modern home was centered on an open-plan, companionable space meant to suit both men and women. This unisex space was understood as semi-public and geared for entertaining and display, rather than as a private zone—whether one lived with a family or alone. Etiquette guru Emily Post's popular book *The Personality of a House*, first published in 1930, supported the notion that relaxation and social interaction were now the essential purposes of a living room. Its design should be flexible enough to accommodate spontaneous plans, like rolling up the rug for dancing, or pulling out card tables for a game of bridge or dinner around the fireplace. Although open fires were no longer an efficient form of heating, they remained powerfully appealing as a source of comfort and symbol of togetherness—thus Dorothy Draper, with her modular tables set for dinner around the flickering fire, could not have been more up-to-date for the late 1930s.

The modernist spirit in design quickly spread from museums to department stores. In 1936, for its special "Forward House" display, Macy's showcased ten interiors, including a "twenty-four-hour apartment" with multipurpose furniture. The display emphasized that each room told a story about its inhabitants and about the moment in which they lived: the colors used in the decor drew on contemporary art and fashion, even current makeup shades. "The rooms in cosmetic colors emphasize the fact that room colors can contribute to personality just as cosmetics dramatize feminine beauty," reported the *Herald Tribune*, underlying the idea that design was a woman's particular arena.[10] The designs in these interiors included everything from furniture to textiles to table settings. Russel Wright's hugely popular line of American Modern ceramic dishes, in up-to-the-minute shades of chartreuse, coral, teal, and gray, reflected his belief that informal, modern living began at the dinner table, the center of the home. It was around the dinner table that guests would gather, and through entertaining that the home would be thrown open to outsiders who would see in it an expression of the owner's individuality.

Entertaining Is Fun!

For Dorothy Draper it was a natural progression from decorating a home to sharing it with guests. Two years after she proclaimed the fun of decorating, she published a companion volume, *Entertaining Is Fun!*—this time with a cover design of bold pink polka dots. "Decorating and entertaining are halves of the same apple," DD wrote. "They are important parts of the art of living."[11] Successful entertaining, she went on, was a matter of spirit and attitude as much as money or menus. To invite guests, whether to an intimate dinner or a cocktail party for two hundred of your closest friends, was a sign that you were putting up a good fight against the pervasive Depression-era "will to be dreary," a gloomy marker of mental failure that echoes the language of Dorothea Brande's uncompromising *Wake Up and Live!* As the country slid closer to war, it was becoming harder to sustain the self-help illusion that bad things lay in the mind, not the world. But for a while, Dorothy Draper could just about convince her readers that a coat of paint and a party would make everything better.

That a single woman could entertain at home at all was a modern innovation. Twenty years earlier, the Live-Aloner who was not a wealthy dowager with an army of staff would have taken it for granted that she couldn't issue invitations. And who to, anyway? She couldn't have invited a mixed group without raising eyebrows, unless she were a bohemian living on the border of respectability in Greenwich Village. Most likely her social life would be monitored by her family, and it would be in the company of parents and siblings that she'd have to find her fun. Until she married, the idea of being a "hostess" simply wasn't for her.

But by 1937 things were different, and the Live-Aloner expected not only to feed herself but to throw open her home to guests. After all, what good was a chic apartment if no one else saw it, and what fun was there in preparing a fine meal if you couldn't share it? In this modern era, "you will find hopeful hostesses in everything from hall bedrooms to penthouses (and printed pyjamas to décolleté gowns) getting ready for guests," Marjorie Hillis wrote in her third advice guide for the solo woman, *Corned Beef and Caviar (For the Live-Aloner).* A cooking and entertaining guide that included

advice on everything from boiling an egg to the etiquette of inviting men for supper, the book was structured around a collection of
menus. These ran the gamut from simple suppers that a girl could
prepare for herself alone, to elaborate affairs that required at least
one maid, featuring dishes like roasted pheasant with "three indis-
pensable sauces" or a cheese soufflé that "has to be prepared with
care and prayer."[12] Taking obvious pride in his extended metaphor,
one reviewer praised the book by calling it "as smart as an hors-
d'oeuvre, as rich in substances as a two-inch porterhouse steak
and as cleverly put together as a club sandwich."[13]

To help write the menus and recipes in *Corned Beef and Caviar*,
Marjorie turned to her friend and colleague Bertina Foltz, a Vassar
graduate from Indiana who had gone to work at *Vogue* after college.
Unusually for the time, but following the lead of her boss Edna Woolman Chase, Foltz stayed in her job after her marriage in 1923 and
kept her maiden name professionally. As a beauty editor at *Vogue*,
Bertina had played a part in easing cosmetics into mainstream
respectability in the 1920s and '30s, endorsing Max Factor makeup
and showing readers how to mimic the dazzle of a Hollywood starlet
with the company's eyeshadow, lipstick, and rouge. From there she
had become the magazine's hostess editor, and her qualifications for
the job of coauthor of a cookbook lay in the sizzle, not the steak—
both authors freely admitted they were more interested in "the fun
in food" than the flavor. The idea of their joint cookbook predated
Live Alone, but on the heels of *Orchids on Your Budget* they dusted
off the plan and turned the book around in less than six months.
When Marjorie wrote in late September to ask if she could have a
little more time to check the proofs, Chambers replied that it was
impossible, given how fast his production team was already working to set the type, print, and distribute the book.[14] With an eye on

Christmas gifts, the publishers wanted the book out by November 24, so it could be offered both alone and in a boxed set with *Live Alone* and *Orchids*, priced $4.50 for all three.

Corned Beef and Caviar inspired women to host everything from conventional dinners and cheap buffet suppers to ladies-only teas or Sunday morning breakfasts, and is more inspirational than instructional. An adventurous Live-Aloner might try her hand at exotic "Bortsch" or "Zabione," stewed okra or white parfait, but the recipes contain little indication of what the finished dishes should look or taste like. The theme, mood, and appearance of a meal mattered more than its flavor—and reviews suggested it was fun to read "even if you have no intention of cooking."[15]

The gender of one's guest, or guests, was of primary importance. In common with many cookbooks of the era, *Corned Beef and Caviar* assumed fundamental differences between what men and women ate, so that a ladies' tea "should, of course, be dainty rather than hearty," featuring nothing more substantial than thinly sliced white-bread sandwiches.[16] Men, on the other hand, needed meat and liquor—especially if the hostess wanted him to stick around. The chapter "Getting the Man with the Meal" offers menus tailored to particular categories of male guest—young or old, teetotalers or drunks, crashing bores or potential Mr. Rights. A man who never touches alcohol is "seldom a true connoisseur of food," and gets a suggested meal of canned mushroom soup, chicken à la Maryland, string beans, and lemon chiffon pie. "We think this menu is TERRIBLE," the authors admit, "but the teetotaler will like it." His counterpart, the heavy drinker, is just as uninterested in food, so his hostess (who is strongly cautioned not to regard him as "a prospective beau") should simply prepare a meal to please herself, "and let him eat it or not as he sees fit." The uncompromising gourmet requires a serious outlay of time and money, and carries a high risk of failure: "Unless you are a Helen of Troy and a Peggy Joyce combined, a gourmet will float out of your life forever on the first dab of whipped cream you give him." These menus may lead to "other adventures," the authors promise, if a hostess plays her cards right. That meant that she must never appear stressed or apologetic; never try to serve a man his "native" dish, whether it's gumbo, chowder, or goulash; and never, never ask him to balance his plate on his knee—the chaise longue supper spells disaster for romance, and should be kept strictly as a solo affair.[17]

The Working Girl Must Eat

Not even the most determined Live-Aloner could entertain every night of the week, of course, but there were few resources that provided menus or recipes for one. Several reviewers noted that *Corned Beef and Caviar* was filling a clear gap in the market by giving working women at least a few ideas for solitary suppers. "Brief as this volume is, it provides assistance along lines no one else has ever deemed necessary to take any pains about," wrote one newspaper, while *The New Yorker* offered a surprisingly down-to-earth assessment, calling the book "an extremely practical little volume" that would be "a blessing to young women making a salary of less than fifty a week, who realize that the second men and parlormaid of the fashion magazines are not exactly their dish, but want savory meals and pleasant parties."[18]

Yet the problem of the solitary meal was not just a question of what to eat. Eating alone flouts more than just social convention: across cultures and eras, breaking bread at the family table is a fundamental human ritual, and a solitary meal is usually a matter of fuel, not fulfillment. "There is no denying that it is hard to make meals for one only seem worth the effort," Marjorie admitted in *Live Alone*. Years later, in an essay about eating alone, food writer Laurie Colwin put her finger on the secret pleasure and not-so-secret shame of these unsupervised meals: "People lie when you ask them what they eat when they are alone," she writes. "A salad, they tell you. But when you persist, they confess to peanut butter and bacon sandwiches deep fried and eaten with hot sauce, or spaghetti with butter and grape jam."[19] But Marjorie's vision of solitary happiness was meant to be one of pride, not secrecy. Was there a way to harness the pleasure of eating alone and jettison the shame—and the grape jam?

First, the family table had to go. Why should the Live-Aloner feel beholden to a piece of furniture that was little more than a bulky reminder of the company she lacked? Marjorie urged her reader to swap the table for a tray and take dinner wherever she fancied: at "a little table beside the fire," on a chaise longue, on the balcony, or in bed (she was a firm believer in the pampering power of breakfast in bed, so why not dinner?). Wherever one ate, it should look like an occasion, the table brightly dressed with cloths, napkins, dishware, glasses, and flowers. If a meal of corned-beef hash and coleslaw was to look like more than "pretty poor pickings," the backdrop needed to be coordinated and chic: "Black-and-tan checked linen . . . yellow pottery, amber glassware, and yellow marigolds in a black bowl," might not solve the existential challenge of dinner for one, but they would help to offset the gloom. Having dressed the table, the solitary diner should also dress herself, not in a restrictive evening gown, but something privately luxurious and impractical, like "a trailing négligée and froufrou" (presumably taking extra care how she ate her soup). Dress for the company you want, not the solitude you have, Marjorie insisted: "the woman who always looks at night as though she were expecting a suitor is likely to have several."

In *Corned Beef and Caviar*, Marjorie and Bertina Foltz offered soup-to-nuts meal plans for solitary suppers, which strove for maximum variety with minimum effort, resulting in some frankly bizarre combinations. The main selling point of "A Dinner Anyone Could Get"—chicken gumbo soup, Triscuits, baked beans, salad, and grapefruit—was that the beans would keep warm in a covered dish during the soup course, and there would be no need to get up and dash to the kitchen halfway through the meal. Lowering the bar even further, "If You Can Only Boil an Egg" and "All Out of Cans" promise to be quick and easy to prepare, even if they will only taste, at best, "perfectly good." The book strained to conceal the gap between the reality of affordable ingredients and the promise of elegant dining; creamed chipped beef, we are assured, is better than it sounds. Readers who belonged to an older generation, or shared its suspicion of canned foods like soup, spaghetti, spinach, and cherries, were reminded that Grandmother lived in inconvenient times, when such delights were not available. On the evidence of her first two books, Marjorie herself relied heavily on these convenient culinary shortcuts—in *Live Alone* she extolled "the great army of canned things" newly available to a Depression-era cook, and dispensed in two pages with actual cooking suggestions. The menus in her cookbook were guided more by style than flavor—"elegance," for instance, is the quality uniting a meal of mushroom beignets, boned trout amandine, wilted cucumbers in French dressing, asparagus vinaigrette, and cheese and biscuits.

The few other cookbooks that addressed time-pressed single women rarely suggested that eating alone, rather than cooking for a family, could be a pleasure. *The Working Girl Must Eat*, published the same year as *Corned Beef and Caviar*, made dinner sound like an obligation. It tried to minimize the effort by making the most of convenience foods—a natural extension, for its author Hazel Young, of her day job at the rapidly expanding General Foods conglomerate. Under the leadership of one of the twentieth century's wealthiest women, Marjorie Merriweather Post, who inherited her father's packaged-cereal company at the age of just twenty-seven, General Foods quickly absorbed brands like Birds Eye, Jell-O, Minute Rice, and Maxwell House. As the company grew, it relied on the expertise of trained nutritionists like Hazel Young to test new convenience foods and find ways to sell them. Young was exceptionally well qualified as a recipe writer, having studied chemistry and nutrition at Colby College and Yale, and, after quitting her job as a home economics teacher, going on to gain a master's degree in food and nutrition from Columbia. Her qualifications dwarfed the hostess-editing experience of Marjorie Hillis and Bertina Foltz, but she was similarly inspired by a problem of contemporary culture, which she believed she had the skills to solve.

At General Foods, there was an in-house store that sold food to employees, and day after day Hazel overheard her single secretary, Virginia, placing the same order over the telephone, for "hamburg and spinach." Finally she asked the girl whether she didn't get bored with her menu, and Virginia replied that it was the only thing she knew how to cook. Hazel began to write out recipes for her young colleague, and soon wondered whether her simple instructions might not help other girls, those her book called the "thousands like her who hold down jobs and also do some housekeeping." Her book held to the principle that there was no instruction too basic, teaching readers how to chop and blend while reassuring them that the dishes would turn out fine, as long as they followed the instructions to the letter.[20]

The cover of *The Working Girl Must Eat* announced its philosophy in both words and pictures. Side-by-side photographs depict a Rosalind Russell-type professional in suit, gloves, and jaunty hat ("Five O'Clock") standing at her apartment door and looking resigned to a dinner of canned spinach and Triscuits. But her Seven O'Clock self, presumably saved by the book, has been transformed into a smiling, apron-clad homemaker, happily laying a small table for two with tablecloth, dishes, and napkins neatly tucked into glasses. "Open it anywhere," the book invites, and the reader can share Miss Seven O'Clock's smile of relief that dinner is served, and solved.

Her smile might not have lasted long, however, once she saw the recipes, arranged in complex, multicourse menus that usually featured a main and side dish, a salad, and a dessert or even two. These at least made a concession to practicality by being arranged in a chronological sequence, so that leftovers from one meal could be incorporated into the next. The question of leftovers and the fear of waste could present acute difficulties for the Live-Aloner with only an icebox rather than a refrigerator. Marjorie Hillis, however, thought the problem was overstated. "Incidentally, we think Live-Aloners make too much fuss about the difficulty of using up left-overs," she wrote briskly. "People with families eat left-overs too, quite as much as you will have to." The secret lay in careful planning, and in resisting the temptation to roast a whole turkey for one.[21]

Like the menus in *Corned Beef and Caviar*, those in *The Working Girl Must Eat* were organized by sometimes mystifying logic, but the latter book did encourage its young cooks to be adventurous—a recipe for curried oysters included a note suggesting several other ways to use the unfamiliar spice, such as to "pep up a lamb stew." Although the oyster dish was simple enough, the menu it belonged to could hardly be called quick or convenient. Its full complement of rice, buttered asparagus, and stuffed celery salad, plus an apple brown Betty for dessert, would have dirtied every pan in the working girl's kitchen, and left her washing dishes for the rest of her night.

In 1940, on the heels of *The Working Girl Must Eat*, the true queen of midcentury convenience cooking made her debut in the pages of then five-year-old *Mademoiselle*, "The Magazine for Smart Young Women." As the author of 1951's *The Can-Opener Cookbook*, Poppy Cannon would become the face of 1950s packaged food in all its Jell-O-and-marshmallow glory, but her popularity was established early on, in these vibrant magazine columns. Cannon understood that a young working girl living alone found her independent life both exhausting and exhilarating, and she did not want to simply rehearse the staid existence of her married older sister. Unlike the poised-professional-turned-placid-homemaker of *The Working Girl Must Eat*, the *Mademoiselle* girl took risks, in her kitchen and her life, and Cannon urged her on to reckless heights. As food historian Laura Shapiro writes, "The heroines of her column were constantly inviting men to brunch or throwing together a spontaneous after-theater supper or staging a wedding breakfast for ten in a one-room apartment—even though they were working girls and had never cooked in their lives."[22] Their ingredients are whipped and sloshed and splashed; there's zest in everything and a sprinkle on top, and flavor is far less important than flair. The real joy of cooking as a single woman, according to this energetic new guru, lay in the anticipation of where a meal might lead—to company, pleasure, or (as Marjorie put it) "Who Knows What?"

The Labor—and Joy—of Cooking

It was not just Live-Aloners who had to learn to shift for themselves in the kitchen in the early years of the twentieth century. By the time the Depression hit, there had been a "servant problem," as the upper classes saw it, for at least twenty years. Employment options for white women, especially, had expanded over the first three decades of the twentieth century, so they increasingly rejected the drudgery of domestic service in favor of clerical, trade, and professional jobs. But in a labor market firmly segregated by race as well as gender, domestic service remained the dominant form of employment for urban African American women into the 1960s. At the same time, the overall number of servants steadily dropped; they made up almost half of all working women at the turn of the century, but less than a third by 1940. World War II, with its rapacious need for women's industrial labor, only hastened the decline. Over the same period, child labor laws were tightened so that girls stayed longer in school, largely thanks to the efforts of FDR's Labor secretary Frances Perkins. Immigration restrictions in the early 1920s further reduced the availability of cheap young maids from overseas, and in an increasingly urbanized landscape, there were more nondomestic work opportunities for women than ever before—spelling a sharp decline for a system of household management that had endured for decades.[23]

American homes were also beginning to look much more like the mechanized and efficient places they are today, equipped with hot and cold running water, gas stoves, central heating, washing machines, vacuum cleaners, and refrigerators. The spread of electricity was as fast as the flames from an overloaded circuit, leaping from novelty to normality in the space of a generation. In 1907 less than 10 percent of American homes were wired, and then only for electric light. By the time *Corned Beef and Caviar* was published in 1938, more than 80 percent of households boasted not just lighting but also electric currents that could power appliances. These innovations were prohibitively expensive at first, but their prices fell steadily until they were within the reach of middle-class households. Small electrical appliances, like toasters, waffle irons, blenders, and mixers, promised to make food preparation fast and fun. Home electricity was pointedly advertised as a technological solution to the problem of human labor. In 1923 one magazine described electricity as a female servant, "Push-Button Mary," that had the immeasurable advantage over her human predecessors of being "wageless and strikeless."[24]

But Push-Button Mary could never be more than a sous chef; someone still had to tackle the actual work of deciding what to eat, when, and how. According to *Orchids on Your Budget*, the Depression made it socially acceptable, even fashionable, for the upper classes to take an interest in food, where previously they would have been sneered at as "kitchen-minded."[25] This was making a virtue of necessity, as many of the women who now faced the task of cooking for their families could no longer afford hired help in the kitchen. But there was no doubt that a profound cultural shift was under way in the meaning and place of food and cooking in middle-class domestic life. The kitchen, once an out-of-sight servants' lair, was on its way to becoming the so-called heart of the home and the engine of social and family life. At the same time, a passion for food and a curiosity about its preparation was becoming an essential marker of cultural sophistication.

During the Depression, the threefold obligation to create cheap, nutritious, and delicious meals fell on the shoulders of wives and mothers as their patriotic duty—which they were now also supposed to find fun and fulfilling. In the day-to-day provision of family meals—where the rubber met the stove—the new, higher standards for food knowledge and interest only added to the pressure on women at home. The woman who came to the rescue of America's home cooks and reassured them they were up to the task was not a trained chef or culinary expert. She was a St. Louis housewife named Irma von Starkloff Rombauer, who spoke to nervous cooks like a trusted friend, and whose 1936 book would soon become a staple of kitchens across the country.

Irma Rombauer's recipe book was the product of the times in more ways than one, born out of both the national crisis and a personal tragedy. At the time of the Wall Street crash, Irma was fifty-two years old and had been married for more than thirty years. Her husband, Edgar, ten years her senior, was a lawyer with political ambitions, and the couple hosted regular dinners and parties at their home in the historic Shaw neighborhood of St. Louis, where they were respected members of the city's German immigrant community. Irma and Edgar lost their first child in infancy, but after that early bereavement had gone on to raise a healthy son and daughter, Edgar Jr. and Marion. The latter recalled that her mother was famous for her beautiful cakes, "masterpieces of delicate sugar frosting with garlands of wild roses cascading over the sides."[26] But the Rombauers' outwardly happy, hospitable life had a dark side. Edgar struggled with depression throughout his life, and in the winter following the Wall Street crash, the prospect of financial ruin triggered a severe relapse. On February 3, 1930, he committed suicide, leaving Irma with just a few thousand dollars in savings and no obvious way to earn a living.

Instead of throwing herself on the mercy of her relatives, Irma summoned her boldest Live-Aloner spirit, resolving to find a way to survive on her own terms. What was she good at? And what did people need? In the mid-1920s, she had offered a popular series of cooking lessons at the local Women's Alliance, so she now decided to try to bring her teaching to a wider audience, gathering her notes into a small compendium of what she called "reliable recipes with a casual culinary chat." No publishers were interested—the timing could not have been worse, with the industry floundering in the wake of the crash—so Irma, undeterred, enlisted her daughter Marion and her husband's former secretary in preparing and printing the cookbook themselves. Marion designed a striking blue-and-green cover depicting "St. Martha of Bethany, the patron saint of cooking, slaying the dragon of kitchen drudgery." The book's title, however, discarded allegory and boldly proclaimed its goal of turning a chore into a pleasure: *The Joy of Cooking.*[27]

The first three thousand copies sold briskly to Irma's friends and local contacts—so briskly, in fact, that they soon needed to print more. For a few years, the book sustained Irma as she published it out of her apartment, while she continued to try to convince a publisher that she was on to something. In 1935 she found her mark. On a visit to her cousin in Indianapolis, Irma met Marjorie's editor and regular correspondent Laurance Chambers, president of the local firm Bobbs-Merrill, over a game of bridge. She told him that she'd been looking for a commercial publisher without success, and Chambers—captive in a bridge foursome— agreed to take on *Joy.* The following year, Bobbs-Merrill published its version of Irma's cookbook. It had expanded to more than six hundred pages, and had lost Marion's whimsical cover art to a no-nonsense yellow and brown design that, on its dust jacket, established the central message of the book: It was all you needed. "As

American as ham and eggs, as modern as China Clippers and television, this is one of the most complete collections of recipes for good food ever assembled," the book promised. Not only that, it was detailed, practical, and thoroughly indexed as well.

But that was not why it sold. During the fall of 1936, Bobbs-Merrill's marketing department pushed *The Joy of Cooking* alongside its other big title, *Live Alone and Like It*, as handbooks to help women weather tough times. The books were frequently reviewed together on the women's pages of newspapers, but their similarities ran deeper than their overlapping audience. Both Irma Rombauer and Marjorie Hillis drew on their own experience to impart advice, and both made it clear that they and their readers were not so different. Irma had battled Bobbs-Merrill in order to maintain her distinctive "action method" of recipe writing, in which ingredients are highlighted as needed in the method, rather than assembled in potentially intimidating lists at the start of the recipe. She also persuaded them to leave in her chatty headnotes, which enticed the reader to try out a new dish and reassured her that it would turn out well. For home cooks, the joy of *Joy* lay in these notes, which made the book feel like an invitation to experiment in the kitchen alongside an encouraging friend. Mrs. Rombauer and Miss Hillis did not claim to be experts, and they did not condescend. Instead, they spoke frankly and with humor about making the best of life at home, even if it looked nothing like the life their readers had once expected.

The Joy of Cooking acknowledged that its reader was operating on a tighter budget and with less help than ever before, yet it generally assumed that she was feeding a family, had no job outside the home, and could put time and thought into stretching her grocery budget and preparing her meals. For the Live-Aloner supporting herself, who might have had little more than a hot plate on which to exercise her culinary talents, the goals were different: speed, simplicity, economy, and with luck, a little flavor. Joy—and *Joy*—could wait. But that didn't mean that Irma Rombauer couldn't lend a hand. In 1939 she published *Streamlined Cooking*, a title that proclaimed the modern spirit of a book that promised "Good Meals in 30 Minutes," using "Canned, Packaged, or Frosted Food." We often think of the 1950s as the heyday of these sorts of convenience foods, but they were already well established as cooking shortcuts by the 1930s, although cooks were usually urged to dress them up with fresh ingredients—at least, if they wanted to impress guests.

Streamlined Cooking was published shortly after *The Working Girl Must Eat*, and also aimed to help this species of cook, "the business woman who hurries home from the office to prepare the evening meal." But in addition, it spoke to the upper-class lady of the house who needed to manage temporarily without a maid, as well as to "the camper, the trailer-dweller, [and] the vacationist in a summer cottage." The meals in *Streamlined Cooking* were not going to show off anyone's culinary prowess, whether for a perfect rib eye or a platter of cucumber sandwiches, as the book made it clear that streamlining was for out-of-the-ordinary scenarios, not regular cooking. By extension, it implied that the single woman's nine-to-five life was similarly unusual and temporary, a reprieve before her real work of domesticity began. For a variety of reasons, including perhaps this implication that the recipes weren't for "real" meals, *Streamlined Cooking* was "a terrible flop."[28]

Books aimed at the busy female businesswoman rarely suggested that men might also find something useful in their pages. *Streamlined Cooking* did suggest that it might be of some use to the husband who had to make dinner because his wife was absent or sick, but if they did cook, men were supposed to look to entirely different guides. Although the working man must also eat, it was assumed he did not eat boned trout. Midcentury cookbooks like 1937's *For Men Only*, by Achmed Abdullah and John Kenny, worked hard to reassure men that their masculinity would survive a stint in an apron. These books insisted that a man only ever cooked as a hobby, preferably over a grill, and that when he did, the results were reliably superior to his wife's daily efforts. His tastes were assumed to run to the bloody, boozy, and bold, and away from such feminine treats as cakes, whipped cream, and garnishes of any kind.[29]

In the bestselling 1943 edition of *Joy*, however, several of the economically minded recipes from *Streamlined Cooking* were successfully repackaged. They looked newly appealing as responses to wartime rationing that restricted the availability of sugar, butter, and meat. Along with the very similar, postrationing update of this edition, published in 1946, it was this version—appealing to both men and women, and written with an eye to convenience and economy—that cemented the book's status as the kitchen bible for American households. It would retain that status through its multiple revisions well into the twenty-first century.

A Lady and Her Liquor

Corned Beef and Caviar made it clear that entertaining was not just a matter of food. With the exception of the occasional ladies-only affair of tea and sandwiches, the assumption throughout was that entertaining included cocktails, and possibly beer and wine too, depending on the menu. When *Live Alone and Like It* first appeared, three years after the repeal of Prohibition, it was no longer an act of rebellion for a single woman to keep her liquor cabinet well stocked. Indeed, according to Marjorie Hillis, it was a marker of a woman's sophistication that she could offer her male and female visitors a glass of sherry, a Scotch, or a properly mixed old-fashioned. But the bar was no place for fashionable, feminine frills: "Worse, even, than the woman who puts marshmallows in a salad is the one who goes in for fancy cocktails," she warned. The recipes Marjorie offered her reader were brief and bulletproof, for straightforward drinks like martinis and Manhattans. "Do not try to improve on them," she ruled. "You can't."[30] But that didn't mean that women's freedom to drink was universally accepted. On her *Live Alone* lecture tour, Marjorie told the story of receiving the whole of chapter nine, "A Lady and Her Liquor," in the mail, after it had been "torn out by an irate reader, who had scrawled over each page, 'delete,' 'delete,' 'delete.' "[31]

Marjorie was less sanguine about women going to bars alone, advising her readers to avoid them in favor of a lounge or restaurant if they really wanted a drink. In the introduction to her memoir *Drinking with Men*, an ode to the joys of becoming a bar regular, writer Rosie Schaap finds it "remarkable—and a little depressing" that so many women, even eighty years on, have internalized the warning from *Live Alone and Like It* that drinking alone in public will make them look "forlorn and conspicuous."[32] But as with many questions of "etiquette for a lone female" in Marjorie's book, this one has more to do with personal comfort than public judgement. In a bar, she argues, a woman alone can't be assured of peace and quiet, can't fully control how she's seen or treated, can't be mistress of her domain. A cautionary tale from her column, about the "young lady who didn't know when to stop," harshly recounts how drunkenness destroys a woman's appearance and composure: "her features slip and blur, her hair straggles, her eyes look vacant, and her dress doesn't seem to set quite right." It's the girl's vacant eyes that are really the sign that things have gone too far—she's all body, no brain, and is no longer in control of her situation or herself.[33]

At the height of Prohibition, when *The New Yorker* paid the young Vassar graduate and minister's daughter Lois Long to be its nightlife correspondent, the writer became emblematic of the flapper, in her loose dresses and looser morals. Flappers took very little seriously, especially drinking, and if they got married—as Long did, in 1927, to *The New Yorker*'s cartoonist Peter Arno— that marriage would be tumultuous, boozy, and probably short-lived (Long went to Reno for a divorce in 1931). In her nostalgic 1940 ode to that "foolhardy, collegiate, naive era" of Prohibition, Long remembered—or didn't, quite—nights drinking hard in the unlikeliest places, like the "respectable maiden-ladies' hotel" that "had a roaring bar in the basement, which you entered through a secret door in the back of the coatroom." Her stories regularly featured narrow escapes from police raids, when she was forced to scramble out back doors and sprint down alleyways in her evening gown. "You were thought to be good at holding your liquor in those days if you could make it to the ladies' room without throwing up," she recalled.[34]

While there was no going back to the teetotal past, the years after Prohibition's repeal saw a widespread effort to restore order by curtailing and regulating women's drinking. The major effort to retrain women's behavior and reassert public morality happened through the all-important cultural force of the movies, compelled since 1934 to follow the restrictions of the Hays Code.[35] In the early years of the Depression, the pressure to make movies morally improving—or at least not corrupting—struck the industry as a luxury for better times. Struggling studios and theater chains needed to pack in audiences, and tales of bloody murder and unbridled desire were reliably profitable. In 1930, the industry's ad hoc, state-by-state system of self-censorship had theoretically been standardized under a code of conduct nicknamed for Will H. Hays, the religious Republican head of the MPPDA, the Motion Picture Producers and Distributors of America (renamed the Motion Picture Association of America, MPAA, in the 1940s). For its first four years, however, the Hays Code was essentially toothless. Its weakness was best embodied in the curves and wink of the most bankable star of that era: brash, busty, brazen Mae West, whose films cheerfully violated both the spirit and the letter of the Code, by mocking the law, celebrating sin, and displaying plenty of "lustful kissing" and "scenes of passion"—not to mention public intoxication.[36]

But by 1934, following the end of Prohibition and under pressure from Catholic groups threatening mass cinema boycotts, Hays and his office had had enough, and put pressure on the studios to enforce the code in earnest. Until the adoption of the MPAA ratings system in the 1960s, the code regulated what stories could be told and how, operating on three general principles: (1) that villains and sinners would not win the audience's sympathy, (2) that laws of man or nature would not be ridiculed, and (3) that "correct standards of life" would be presented. These ambiguous principles were harder to enforce than the specific rules, which banned concrete elements like drug use, criminal acts, and disrespect of religion or the American flag. By far the longest list of taboos, however, was sexual. Movies in general were supposed to uphold "traditional" marriage, which meant that depictions of, or references to, homosexuality, interracial relationships, adultery, and prostitution were off-limits. Female independence was a particularly dangerous proposition. The single woman had to be brought into line, even if it was right at the end of a movie that had seemed, up to that point, to celebrate her freedom.

Directors therefore had to get creative if they wanted to push the boundaries of women's lives and relationships on-screen. In the screwball romances of the late 1930s, women's drinking often stood in for sexual indiscretion: drunk women misbehaving, and their regrets, allowed filmmakers to flirt with taboos and hint at what might happen if they followed their desires. In *The Philadelphia Story*, champagne flows through the story like a mischevious sprite, whose role is to reveal the characters' true desires. The film was one of a popular minigenre of so-called comedies of remarriage, in which a formerly divorced couple wittily reunites, often after the woman has tried a little Live-Alone and found she doesn't like it. Cary Grant made the role of the repentant, sometimes reformed husband his own in a string of such movies: 1937's *The Awful Truth* and 1940's *His Girl Friday*, as well as *The Philadelphia Story*, in which the remarriage depends on the woman's drunkenness and the man's abstinence. In a silent prologue, Grant's C. K. Dexter Haven is shown leaving the mansion he shares with his wife Tracy Lord (Katharine Hepburn) and raising a fist against her, before reconsidering and merely pushing her to the ground. When the story begins in earnest, two years later, Tracy is about to marry the uptight George Kittredge, when Haven reappears to win her back. We're told that it was drink that drove the couple apart—or rather, Tracy's Puritan intolerance for her husband's "deep and gorgeous thirst." Haven says that it would be good for Tracy's "foot to slip a little," by drinking too much herself, in order to humanize her and make her more sympathetic to his weakness—as well as to conquer her sexual frigidity (in one of the film's most vicious speeches, the hero accuses his ex-wife of belonging to "a peculiar class of the American female—the married maidens," who are too proud and prudish to have sex with their husbands). The perfectly proper, upwardly mobile George is content to worship at Tracy's feet, but her father, Haven, and Jimmy Stewart's infatuated Mike all conspire to shake her down from her pedestal. When Tracy and Mike escape a lavish party the night before the wedding—she in a watery Adrian gown with sequined epaulettes, and he in tie and tails, bottle of champagne in hand—it's a scene that places the society queen and the struggling writer on a newly equal footing through the leveling power of drink. Their ardent conversation, dance, kiss, and late-night swim stand in for a sexual dalliance. The next day, interrogated by Tracy's precocious little sister, the hungover pair are forced to clarify exactly what happened. Although at first she's horrified that Mike carried her to bed, Tracy is then even more incensed to learn that he left her there alone: Was she so unattractive? "You were *very* attractive," he protests, "but you were also a little the worse—or better—for wine, and there are rules about that." George, the middle-class stick-in-the-mud, is shocked by the rest of the group's ability to shrug off Tracy's wild night. "A man expects his wife to behave herself, naturally," he protests, leaving Haven to twist his words in the rejoinder, "A man expects his wife to behave herself *naturally*." George leaves when Tracy refuses to swear off drinking forever ("there was something about that girl, that Miss Pommery '24, I quite liked," she admits) and her ex-husband slips in as a substitute groom. Where the proper Tracy Lord was an ice queen, Miss Pommery '24 is flesh, blood, and feminine sympathy.

The idea that a little too much wine could soften a proud woman into a loving wife was one way in which the drinking culture—at least in upper-class circles—expanded to include women. After repeal, the demon drink was transformed into a symbol of style and modernity, shared by men and women, like the living room of the modern home. The cocktail, which in the 1920s had been a way to sweeten the bite of bootleg booze, became instead a chic accessory, thanks to figures like Harry Craddock, the British-born bartender who made his name shaking up drinks at New York's Knickerbocker Hotel until Prohibition chased him back to London and the Savoy. After presiding over the bar there for several years, he published *The Savoy Cocktail Book*: "A complete compendium of the Cocktails, Rickeys, Daisies, Slings, Shrubs, Smashes, Fizzes, Juleps, Cobblers, Fixes and other Drinks known and vastly appreciated in this year of grace 1930, with sundry notes of amusement and interest concerning them together with subtle observations upon wines and their special occasions." After repeal, an American edition reproduced Craddock's recipes and notes in an effort to establish "proper" versions of old and new concoctions, and to instruct readers on how to prepare and serve them. *The Savoy Cocktail Book* promised to reestablish class boundaries after the crash had smashed them, offering an "elucidation of the manners and customs of people of quality in a period of some equality." Knowing how to mix drinks, and how to hold them, became a convenient way to identify "people of quality."

Although she sounded like an old hand by the time she wrote chapter nine of *Live Alone*, "A Lady and Her Liquor," Marjorie Hillis was in fact fairly new to drinking. In an edition of her syndicated column titled "How Many Martinis?" she explained, "I am a minister's daughter and 10 years ago I had never had a drink." The only taste of alcohol she'd had by the time her parents died was a sip of wine or beer on European vacations, "taken in the same sight seeing spirit as art galleries and cathedrals." The column is yet another hint of the abject failure of Prohibition, if a practically teetotal minister's daughter dates her drinking life to around 1926, right in the middle of the great dry experiment. Ten years on, "I am an orphan and a business woman, and my cellar (under the shelf in the kitchenette) is as well stocked as my larder." Legal or otherwise, drinking represented liberation from old social and familial constraints. For a single woman it was also a statement of financial independence: stocking a home bar wasn't cheap. To invite guests and not offer a highball "seems like another form of sponging"—the worst social crime to be found in *Live Alone and Like It*. But it wasn't just a commodity—alcohol was cultural currency as well. "I like to be able to discuss the comparative merits of tequila and vodka along with those of Mussolini and Hitler or Duranty and Hemingway," Marjorie wrote. The true Live-Aloner should be able to hold court freely with men, whether the conversation turned to dictators or distillation.[37]

The majority of cocktail writers, then as now, were men—some bartenders like Harry Craddock, and others writers who cultivated bon vivant reputations, infusing their books with jet-setting glamour and masculine authority. The flapper, reckless goddess of the speakeasy, was a consumer of drinks, not a connoisseur. But in a post-Prohibition world, women would have a new role to play, as public regulators of drinking and drunkenness. As Americans prepared themselves to welcome alcohol back into polite society, several new guides set out to teach the finer points of domestic imbibing. A pair of books by women took the lead in setting their readers on the responsible course. Virginia Elliott's *Quiet Drinking*, published in 1933, was a restrained contrast to her previous, coauthored book *Shake 'Em Up!*, published "in the 12th year of Volstead, 1930." *Quiet Drinking* looked beyond the riotous cocktail, offering advice on beer and wines, as well as the best food to serve to soak up the booze—a notion quite alien in the speakeasy years. Choosing a favorite beer, according to Elliott, was a distinctly sober business: "Buy a bottle of each beer that is sold in your locality, then sit down calmly and seriously and taste them, chewing a bite of bread between each brand, until you find one most pleasant to your taste."[38] There is something appealingly purist about this almost monastic pursuit of flavor, which pays no attention to advertising or branding and trusts only in the individual taste of the drinker. Wine was an even greater mystery, since Prohibition had wiped out a nation's oenophile expertise, and as the author firmly decrees, "Consuming glass after glass of red ink in a speakeasy or Italian restaurant is not wine drinking."[39] Unless the reader has lived abroad, or belongs to a fortunate family that amassed a serious wine cellar before Prohibition was enacted, his or her wine knowledge was assumed to be nonexistent. At the time the book was published, anyone wanting to embark on the extensive (and expensive) business of wine self-education still had to persuade his or her doctor to write a prescription for a case.

Quiet Drinking doesn't openly admit to a fear of drunkenness, but in its emphasis on educating one's palate, serving drinks attractively, and always offering food to guests, the book makes clear that a sophisticated soirée no longer involved bathtub gin and swinging from the chandeliers. The line between tipsy and blotto was a fine one, which women, especially single ones, needed to walk vigilantly. In *Live Alone and Like It*, Marjorie waxed unusually poetic about the pleasure of alcoholic wooziness, that delicate state "when you arrive at the dinner-table, heaven knows how, and are aware that everything beyond the table is vague, like a semilighted stage-set, while the shirt-fronts of the men and the white shoulders and jewels of the women are more acutely accented than ever before." Things snap into focus, however, when the line is crossed: excesses like "shrill voices, familiarities, vulgar stories" are condemned as "frankly, disgusting."[40] Prohibition's anything-goes attitude was firmly in the past.

Virginia Elliott's contemporary Alma Whitaker—a *Los Angeles Times* columnist who in the early 1920s was an evangelist for the pleasures and health benefits of smoking—spent much more time on the risks of domestic drinking in her 1933 book *Bacchus Behave!* Her first chapter was one "In Which We Discuss Nectar and Manners," followed by "Simple Rules for Righteous Behavior." If readers forgot the central message (as they might, after the intervening chapters on cocktails, whisky, gin, brandy, liqueurs, wines, rum, champagne, and beer), they were brought back to the behavioral point, with the chapters "On Being a Good Guest," and "Customs to Frown Upon." The freedom to drink, according to Whitaker, was a fragile privilege, and a serious responsibility. "The success of the Repeal of the Eighteenth Amendment can be materially aided by your own scrupulous personal conduct," she wrote.[41] Post-Prohibition, liquor was no longer a scarce treat to obsess and fight over, like children with cheap candy. It was time for Americans to grow up, and consign the "appalling mixtures" and "reckless indiscretion" of the previous decade to the embarrassing past. All the sneaky trappings of the Volstead era, like the surreptitious hip flask, were suddenly "déclassé," decreed Whitaker, and hosts who had turned a corner of their home into an illicit bar were urged to "wall it up as you would an ancient crypt, for future historians to discover—and shudder over."[42]

The Depression-era turn to the domestic sphere benefited single women by allowing them to claim control over their worlds and close the door on what they didn't want to be or do. Yet for the successful Live-Aloner, the solitary ménage was by no means a hermitage. On the contrary, it could be a site of creativity and reinvention, a welcoming social space, and so much fun that she never even thought to miss the husband and children who weren't underfoot. But she needed to be on her guard, so that the guests she'd invited—especially the men—didn't overindulge and misbehave. It was a balancing act that, writ large, dominated the day-to-day existence of the Live-Aloner as she worked to guard her independence. To enjoy her freedom, but not too much. In the years to come, she would learn that her presence in the culture, and especially in the workforce, would always be ripe for backlash.

5

WORK ENDS AT NIGHTFALL

Careers for Seven Women

In April 1938, Marjorie Hillis first shared with her publishers her cherished idea of a book of verse, which she originally called *If Women Must Work*. It was constructed as a long narrative poem, *Careers for Seven Women*, broken up with a series of sonnets. It would tell the story of seven friends with different jobs and attitudes toward work, and attempt to dramatize the challenges and compromises that met working women at every stage of their careers.

Inside the publishing company, the new project met with a distinctly tepid response. One of the first readers admitted that she didn't have a strong grasp of the mechanics of poetry, but nevertheless thought the lines didn't scan properly, and seemed "labored and uninspired," although she was at a loss to know how it could be fixed. The rhymes and language were simple, and for the most part lacked the "sparkle" that this kind of light verse needed—although there were plenty of "epigrammatic and quotable lines."

A second internal report deemed the sonnet series "exceedingly uneven," and Marjorie would eventually drop them after her brother, Dick, read the manuscript and concurred. The narrative poem, on the other hand, was "distinguished by the sort of knowledge and understanding of feminine character, biting yet sympathetic, that one has come to expect of the French." Marjorie Hillis was no Dorothy Parker, this reader noted, nor even "a Margaret Fishback," the copywriter-poetess whose career was then at its height. But her poems were "human," her characters "recognizable," and the result appealing, if "neither deep nor important."[1]

Despite these reservations, the publishers thought the book could be a modest success with Marjorie's eager fans, more for its subject matter and the author's name than the brilliance of its poetry. The press release emphasized that the author was an authority on the "hopes and heartaches, ambitions and disappointments" of working women, and that her characters represented types that would be reflected in real women across the country. Through "the unusual medium of verse," the release added rather nervously, the author was able to dramatize a different side of their lives—those "spiritual and psychological needs" that were not being met by economic independence alone.

Work Ends at Nightfall was published on August 31. Three days later, Marjorie sent an anxious cable to her publisher about the lack of press attention in New York, and proposed either sending the in-house publicist out to meet personally with reviewers, or engaging an external publicity person, at a shared cost, to try to push her own ideas for promotions and news stories—she was ready with the names of two such "go getters." She had already supplied a list of previously supportive reviewers who might be called upon to say something in praise of the book. But nothing much could move it.

By November, after the British publisher of her earlier books had politely declined this volume, hopes for its success were fading. It had sold about five thousand copies by this point—"not bad for a book of verse," her publisher acknowledged—but it wasn't going to get close to any bestseller lists. There was some small comfort for Marjorie when an acquaintance asked to set the poem's "lullaby" verses to music—but one small song was no match for the chorus of praise she'd previously enjoyed.

Laurance Chambers defended the company against Marjorie's disappointment. "Every one in our organization was keyed up over it, and we worked like sin," he insisted in January, laying out how much they'd overspent on advertising that hadn't resulted in sales. It was always a gamble, he reminded her. "Selling poetry is a tough job except where the critics recognize the author as a poetic genius (and by no means always then)." In the final reckoning, the fault wasn't in the publisher's lack of effort, but in the lack of enthusiastic readers. "So please don't kick us. Kick the dear public."

Nevertheless, there were no tie-in department store displays for *Work Ends at Nightfall*, nor did Marjorie set off on a nationwide promotional tour. (One display ad for Macy's did do its best to capitalize on the lucrative potential of a new Live-Alone book, declaring: "Read Marjorie Hillis's new book 'Work Ends at Nightfall,' and you'll rush right out and buy yourself a new housecoat. Sketched is a colorfully embroidered slipper rayon satin in black, wine, royal and blue. 7.98.") The subdued publication was not exactly surprising, as the new book was a departure in tone as well as form. For the first time, the *Live Alone* queen seemed to be casting serious doubt on whether independence really was a route to happiness.

Poetry was not a new pursuit for Marjorie, who had written verses for *Vogue* and for various newspapers when she was younger—and it also wasn't as strange or noteworthy then as it would be today for a journalist to produce, essentially, a novella in verse. Poetry, of an accessible, conventional sort, was still widely read, and it was a truism that there were certain kinds of intimacy and ambiguity and emotion that a writer couldn't attain any other way. The publisher's advertisement relied on this idea, touting the book's use of "the universal language of poetry" to reveal the "unspoken thoughts" of working women "with beauty, frankness and understanding." The reviewer for the *Los Angeles Times* likewise saw no particular obstacle in the form: "Marjorie Hillis has gone poetic on her readers, and they'll like it." Even "those who shy away from poetry," he (or she) reassured his readers, "need not shy away from her."[2]

Two weeks after the book appeared, Marjorie celebrated at a joint party thrown for her and the novelist Dawn Powell, who had just published a new novel, *The Happy Island*. Powell shared a publisher with Marjorie's rival Dorothea Brande, and although Marjorie's satire was gentler, both writers were frequently likened to Dorothy Parker. Their books cast a sidelong, skeptical glance at New York society and women's place in it; the *New York Herald Tribune*'s book columnist explained of Powell's novel: "Happy Island means Manhattan, and the title is writ sarkastic [*sic*] . . . It illuminates the desperate situation of people who hate New York and can't stand living anywhere else—besides which, nowhere else could stand them either . . ."[3] Marjorie's characters in *Work Ends at Nightfall* were not as glamorous as Powell's cast of café-society denizens, but both authors were concerned with questioning New York's reputation as the natural and most congenial habitat of the independent woman, especially, in Marjorie's case, one who was no longer quite young, and who felt herself lacking the energy to continue making the compromises the city so relentlessly demanded.

The seven friends in *Work Ends at Nightfall* meet after work "in one of those dim restaurants / Where chiefly women gather," a claustrophobic and unglamorous place full of "milling femininity" and "minor dramas." First to arrive are Eileen and Nancy, an advertising executive and a photographer, who order a daiquiri and a Scotch and soda and await the others. Next is Kate, "plain, dun-colored" and eager to please, a columnist who is married to a man she doesn't love—and is torn between triumph that she has a man at all, and misery that he is so unpleasant. Claudia, a stylist, is a quintessential Live-Aloner, "slim and composed" and the happiest, or most self-satisfied, of the group, while Irene, "a dainty, fluttering woman," is a stenographer whose hopes for a romantic future are fading. Last to arrive are Martha and Mary, bearing biblically appropriate names: a selfless, religious social worker and a besotted mother. The balance of jobs the seven share is somewhat unrealistic—five are professional, and only two (Irene, the stenographer, and Mary, who works in a gift shop) do the kind of routine, low-paid jobs that actually occupied most working women in the 1930s. The Depression benefited women workers in several ways, but it took its toll on those who had managed to fight their way into prestigious fields like law, medicine, and higher education. The decline in opportunity was small as a percentage of those fields, because they were still so male dominated, but it represented a larger decline in possibility. As one historian sums it up, "by 1940, only one woman job holder in ten could be classified as a professional; the remaining nine were clustered in clerical, sales, manufacturing, and domestic service."[4] Five out of seven is clearly no one in ten—though perhaps Marjorie might protest that among such a small and sinking band, it would hardly be surprising for professional women to cling together once they had found one another.

All the women in the poem are interested in discussing their working lives, but their rivalry is obvious in the private reflections they make when another speaks. When Irene, the stenographer, complains that "Such work as ours is hard," the others immediately think, "Your work and mine are surely not the same."[5] Irene is desperate for solidarity from the other women, but her job places her below them in prestige, and they don't want to equate her labor with their careers. Despite popular culture's promise of office romances, Irene has discovered that it isn't there, beside a desk, that "A man chose a woman to take in his care."[6] When her workday ends, there is nothing for her but to go home, alone.

The poem suggests that there is a particular pleasure and privilege to work that *doesn't* end at nightfall, represented by stylist Claudia eyeing the new fashions on the restaurant-goers and journalist Kate keeping her eye out for stories. Marjorie herself described this thrill in her own work as a writer and lecturer, of not knowing where business ended and social life began, "as everything I did opened up some new channel and it was all exciting."[7] Kate admits that they are guilty of letting their work "engross" and "absorb" them to the exclusion of other pleasures, and Claudia agrees:

> *"Women don't know when*
> *Their work should end, their private lives begin;*
> *Or sometimes it's the private lives that win.*
> *We need more balance."*[8]

For Eileen, the wealthy advertising executive, the problem is that work is still new enough for women that they haven't yet learned to take it for granted, or fit it easily into their lives, as men do.

Marjorie Hillis's parents,
Newell Dwight Hillis and Annie
Louise Patrick Hillis, were both
Midwesterners. They met at Lake
Forest College near Chicago and
married in 1887. *(Courtesy of the McHenry
County Historical Society)*

When Dr. Newell Dwight Hillis
arrived in Brooklyn in 1899 to
lead Plymouth Church, admiring
newspaper reports described
his intense gaze and forceful
personality, and he became a local
celebrity. *(Library of Congress Prints and
Photographs Division)*

Marjorie Hillis embraced the role of Live-Alone ambassador, signing books and addressing audiences across the country. Her ideas were very different from her father's, but she inherited his charisma and skill at public speaking. *(Courtesy Lilly Library, Indiana University, Bloomington, Indiana)*

"Live Alone and Like It" soon became pop-culture shorthand for female independence. Claudette Colbert, playing Gary Cooper's unhappy wife in the 1938 comedy *Bluebeard's Eighth Wife*, reads the book as she contemplates her escape. *(Courtesy Lilly Library, Indiana University, Bloomington, Indiana)*

The cover of Marjorie Hillis's first bestseller, *Live Alone and Like It*, implied that a single woman's indepedence would be rewarded with male attention. But the book itself made clear that men were not essential to her happiness. *(Courtesy Lilly Library, Indiana University, Bloomington, Indiana. Reprinted with the permission of Scribner, a division of Simon & Schuster, Inc. All rights reserved. From: 1936 Book cover edition of* Live Alone and Like It *by Marjorie Hillis. Copyright © New York: Scribner.)*

Department-store shoppers were encouraged to purchase the stylish accessories for a Live-Alone life along with the book. In San Francisco, a window display invited shoppers to "relax luxuriously in this pink and frothy NEGLIGEE." *(Courtesy Lilly Library, Indiana University, Bloomington, Indiana)*

Marjorie's publisher Bobbs-Merrill enjoyed another success in 1936 with Irma Rombauer's *The Joy of Cooking*, which the St. Louis housewife wrote to support herself after her husband's suicide. By the 1950s, it was a household staple. *(Schlesinger Library, Radcliffe Institute, Harvard University)*

As Kitty Foyle in the 1940 film, Ginger Rogers played the quintessential "white-collar girl" and gave voice for young working women's struggles to balance independence and romance. Her signature white-collared dress became iconic. *(RKO Pictures, 1940)*

In one of her last features before she left *Vogue*, Marjorie Hillis profiled the famous interior designer Dorothy Draper in her chic "bandbox" apartment, which the divorcée shared with her daughter and her Dalmation. *(Peter Nyholm/Vogue, November 15, 1936 © Condé Nast)*

She's a NICE GIRL

but she COMMUTES

SHE plays the piano and speaks excellent French but her habit of commuting is one her friends can't overlook. Leaving theatres and parties early to catch a train is a nuisance as well as inexcusable—when she could live in Tudor City and see things through to the end. There is more time at the other end of the day too, if you live in this quiet community—only a few minutes' walk from all that makes life interesting as well as profitable. Tudor City is high, quiet and airy, on the East River front—with its own shops, restaurants, parks, garage, even a miniature 18-hole golf course . . . as well as maid, valet, laundry and meal service. A wide variety of apartments at reasonable rentals. Renting office at the East end of 42nd Street. (Vanderbilt 8860.)

Your choice of 147 different kinds of apartments in 7 buildings. Hotel apartments, 1, 2 and 3 rooms: $900—$2700. Housekeeping apartments, 1 to 6 rooms: $800—$3900. Additional apartments ready this Fall.

FRED F. FRENCH MANAGEMENT COMPANY, INC.
551 Fifth Avenue, New York City Vanderbilt 6320

LIVE IN TUDOR CITY
AND WALK TO BUSINESS

Tudor City, where Marjorie's Live-Alone theories were born, was heavily marketed as a chic alternative to suburban living. A playbill advertisement targeted theatergoers tired of rushing out to make the last train. *(Manuscripts and Archives Division, New York Public Library)*

The 1939–1940 World's Fair in New York inspired Marjorie Hillis's fifth book, a guidebook aimed at women visiting the city alone. The Fair's own publicity showed it off as a stylish destination for adventurous female travelers. (Manuscripts and Archives Division, The New York Public Library)

During the fair, the newly married Marjorie Hillis Roulston chaired the Brooklyn branch of the National Advisory Committees on Women's Participation, which culminated in a special "women's week" in May 1940.
(Manuscripts and Archives Division, New York Public Library)

When Marjorie Hillis married wealthy widower Thomas H.
Roulston at the age of 49, she submitted as gracefully as she could
to the media's gloating. Her happiness, she said, outweighed any
embarrassment at having finally capitulated to matrimony. *(Wide
World Pictures)*

By 1967, when her final
book was published,
Marjorie Hillis looked
like a wealthy dowager—
but her advice for single
widows and grandmothers
still insisted on a life full
of pleasure and fierce
independence. *(Photo by Frances
McLaughlin)*

In an interview with the women's page of the *Baltimore Sun* after
the book's release, Marjorie referred to her characters as though
they were case studies to explain her belief that taking pride in her
appearance had the power to shape a woman's happiness. "Take, for
instance, Claudia and Eileen in my last book, *Work Ends at Nightfall*,"
she said. "They were successful because they were meticulous—or
I might say, because they lived meticulously. Kate and Irene didn't
bother, and just let themselves go, so as a consequence they got the
second best from life instead of the best, which they desired."[9] Claudia, the stylist, is the happiest of the seven in her small apartment
in a remote, shabby neighborhood. Her happiness gave Marjorie
a way to prove her point that domestic surroundings had a powerful effect on happiness, and the author equates Claudia's pride in
her three rooms to Mary's in her sleeping child. Claudia has chosen and knows every object in the apartment, so that "Every little
charming part / Of her rooms, made up a chart / Of the travels
of her heart."[10] Eileen, by contrast, is successful enough to afford
a high-floor apartment reflecting the height of her ambition, but
its beauty has been purchased, rather than curated. Her expensive
"deep, pale rugs" and "calla lilies in a crystal vase" give Eileen less
happiness than Claudia's quirky statues and paintings.[11]

Kate, despite finding her job as a journalist rewarding, finds her
personal life miserable. Although she has long enjoyed "the pride
plain women feel / At winning any man," her "morose and critical"
husband makes her home life miserable. Single Nancy, meanwhile,
believes that "If you're lonely, there is laziness behind it,"[12] and has
almost too much male attention. She devotes herself to romance so
determinedly that she neglects her home, which is a "workmanlike
and bare" studio.[13] One of the manuscript readers picked up on
a contradiction—or perhaps hypocrisy—undermining the character. "It seems as though the author wasn't quite sure what Nancy

proved. She tries to make Nancy's promiscuity a natural thing, and then turns around and condemns her freedom as license."[14] But Nancy's problem isn't too much sex, but too little care of herself.

Along with Claudia, Mary, the mother, is the most fulfilled of the seven, although her satisfaction is chillingly expressed as relief that she can now sink her ambitions into her child, rather than try to fulfill them herself: "All your broken wishes will / Mend themselves and live in her," she thinks, as she watches her baby sleep.[15] Her husband, "stirred / By her sweet frailty," treats her like a child, and she has mastered "the useful gift / Of helplessness"—hardly a victory to celebrate.[16] Martha, the social worker, feels empathy for the others but wants to find a definite answer to which way of life, work or marriage, is better for women. She finds herself, on her way home, in an ornate chapel, where a glimpse of the nuns comforts her with the reminder that there is no one way of life that will make every woman happy, and that each of them must find her own way to make her life count.

We Need More Balance

Work Ends at Nightfall gave Marjorie an opportunity to dramatize the challenges for working women that weren't simply a question of money and budgets, as she'd discussed in *Orchids* and elsewhere. Her ambivalence about what it meant—and what it cost—to be a "career woman" reflected the culture at large, which was still not prepared to truly embrace women's professional ambitions, nor to make the allowances that would enable them to combine work with family life.

Marjorie didn't see her own job at *Vogue*, much less as a full-time writer, as simply a way to support herself. After her parents died and her family obligations faded, she began to derive a stronger sense of identity from her status as a career woman. "I had never taken it very seriously," she recalled later, while her pious and bookish family "had never taken it seriously at all." But she valued *Vogue* more as her status there rose, after she'd become accustomed to the "free and easy" attitudes of the younger women and "very, very fancy young men," with whom she worked.[17] Even at the deepest moments of family crisis, she did not leave the magazine until her books were truly successful, launching her on a new and higher-profile career.

Historian Alice Kessler-Harris has long argued that the division of women into workers and nonworkers is ideology, not reality, and that women have always worked, whether or not they have received a salary. It was only when the self-contained homestead, as a site of labor and production, gave way to factories, stores, and offices, that women's domestic work was separated and sidelined. Running a household and raising children were reconfigured as a blend of moral duty, pleasure, and spiritual fulfillment—a blessing set against the curse of "real," paid work. The veneration of the domestic sphere cast a long shadow over the labor of women who wanted or needed to earn a wage; the so-called "Mommy Wars" remain a convenient shorthand for the way women are encouraged to face off against one another's choices with a mixture of envy, pity, and contempt. The cultural divide between "stay-at-home" and "working" mothers obscures the larger structural reality: that women's "free" domestic labor has always had an economic value, and is fundamental to the working of capitalism.[18]

Marjorie's approach to the still-vexed question of "work-life balance" was forward thinking in that she refused to frame it as a trade-off between work and "life." Instead, she called women who worked outside the home "two-job women," for whom the variety—if they were efficient—could make both jobs more enjoyable. Men who insist on their wives staying home are portrayed in her books as old-fashioned fogies, who fail to appreciate the benefits of a wife's job to both partners: "Our personal opinion is that the average wage-earning woman is more interesting and keeps younger and handsomer than if she stayed home, whether she really likes working or not." Her advice for women in the workforce who were there by necessity rather than choice was refreshingly straightforward: "don't worry too much." Being in an office all day would only make home feel more charming—and the children would be fine.[19]

But in this blithe opinion she was swimming against the tide. Married working women faced discrimination and negative public opinion throughout the 1930s, not to mention outright bans on their participation in several states and industries—and the notion that working women were taking jobs from unemployed men was persistent throughout the Depression. But despite this, the number of women working outside the home grew steadily over the course of the decade, and included many who had families. In *Orchids on Your Budget* Marjorie cites a figure of "something like ten and a half million" women in the workforce, which by the 1940 census had climbed to 13 million, or a little over 25 percent of all women over the age of fourteen.[20] The proportion of married women working increased nearly 50 percent over the course of the decade.

We might assume that for these women, working was not a choice but a necessity. Yet a surprisingly large proportion of them (40 percent in 1940) had husbands who were bringing home a reasonable income, more than a thousand dollars a year. How far that stretched depended on many different factors, particularly how many mouths there were to feed, but it suggests that a significant number of women were following Marjorie's advice and looking for work in order to get a little extra pleasure in their lives, hoping to earn enough to allow for more "trimmings" than their husband's salary would cover by itself. However, we should be wary of this notion of women's work as supplementary—Marjorie only had to look in the mirror to know how essential it was to her sense of self, even though she could have survived quite well on the inheritance from her family. The roots of the entrenched gender-based pay gap lie in this idea that wage work for women is a choice, not essential to their identity as it is for men. In the Depression, as in the wake of the 2008 recession, it was women who gathered up the scraps from the shattered economy, piecing together part-time and temporary work that men couldn't or wouldn't do. Because the jobs that are always there—tending to the sick, the elderly, and small children; cleaning private or public spaces; soothing and managing the needs of wealthier people, travelers, or restaurant diners—are the jobs for which women are presumed to have natural aptitude, even desire.

In earlier eras it was widely assumed that for white, middle-class women there was a basic trade-off between work and family: you could have one or the other. But during the Depression, American women could look to a new role model in the First Lady. Female voters had played a crucial positoin in President Roosevelt's 1932 election, and his wife Eleanor represented a version of marriage and work that was unlike anything anybody had seen in that position before. Through her lectures, columns, and books, through her regular all-female press conferences, and through her highly visible public persona, Eleanor Roosevelt set an example to the nation that women's contributions were valuable. She showed American women that they had the right and responsibility to participate in the economic life of the nation, whether they were married or not. She fought the idea that a wife, mother, or Live-Aloner was a social and economic burden rather than an agent. In 1936, because of the First Lady's activity outside the home and her engagement with the world, Marjorie Hillis called her the "perfect example of the live-aloner, despite the fact that she has a husband and children."[21]

Mrs. Roosevelt regularly drew connections between women's domestic lives and their political potential. "When we come to finances we realize that after all, all government, whether it is that of village, city, state or nation, is simply glorified housekeeping," she wrote in 1932.[22] Her book *It's Up to the Women*, published the following year, expanded this theme and drew on her past efforts as an advocate for women's suffrage to insist that women could and should play a role in public life. Her notion that women's ability to manage a family budget qualifies them to be stewards of the national economy has been reiterated by female politicians ever since, even by Sarah Palin, hardly an obvious heir to Roosevelt, during the 2008 presidential campaign.

The 1930s saw women answering the First Lady's call and taking an unprecedentedly high-profile role in national political life. The most prominent among them was Labor secretary Frances Perkins, the first woman appointed to a cabinet position and a champion of Social Security and minimum-wage laws that transformed the lives of millions. By the time President Roosevelt invited her to join his cabinet, Perkins was a veteran of the fight to improve America's working conditions. It's easy to forget how recent, how inconsistent, and how fragile are our supposed rules about work—the regular time off, the predictable schedule, the idea that children and teenagers should be in school, not in the workplace. In the fight to treat workers as people, Perkins faced powerful opposition from captains of industry who had grown rich treating them as machines, and saw no obligation to care for machines that had broken down. Yet even the protections introduced under the New Deal were patchy and piecemeal: Social Security, when it finally arrived, did not extend to domestic or farm laborers—meaning that the benefits were largely unavailable to the African American women and men who were clustered in those jobs. Fixed schedules, fair pay, and a secure future were still privileges determined by race as well as gender.

As a prominent public figure, Frances Perkins was a powerful symbol of what a woman could achieve independently. Unlike the First Lady, whose role remained tied to and contingent upon her husband, Perkins's husband had no public role. She married economist Paul Caldwell Wilson in 1913, but insisted on keeping her name—a controversial measure at the time. The couple had one daughter, Susanna, and the marriage endured despite Wilson's increasingly severe bouts of mental illness and frequent spells in institutions. Susanna also suffered from what was probably bipolar disorder, and Perkins supported her family alone.[23]

Perkins's decision to keep her birth name on her 1913 marriage certificate anticipated the formation a few years later of the Lucy Stone League, a coalition of women inspired by a nineteenth-century suffragist who kept her name when she married in 1855. The founder of the modern league, Ruth Hale, went to court in 1921 to demand that the government issue her a passport in her own name and not that of her husband, journalist Heywood Broun, who supported her crusade. Hale refused to accept the compromise of a document that listed both names, and canceled her travel plans, but soon afterward, she succeeded in becoming the first married woman to have a property deed issued in her own name. She was joined in her fight by other prominent literary women, including Jane Grant, cofounder of *The New Yorker* with her husband Harold Ross, and writers Fannie Hurst, Zona Gale, and Anita Loos, author of *Gentlemen Prefer Blondes*. Thanks to the fame of its members, and of the Algonquin Round Table, to which many of them belonged, the league and its battles achieved cultural prominence in the years just after the passage of the Nineteenth Amendment, when interest in women's rights was at its height.[24]

There were many battles still to fight. A married woman, for much of the twentieth century, could not register at a hotel under her own name, nor open a bank account or a store account. She could not take out an insurance policy or a copyright, could not receive a paycheck or register to vote, and could not get a library card.[25] The Lucy Stoners' fight was rooted in the belief that marriage ought not to mean that a woman disappeared from the public into the private sphere. They battled the remnants of coverture laws that clung on in the modern world, and declared that they could still remain, after marriage, the people they had been before. Their motto made that idea plain: "My name is my identity and must not be lost." As its scope expanded beyond naming rights to women's broader civil rights, the Lucy Stone League operated as a precursor to NOW (National Organization for Women) and other influential women's rights organizations of the second wave.

Although the Lucy Stoners were married, they shared a common cause with Marjorie Hillis's coalition of Live-Aloners, in their determination to take their place in society on their own terms, and define for themselves what marriage or singleness meant. In their different ways, they resisted the long-standing assumption that marriage constituted an absolute divide between women, and that married women ought to retire gracefully from public life once they had crossed over, finding fulfillment and self-expression only in the home. Both Lucy Stoners and Live-Aloners recognized that true independence for women did not simply mean rejecting family ties. It meant standing up for the life you wanted to lead, even if society said you were greedy, that you wanted too much.

On the Side of the Underbitch: *Kitty Foyle*

Much of the appeal of Marjorie Hillis's *Live-Alone* books lay in the author's ability to cross generational lines, and speak with a voice of authority about single life without sounding like a lecturing aunt. Some of that authority no doubt derived from the generation to which she belonged, along with women like Frances Perkins, Eleanor Roosevelt, and Edna Woolman Chase, that had come of age amid the ferment of the women's suffrage fight. As a twenty-something working woman in New York, Marjorie would have witnessed firsthand the renewed energy and excitement of the campaign as it surged toward victory in the state in 1917, and the nation in 1920. Her young adulthood mapped a broad progressive journey from the family-centric philosophy her mother articulated in 1911, through the suffrage victory and the reckless years of the flapper, until she arrived in her mid-forties at a point of confidence in women's abilities but no complacency about their rights and the progress still to be made.

For women of the generation below Marjorie, the age of her nieces who were children when the vote was won, such complacency was more common, as things seemed to be getting better and better, at least for women who enjoyed the privileges of class and race. Their chances of finishing high school and entering college climbed with every passing year—during the 1920s, the number of young Americans enrolled in college shot up an astonishing 84 percent, and at first almost half of them were female. It was not a question of gaining access to the workplace, for these women—it was how to behave when you got there that troubled them. Without a clear goal to fight for, they questioned who they were, and who they might become.

The single girl of this younger generation could learn plenty from *Live Alone and Like It* and *Orchids on Your Budget*—from the practical advice of how to decorate and dress on a budget, to the more profound lessons about learning to value her own choices and hold on to her independence. But Marjorie didn't spend a lot of time on the specific problems of the young white-collar worker, who had to work in close proximity with men who were often married, and needed to navigate the sexual politics of offices regulated only by people's good behavior, not by any rules or laws designed to protect the vulnerable. She could consult a wealth of new guidebooks like *Manners in Business* (1936) and *How to Be a Successful Secretary* (1937), which told her how to dress (modestly) and how to behave around her male boss (efficiently but not flirtatiously). Secretly, though, she yearned to know what was really at stake—how far could a modern girl exercise her freedom, and what was the worst that could happen if she let down her guard around men?

For those questions, she turned to Kitty Foyle.

This quintessential midcentury working girl, a fictional character who became an icon, was created by a man: Christopher Morley, a gregarious writer-about-town in the 1920s and '30s. Of Marjorie Hillis's generation, he was born in Haverford, Pennsylvania, in 1890 and worked for most of the major literary and journalistic outposts of the day, but he was unusual for a literary man in being a happily married father of four. Morley loved literature, his family, and Sherlock Holmes, and was one of the founders of the Baker Street Irregulars, a still-thriving semisecret fan club. None of which quite explains how, in 1939, he came to create Kitty Foyle, an outspoken girl of "healthy, lower-class, humorous Irish-American stock," who became the emblem for an entire genera-tion of the struggles of the independent working girl. A skeptical *New Yorker* reviewer doubted whether he, or any other male critic, could really judge whether Morley had managed to get inside his heroine's mind, an effort he nevertheless called "a brilliant stunt."[26] But readers flocked to the novel in their thousands. Some-thing about Morley's Kitty struck a raw nerve.

Whether or not she's an entirely plausible woman, Kitty is a great storyteller. The novel is the story of her life, told in a backward glance from the ripe old age of twenty-eight, and laced with morbid bitterness. At the time of telling it she's a Live-Aloner, but she most decidedly doesn't like it, spending her evenings reminiscing and "pac-ing round this damned apartment until I'm glad it's not a penthouse, I might have taken a dive." Her melodramatic tone is often uninten-tionally funny, crying out for a husky Joan Crawford voiceover, but her unhappiness is real, and believably darkened by the state of the wider world in 1939. That world presses in insistently through the newspapers and the radio, two of the things Kitty says are guaranteed to get her "jittered," along with business, liquor, cigarettes, and sex.[27]

Kitty is a decidedly modern creature, who has come a long way from her roots in old-fashioned Philadelphia, the daughter of a respectable working-class Irish family. Her widowed father relies on the labor and goodwill of Myrtle, the family's African Ameri-can housekeeper, a stock figure who dispenses homespun wisdom in painfully rendered dialect. Kitty, immersed in the racism of her day, cherishes her while still treating her as fundamentally other, a member of a kindly but less-than-human species who thinks and feels and knows things quite differently from white folks. Morley never suggests that Kitty ought to recognize a shared identity with Myrtle as a put-upon working woman—no gendered connection can transcend the gulf of race and class.

At the heart of the novel is Kitty's long-drawn-out and doomed love affair with Wynford Strafford VI, the scion of an Old Philadelphia banking family and a cricketing acquaintance of Kitty's father. Wyn is a directionless charmer in the mold of Cary Grant's C. K. Dexter Haven in *The Philadelphia Story*, also set amid the fabulously wealthy and snobbish aristocrats of the Philadelphia Main Line. Taking a shine to Kitty, Wyn enlists her in an effort to start his own local version of *The New Yorker*, but the magazine fails in the face of Philadelphia society's total lack of interest in the sophisticated modern world. Kitty gets a new job in New York, and Wyn reluctantly enters the banking business as he's been expected to all along—and marries, in the end, a girl of his own class. Wyn's wealthy relatives speak of girls like Kitty rather as she herself thinks of Myrtle, as a different species: "The modern girls are so courageous, I think it's wonderful how enterprising they are," says Wyn's mother at one point. But it's clear she doesn't want one in the house.[28]

Despite the barrier of class, Kitty decides not to hold back from a sexual relationship with Wyn, fueled by his money and a lot of bootleg liquor. When she discovers that she's in trouble ("Female plumbing is just one big burglar alarm"), she plans to tell Wyn, until discovering that he's engaged to a more socially suitable girl. Luckily, her glamorous, female French boss knows exactly what to do. Once she's on the other side of the abortion, Kitty's emotions are mixed but unrepentant. "I felt sorry, and selfish maybe, and like I'd lost something beautiful and real, but I couldn't feel any kind of wrongness, I did what I had to do."[29]

It was not Kitty's doomed romance with the milquetoast Wyn that made the book a cultural phenomenon. Instead, it was her outspoken defence of the life and morals of the "White Collar Girl"—a phrase Morley did not coin but which his character came to embody. The "WCG," as Kitty calls her, was a stock cultural figure in the 1930s, beset on all sides by advice, suspicion, fantasy, and warning. The popular novelist Faith Baldwin made a fortune writing stories about white-collar girls who were torn between professional independence and romantic happiness. Many of her stories were made into movies, like 1936's *Wife vs. Secretary*, starring Clark Gable and Jean Harlow, and she took pains to twist the clichés about working girls to interesting, if not exactly feminist, ends. 1932's *Self-Made Woman*, for example, features a single thirty-year-old woman who is torn between two men as well as her career, and has to ask herself, "Is it worth sacrificing a man of your own and children to be a successful business woman?" When *Live Alone and Like It* was sold to Universal Pictures in 1936, it was Faith Baldwin who was contracted to write the screenplay.

Like Carrie Bradshaw in the 2000s, "Kitty Foyle" became, for the next twenty years, shorthand for a particular type of girl: independent but still romantic, a young striver who dissects and debates her own life even as she's living it. Formulating her theories along with her best friend Molly, who works in the furniture section of a large Chicago department store, Kitty becomes an observer, a sympathizer, and eventually—at least in her imagination—a spokeswoman for the wrongs done to young women in the name of modernity and progress. The WCG is underpaid and undervalued, and her long work hours leave her too exhausted to create the life she wants, with room for pleasure, love, and a sense of purpose. Kitty and Molly come up with a working sketch: "There's millions of them, getting maybe 15 to 30 a week, they've got to dress themselves right up to the hilt, naturally they have a yen for social pleasure, need to be a complete woman with all a woman's satisfactions, and they need a chance to be creating and doing."[30] But the hours they work mean that their private life is a "rat-race," and they see themselves as "sharecroppers"—a loaded comparison to make at the tail end of the Depression. It wouldn't be so bad if they had a share in the profits, or thought the crop worth raising: "it must be nice to feel some of that ground you sweat on belongs to yourself."[31]

With no money to spare for a meal at a diner or even a slice of pie at the Automat, the career girls get by on coffee and cigarettes. No cream, Kitty notes, "because that adds just one more complication; and no sugar because it's fattening." They take their coffee black, simple and strong, but its bitterness has affected them. "Something of the strong taste of black coffee has got into our thinking."[32] And when caffeine won't cut it, there are stronger drugs available, Kitty shrugs. "Lots of career girls have got raises for their ambition that was really benzedrine sulphate."[33]

But despite Kitty's—or Morley's—bleak view of the plight of the WCG, the professional opportunities open to young single women during the Depression were abundant. For the women who were able to access the office—who were white, educated, and able to speak unaccented English—they were not just a paycheck but a source of pride and identity. They were also some of the opportunities least affected by the downturn. This was partly because women could be paid less, as it was assumed they had no family to support, and partly because the nature of work was changing, and the white-collar sector was expanding enormously. As companies grew and merged in the early twentieth century, the logistical challenges of managing production and distribution of goods called into being a whole new class of managers and organizers, whose job it was to issue instructions to those below them and report to those above. Once a place where a boss would have had worked side by side with a small, all-male group of trusted clerks and secretaries, offices were now vast hives, in which the multiple tasks of the clerks were separated out and divvied up by gender. But even if the work inside them was rote and repetitive, offices were desirable places to work: they were clean, safe, respectable, and offered the opportunity to meet eligible men.

Given the growing dominance of the corporate office, Kitty is a somewhat unlikely representative of the WCG. She works for a glamorous woman in a small office marketing luxury cosmetics, getting to exercise creativity and her own kind of power by persuading her shoppers that they're making their own choices, "when actually they're simply falling in line with what some smart person has doped out for them."[34] Her boss, Delphine, understands the feminine economics of the Depression quite plainly—"when people are not sure of necessity they crave for luxury." Or in Kitty's plainer words, "There won't never be a slump in a business that makes people feel pleased about themselves."[35]

It's through her friends and acquaintances that Kitty formulates her darker theories about the WCG's fate. One friend gets a short-lived job in a small office that's more typical of the kind of work young women were doing in huge numbers in the 1930s: "It was one of those jobs where you are stenographer and switchboard and receptionist all at the same desk, and probably have to teach the billing clerk to take No for an answer."[36] The sexual menace implied here is lightly presented, but it was a reality for working girls. What found its way into popular culture as the "office romance"—with the office girl usually positioned as the temptress, luring the boss away from his stay-at-home wife—was more often a daily battle against sexual harassment—a concept that wouldn't enter the law or the lexicon until the 1970s.[37]

At the end of the novel, Kitty has a dream that reveals the wider importance of her WCG theories. She's at a White House press conference near the president, though sitting hidden under a piano. Undaunted, she gets up to make a speech, seizing her "everlasting chance" to tell the world "how the White Collar Girl feels about things and what a bloody mess and etcetra [sic]." She tells Molly later that she did want to speak for them—"your poor damn sharecroppers in the Dust Bowl of business." She wanted to tell the president about their courage, as they move around the city, "putting up a good fight in their pretty clothes and keeping their heebyjeebies [sic] to themselves." But she finds that when it comes to the crunch, she can't pronounce the crucial words, "White Collar Girl."[38]

Even without getting the words out, Kitty Foyle managed to speak for her courageous, neglected sisters. The novel was a smash hit. In April 1940 the publisher Lippincott took out an ad in the *Saturday Review* touting the book's fifteenth printing, upcoming movie adaptation, and a seven-page photo spread in *Life* magazine. This spread posed a model who resembled the film's star, Ginger Rogers, around New York City: in a drab diner and at her desk, outside her all-women residence and dressed up for a night out, leading the reader through the daily grind of (a spectacularly glamorous) WCG. Kitty Foyle was hailed "Not a Book but a

Woman"—like the Live-Aloner, a symbol of the times who quickly outgrew her pages.

The novel had been snapped up by RKO Pictures as a vehicle for its star, Ginger Rogers, and a way for her to break out of her fleet-footed two-step with Fred Astaire, which was starting to feel like the same old dance. It worked, at least this time: Rogers won a Best Actress Academy Award for her portrayal of Kitty, in an adaptation that waved the wand of Hollywood glamour over the book's blunt, working-class heroine. Most reviewers saved their praise for Rogers; *The New Yorker* headlined its review "Ginger's White Collar," and hailed her performance for its "air of spanking gaiety" and "promise of piquant insecurity and dainty audacities," which seems to be a prim way of alerting readers that they wouldn't get to see screen-Kitty getting up to quite the same sexual antics as the girl in the book.

Laboring under the Hays Code, the film cleaned up Kitty's romantic backstory, having her marry Wyn and give birth to a legitimate child, only for the baby to die and the couple to divorce. This makes Kitty's experience far more tragic than her secret but unrepented abortion in the book, and the film ultimately turns the story into a melodramatic love triangle, with Kitty forced to choose between Wyn, who won't leave his wife but offers her a long-term affair, and Mark, a dull doctor she doesn't love. Her white-collar life generates no political awareness or determination to share the fate of her sisters with the world. Indeed, the film took the larger concept of the white collar and reduced it to a literal accessory on Rogers's on-screen outfit, which became known as a "Kitty Foyle dress." Created by the designer Renié, who went on to win an Oscar for the far more flamboyant costumes of Elizabeth Taylor's *Cleopatra*, the Kitty Foyle dress became a staple of 1940s wardrobes. A dark, often navy-blue, short-sleeved shirtwaist style, with contrasting touches of white at the cuffs, buttons, and of course, the collar, the dress was enormously popular with working women who could exercise their thrift and ingenuity by adding those fresh white accents to a dress they already owned, and bask in a little of Ginger's reflected glamour. In a happy coincidence for the film's producers, the high contrast of the white collar brightened and flattered an actress's features on screen, giving her a sort of upside-down halo—an irony that might have given Kitty herself a good laugh.

The professional and sexual adventures of working girls like Kitty would remain a staple of popular culture into the 1940s, with twists that could make the stories romantic or tragic depending on the circumstances. Although in most cases her sphere was limited to the office, there was one incarnation of the WCG who was allowed to get out from behind her desk and have adventures in her own right. This was the "girl reporter" turned amateur sleuth, like the titular Torchy Blane, played by three different actresses in a series of nine popular movies released by Warner Brothers between 1936 and 1939, with titles like *Smart Blonde* and *Torchy Gets Her Man*. In 1940's *His Girl Friday*, Rosalind Russell made her an icon, in her role as Hildy Johnson, the whip-smart reporter who can't quit her story, the business, or her ex-husband boss. Through Hildy, women could imagine a working world in which they had the respect of male colleagues, made decisions for themselves, and used their wit and brains to make a difference in the world, just like a man—no surprise, as the Hildy character was originally male. The film, and especially Russell's performance, still offers a potent vision of women's professional power and potential.

6

MAD ABOUT
NEW YORK

Marjorie Hillis wrote *Live Alone and Like It* for all the girls and women who, like Kitty Foyle, dared to leave their hometowns for the thrilling, anonymous city, a city that was an idea more than a place. The book's case studies might play out in Chicago, Boston, or St. Louis, but the arc of each story remained the same: a young, or not-so-young, single woman escapes the scrutiny and expectations of her family by moving to a place where her unfortunate singleness can be made over into a lifestyle choice. Wherever they actually lived, the myth of urban reinvention, the city as a place of opportunity and anonymity, resonated with readers. But it was New York where the pattern was laid. As a hybrid of New World energy and Old World glamour, New York shaped the look and the ethos of the twentieth-century American city. During the Gilded Age it was defined by the extremes of fabulous wealth and the abject poverty into which it crammed its dreaming newcomers, who came in waves from Europe and China, the Caribbean, and the rural South, fleeing abuse or exclusion or poverty, or simply chasing a dream. For those women who were allowed through the door, the city's proliferating offices, factories, schools, hospitals, and department stores held out a chance at respectable work, romance, and reinvention.

During the 1930s, the physical appearance of New York City changed dramatically, and was captured in the photographer Berenice Abbott's 1939 book *Changing New York*—a striking record of new buildings under construction, older structures awaiting demolition, and the men and women who witnessed the changes without, perhaps, quite seeing them. The city's first skyscrapers, like the Flatiron and Woolworth buildings, had been built in the neo-Gothic style, with its frills and adornments in stone. But when the Chrysler Building's gleaming Art Deco arches rose above the city, heralding the new decade, its aesthetic was triumphant. In the cabarets designed to look like cruise ships, in cars and women's dresses, in the fourteen buildings that made up Rockefeller Center and finally opened at the end of the 1930s, the new New York style—sleek, steely, and streamlined—was visible everywhere. New bridges spanned the rivers; new subway lines linked far-flung neighborhoods, and a sense of expansive growth marked the city— even as, at street level, its citizens still struggled to get by.

The World's Fair in Flushing Meadows Park ran from April 1939 to October 1940 and formed a capstone to the disparities of the 1930s. Attended by forty million people over eighteen months, it was planned as a triumphant sign that the city was emerging from the Depression, under its slogan "Building the World of Tomorrow." At the same time, it looked backward at the nation's founding, and the 150th anniversary of George Washington's inauguration on Wall Street, with an enormous statue of the first president looming over the grounds. The twelve-hundred-acre grounds in Queens were, Marjorie Hillis wrote, "crammed with inventions and discoveries and designs and theories to make the future a better and more exciting and beautiful place."[1] Divided into seven zones separated by sculptures, reflecting pools, and fountains, the fair showcased everything from food and amusement to examples of scientific, business, and technological advances. President Roosevelt's opening of the fair was the country's first television broadcast, an appropriate marker for this fantasia of global innovation and harmony, shadowed by the approach of global war.

The Woman Vacationist

In January 1939, Marjorie had written to Laurance Chambers with the news that "I find myself, all of a sudden, in the midst of another book and one over which I'm quite excited." She hastened to reassure him it wasn't another book of poetry. This would be a practical book, the size and format of *Live Alone*, featuring case histories and advice. Explaining that during her extensive lecture travels, she'd heard from "business women and teachers all over the country" that they planned to visit the upcoming World's Fair in New York, the new book could be pegged to the grand opening at the end of April. She enclosed chapter outlines and had the title ready to go: *New York, Fair or No Fair: A Guide for the Woman Vacationist.*

Chambers was delighted, and even though he thought the competition for similar books would be stiff, he was confident that Marjorie's slant would be unique, and that the interest in the fair would sell the book widely. His readers' reports were generally positive, accompanied by the now-familiar gentle eye roll at her financial optimism: "As usual Miss Hillis is fooling no one with her contention that she is outlining an economical vacation because there is nothing economical about it," wrote one reader. "However, economy and dullness often go hand in hand and there is nothing dull about this guide."[2] The book's sales approach was to capitalize on the fantasy that the book offered—so central to the appeal of Marjorie's earlier books—and to suggest that reading it was almost as much fun as a trip to the city.

New York, Fair or No Fair is a hymn to the city where Marjorie was not born, but made. Although intended as a practical guide for visitors, it was as much a celebration of a New Yorker's love for her home, full of Marjorie's personal voice, her memories and her prejudices, and her exhilaration when faced with the sheer *fact* of the city. "Its air has a zest and sparkle that make my mind tingle," she wrote in the jubilant introduction. "Its hum starts a rhythm of thought in my brain. An idea floats in every puff of wind, a picture shapes itself in every spot of sun or shadow, an adventure waits around every corner and beckons down every street." The city can be champagne and the striking-up of the band, or it can be whisky and curling up by the fire: "Nowhere else, except perhaps on a mountaintop, can one feel so securely snug and remote, so sure of being able to live one's life as one wants to, as in a New York apartment where you never see your neighbor and choose your friends because you like them and not because they live around the corner."[3]

Although the city typically allowed newcomers to escape their families, Marjorie's curiosity and love for New York were closely bound up with memories of her father. Writing more personally than she had in any previous book, she describes her father's embrace of his adopted city after their move from Illinois, his unflagging energy and curiosity, and his determination to show the city off to his children. When she directs her readers to walk over the Brooklyn Bridge at dusk, she recalls taking the same walk in reverse with her father, through the Lower East Side and back to their neighborhood under the shadow of the bridge on the Brooklyn side. They would always pause in the Jewish quarter of lower Manhattan, she writes, "to peer into the windows of a synagogue, where the men wore hats, the women shawls, at their devotions." For the middle-class daughter of a Presbyterian minister, both the religion and the poverty were foreign and fascinating: "We walked down the Bowery, under the clattering El, passed pawnshops and missions and cheap rooming houses, to the dreary entrance to Brooklyn Bridge." Once up on the bridge, the view of the city opens up into "the loveliest panorama."[4] This sigh of longing is typical of a book that presents New York as, like that panorama, at once dazzling in its beauty and frustrating in its scale. "I've had space only for the Musts—and they are all that you'll have time for in any short vacation . . ." Marjorie laments at the end of the book, hoping only that her readers will come to feel as she does, simply "mad" about "this amazing, fast-moving, exciting, beautiful, colorful, Arabian Nights city."[5]

Firmly aimed at the well-to-do female visitor, *New York, Fair or No Fair* doesn't offer much more than a curious glance at the parts of the city populated by people without the means to get lunch at Hampshire House, a taxi to the theater, or a jaunty silk turban at a Lexington Avenue boutique. But Marjorie did make a few concessions to travelers on a budget, and to those out-of-town solo women who might feel wary of staying in a hotel room alone. She advised staying at one of several "feminine hostelries" that were an affordable place to live for a week or two: the Allerton on East Fifty-Seventh Street; the American Woman's Club a little farther west; or, most famously, the Barbizon, on Lexington at

Sixty-Third Street. At the Barbizon, the visitor would encounter an "attractive clientele made up largely of bright young things in search of a career."[6] For several decades it was a coveted address for a young woman on her way—provided she had the references and connections to get in. Applicants were judged by their family, but also their appearance, demeanor, and wardrobe. On the twenty-second floor of the hotel was the national headquarters of the Junior League, an organization of upper-class young girls twenty thousand strong, united by their social status "and an urge, sometimes vague, toward charity."[7] Dorothy Draper, not yet the famous tastemaker of the city's leading hotels, had made over the headquarters as a tropical retreat in the Manhattan sky, with white-washed walls, blue carpet, glossy-leaved rubber plants, and orange velvet chairs, the acid-bright scheme that would become her signature. The Junior League was indicative of the status of the girls the Barbizon wanted; both Hillis daughters were members.

On the lower floors, cramped pink-and-green dormitory rooms sheltered aspiring models and actresses, and a roster of future stars passed through before they were famous: Grace Kelly, Joan Crawford, Lauren Bacall, Liza Minnelli, Candice Bergen, Cloris Leachman. The girls got afternoon tea for free and could load up on finger sandwiches if they didn't have a generous date or their paychecks couldn't cover a trip to the Automat for lunch that day. There was a gym and a swimming pool, a library, and two lounges where the residents could bring their male guests for conversation and a little light flirting until the manager appeared to kick them out at ten o'clock.

The Barbizon was where *Mademoiselle* magazine housed its summer guest editors, including Sylvia Plath in 1953, who ten years later would thinly veil the Barbizon as the "Amazon" in her novel *The Bell Jar*, calling it a place populated by "girls my age with wealthy parents who wanted to be sure their daughters would be living where men couldn't get at them and deceive them."[8] When Kitty Foyle arrives in New York, she lives at the "Pocahontas," a dreary dormitory for women that offers room and meals for just a few dollars a week, and represents a rather less glamorous version of the Barbizon. "It sounds like a cat house," Kitty says with characteristic bluntness, "but that's what the West Side called an economical apartment hotel for dames only."[9] Models at Eileen Ford's agency were housed there from the 1940s, but it was also a training ground for more pedestrian, if polished, employment, with Katharine Gibbs's "posh secretarial school," as Plath called it, taking up several floors in the building. It remains a signature of its era; in Marvel's series *Agent Carter*, set in postwar Manhattan, the protagonist Peggy (after passing muster with the snooty staff) takes a room in yet another fictionalized version, the Griffith Hotel.

One of the chief selling points of these women's hotels, for long-term and short-term shelter, was the community they offered, which even Marjorie Hillis acknowledged was useful for a solo traveler: "I make no claim that it's particularly gay to eat alone in any strange city," she wrote.[10] If for some reason breakfast in bed, her ever-reliable first choice, was neither available nor desirable, a bacon roll might do very well for breakfast at any of the many branches of Schrafft's—where "the timidest female would feel perfectly comfortable alone," and her soigné sister "couldn't complain of a girls' boarding-school atmosphere."[11] No real New Yorker would have needed this explanation. For most of the twentieth century, until the restaurants vanished from the city's streets in the 1980s, Schrafft's was a byword for female-friendly dining, a chain of affordable but genteel establishments that filled the gap between masculine taverns and expensive French restaurants where one dined strictly à deux. From the 1920s and intermittently for the next forty years, *The New Yorker* could run jokes under the heading "Overheard at Schrafft's" and trust that every reader would recognize the particular brand of woman they featured: respectable, rotund, and always mildly displeased about something or other.

According to restaurant historian Paul Freedman, Schrafft's was one of several restaurants that attempted in the early twentieth century to fill the gaping middle in New York dining, catering to the middle class, at middling prices, in the middle of the day. But women needed more than a place that was open and affordable, especially in an era when their unaccompanied presence in public spaces was still a novelty. Schrafft's at first did not serve alcohol, and in keeping with assumptions about women's eating preferences presented a dainty menu long on ice cream, fruit salad, and cucumber sandwiches. The formula was a hit and offered a haven for women on lunch breaks, in the middle of shopping expeditions, and otherwise in need of a respite from male-dominated society.

The longevity and success of the chain has been attributed to its founder, Frank Shattuck's "fanatical" dedication to quality control, which ensured that every branch in the empire (by 1950, more than fifty in New York State, and more in Boston, Philadelphia, and across New Jersey) felt as welcoming and elegant as the original city branch in the heart of Ladies' Mile. Shattuck employed women as managers as well as waitresses, and gave them a modest share of the profits and maternity leave. No feminist and certainly no progressive—he banned "foreign"-sounding foods, and the restaurants discriminated against nonwhite patrons—Shattuck nevertheless realized the enormous, untapped commercial value of women as consumers.[12]

Like Schrafft's writ large, Marjorie Hillis's New York was a feminine place. Most of her book was aimed at helping women navigate it in style and comfort, which meant dressing the part and being sure to take as much time as necessary for rest, recovery, and the kinds of body, face, and hair treatments that some people might call self-indulgence, but that Marjorie called simple common sense. The girl who left no time in her sightseeing schedule for a wash and set, a manicure or a massage, or no room in her budget for a stylish new hat, was doomed to find the city exhausting and sadly lacking in the unexpected-dinner-date department. A truly smart woman was always prepared for such a possibility. "My own optimistic opinion is that it's foolish to go anywhere, ever, for more than twenty-four hours without full evening regalia," Marjorie advised. "You never know what might turn up, thank Heaven, and I, for one, would a lot rather bring a dress I didn't wear than refuse a party because I hadn't brought the right clothes."[13] The successful case studies in *New York, Fair or No Fair* were those who planned ahead just enough to make the most of their stay, like the resourceful Miss R., a Southern belle who shocks her family by announcing a solo trip to New York. Well aware that "knowing nothing at all can get you far, especially if you're small in stature and have large brown eyes," Miss R. doesn't bother to study up on the subway map or the opening times of museums. Instead, she prepares for her trip by packing her prettiest clothes and gathering a list of men she can contact in town—"friends or relations of her worried acquaintances"—and on the train divides them into an *A, B,* and *C* list according to their availability and eligibility. She doesn't get much further than the *A*-list of the young and unmarried, and comes home convinced of the friendliness and hospitality of the dangerous northern city.[14]

If a visitor was caught short without her full regalia, she could seek out expert advice. "Call *Vogue* about clothes or jewels," Marjorie suggested, loyally. "The editors are out in the shops constantly. They know what's new and who has it."[15] Or she could enlist a guide, a sign of the city's flourishing entrepreneurial spirit: Marjorie recommended three college girls who ran tours out of the former home of the poet Edna St. Vincent Millay, the skinniest house in the city—75½ Bedford Street in Greenwich Village. These possibilities aside, a taxi driver could be as good a tour guide as anyone. In her "paean" to this New York stalwart, Marjorie listed among the cabbie's invaluable services the ability to "[find] places when you only half know the address, [get] bags, bundles and intoxicated gentlemen through doors, and [abet] romance."[16]

If her reader's trip was geared to work rather than romantic adventure, there was also an expert waiting for her. Career Tours, a sign of both the novelty and the necessity of paid work for women, took visitors behind the scenes of a welcoming workplace. They were organized by the American Woman's Association, headed by Anne Morgan, the philanthropist daughter of J. P. Morgan, and were headquartered at the Science and Education building at the World's Fair. The tours—some 135 of which had been scheduled by late May 1939, before they officially began in June—started from the association's midtown offices. Their purpose was to "provide opportunities for business women who have come to New York for the fair to visit also metropolitan places of business in which their own professions are practiced," according to one newspaper. The Career Tours Committee kicked off its activities with a ceremony at the fair on June 5, featuring a speaker who had been selected as the "Woman of 1939" out of nominations from the public, a diverse field that included Margaret Sanger,

Eleanor Roosevelt, Helen Keller, and Edna Woolman Chase. In the end, the jury honored a real-life "girl reporter," *New York Times* journalist Anne O'Hare McCormick, for the "accuracy and brilliancy" of her reporting from "the troubled European world," and for having "helped to establish the woman correspondent as a settled institution."[17] The organizers published a commemorative book, but lest anyone be swept away by the celebratory mood, the president of the National Federation of Business and Professional Women used the occasion to sound the alarm to her audience that "a wave of public hysteria" was pushing back against married women's right to work outside the home. "If we deny women freedom of opportunity we will only create a parasite class," she warned. It was a prescient observation, anticipating the backlash against working women that would, after World War II, expand to encompass single as well as married women, and which would take a new feminist revolution to overturn.

On the whole, however, Marjorie's New York was a city of pleasures, not professional or cultural obligations. Her attitude toward the Riverside Park monument of Grant's Tomb was typical of her approach to all statues and "sights": "Look at this one if you want to, but don't say I told you to."[18] Statues, after all, were not why anyone came to New York. She knew that her reader was there for the unique thrills that her hometown couldn't offer, and directed her to restaurants like the one in the newly transformed Hampshire House on Central Park South, where her friend Dorothy Draper had made over the decor "with great éclat."[19] The Algonquin offered both an affordable lunch and the opportunity to gawk at the "celebrities" who gathered in the dining room—even if they, or their tables, unfortunately "can't be tagged, like the animals in the zoo."[20] The mystique of the Algonquin Round Table, forged by Dorothy Parker and her journalist friends back in the 1920s, was still a potent draw. Celebrities were as much a part of the appeal, even of the point of New York, as the "superfine" collection of paintings at the Met or the "glamour of Broadway," which "radiates across the country"[21] —or indeed, the World's Fair itself.

Nightlife City

The glamorous nightlife that was bringing tourists flocking to New York in the late 1930s was a new staging of a constantly evolving scene, ushered in with the end of Prohibition. It didn't appear overnight. Repeal was official at 5:30 p.m. on Tuesday, December 5, 1933, when Utah finally voted to ratify the Twenty-First Amendment— smack in the middle of cocktail hour, but nobody danced in the streets. There were no parties like those boisterous, last-gasp affairs that marked December 31, 1920, Prohibition eve; the *New York Times* reported that the city celebrated "with quiet restraint," while the *Herald Tribune* took a dig at the law's failure. "There was no novelty about drinking," it pointed out, "so the citizenry, by and large, stayed at home."[22] Alcohol had become so central to the city's public life during the previous thirteen theoretically abstinent years, that the chief concern of most New Yorkers after repeal was whether legal liquor would cost more than bootleg sauce.

As much as anything, repeal was an effort to lift the nation's gloomy spirits at the end of a terrible year, in which the economic mood kept dropping to new lows, then finding room to fall even further. Despite the muted celebrations that accompanied the change in the law, repeal did herald a new era in New York City's life of leisure and pleasure. Prohibition had wrenched apart the pleasures of drinking and dining out—restaurants without wine were dreary places, and nobody went to speakeasies for the food. But after repeal, the underground drinking dens that packed in the scofflaws and drained their pockets lost their grip on the market, along with the mafia that had controlled bootlegging and bars from Greenwich Village to Harlem. Those who could afford to eat out, and to wash their steak down with wine, now wanted to show off to the world. Within a few short years New York had reestablished itself as a place where restaurants and cabarets offered a spectacle to rival Broadway.

The Hotel Astor's 1933 New Year's Eve party was an early sign of where things were heading. Despite a steep cover charge, hundreds of people showed up determined to out-swank their neighbors. "Twelve months ago, high hats were decidedly in a minority," noted a reporter for the *Baltimore Sun.* "Today, toppers are in the ascendancy. The black-tie tuxedo has once again become informal, and full evening dress, with the white tie and tails, is in full force for evening appearances in public." It looked like a movie, or like magic, since "no one seems to know just where the money is coming from."[23] In the mid-1930s, New York nightlife was all froth and fantasy. Café Society, a mirage between Depression and war, lit up Broadway at night in lights as bright as the midnight sun.

The champion of this revolution was a Swedish immigrant and impresario named Nils T. Granlund, known as N.T.G., who showed a flair for publicity and promotion from an early age, advertising local revues and writing a society column before he was out of his teens. As the publicity man for the Loew's theater chain in the 1920s, N.T.G. invented the modern movie premiere and the film trailer. His tactics were resolutely populist—when he needed to draw a crowd to a languishing venue, he knew that nothing worked better than a chorus line of underdressed dancers.

(The title of his 1957 memoir, *Blondes, Brunettes and Bullets*, gives a taste of his style.) After repeal, N.T.G. saw that there was better money to be made by offering an extravagant but not out-of-reach night out to hundreds of guests, rather than gouging a reckless few. He began transforming hotels' languishing ballrooms into spectacular restaurants with cabaret entertainment, and throwing open the doors to hundreds of gawping diners, both locals and, increasingly, tourists. His Swedish-themed Midnight Sun cabaret, followed by the Hollywood and the Paradise, set the tone, decked out in chrome-bright polish and swooping Art Deco curves to evoke the sleek lines of a cruise ship.[24]

If you weren't able to conjure up the cash to indulge in person, the radio and movies let you peek in the window. Radio stations broadcast big-band showpieces live from hotels and cabarets, while Hollywood packaged up and sold the cabaret back to its live audiences via a new wave of song-and-dance movies. Busby Berkeley's hits *42nd Street* and *Gold Diggers of 1933* leaped clear off the New York cabaret stage into a fantasy world of their own, while Fred Astaire and Ginger Rogers, in movies like 1935's *Top Hat*, danced their way to romance across the gleaming openness of a "Big White Set," a style for which the studio RKO Pictures became legendary. These elaborate sets in turn became an inspiration for the interior design of cabarets and for women's evening fashions. There was a rage for floor-skimming silver and gold gowns in silk, lamé, and sequins, the work of designers like Adrian and Madeleine Vionnet, which blazed to life on the black-and-white screen, draped over the angular and athletic bodies of starlets like Katharine Hepburn. The wavy, platinum blonde hairstyles worn by icons like Jean Harlow, and innumerable imitators, were also a trick to catch the light and the camera's eye. And of all the drinks that could now be openly ordered, none matched the sparkling mood like champagne.

But no matter how elegant her gown, the Live-Aloner could not sweep onto the dance floor without a partner. Single women were unwelcome at the ritziest night spots—the Stork Club, El Morocco, and the Colony—as New York's see-and-be-seen night-life was still an exclusive affair. Bouncers—often ex-gangsters and semi-reformed bootleggers—kept the genders strictly balanced and guarded the door against lone females and so-called hen parties. Even if they were visiting from out of town and paying to stay in the best hotels, unaccompanied women could find themselves excluded from the public lounges and stylish ballrooms of those very hotels.

The prejudice against lone females in public was enough of a problem that for a few years in the late '30s, an agency known as the Guide Escort Service operated in New York to unite wealthy "extra women" with underemployed men (and part them from their cash). The rent-a-gent service was founded in 1935 by a young and imaginative midwestern transplant named Ted Peckham, who saw an opportunity when he overheard two wealthy dowagers at the Plaza Hotel complaining that they couldn't go out on the town alone. The idea that rich women were sitting idle at nights and young, presentable men like himself were stuck indoors due to a lack of funds struck Peckham as unjust, so he summoned his considerable charm to persuade the manager of the Waldorf-Astoria to back his escort scheme. With the help of publicity from the *New York Times*, where he was working in the subscription sales department, Peckham's agency took off. It was so successful that he traveled to Paris, London, Vienna, and Budapest to launch overseas branches, saving jet-setting single American women the indignity of being turned away from the most glamorous spots in the world.[25]

In *New York, Fair or No Fair*, Marjorie Hillis gave Peckham's service a glowing review, describing it as though it were an opportunity to star for an evening in your very own Hollywood spectacle.

"The young men have college educations, perfect manners, and impeccable evening clothes," she promised. "They will take you where you want to go, dance with you or not, as you prefer, and be faultless companions. What's more, if you feel that you'll be happier accompanied by a Kentucky Colonel, a French Marquis, or a Hungarian Count, he will be supplied."[26]

Unfortunately, when Ted Peckham read this endorsement, he was waiting outside a courtroom in Manhattan to hear the fate of his business, which had fallen afoul of the city's licensing commission. Officially, he'd been hauled up for operating an employment agency without the proper license, but to his accusers, his offense was not bureaucratic but moral. "Activities of this nature lead to all sorts of indecencies and immorality," the city's deputy licensing commissioner argued in court. "The escort is not known to the woman and may not be reliable. Neither party has ever met before." He went on to suggest that it was not just the women who were at risk: "It is also possible that the woman who hires the escort may not be of the proper type." And finally, the city's nightlife in itself was deemed suspect, as was any woman who wanted to enjoy it: "The escorts and those who hire them stay out all hours, day and night, visiting cabarets and night clubs and God knows where." On June 7, 1939, Peckham was fined $250 and ordered to shutter his business.[27]

"Café Society" and 1930s Harlem

It was not just single women who found the doors of the Stork Club closed to them. The nightclub, along with most of the big nightlife venues at the time, was strictly racially segregated. In 1938, a left-wing impresario named Barney Josephson became the first nightclub owner to banish that policy from his new club in Greenwich Village, which he named Café Society, on purpose to poke fun at the uptown snobs who thought the only place minorities belonged was in the kitchen, or in the band. His club was a place where liberals, activists, artists, and intellectuals gathered, and its roster of talent shimmered. It was where, in 1939, Billie Holiday first sang a song called "Strange Fruit," and it launched the careers of stars like Lena Horne, Hazel Scott, Paul Robeson, and many more. It was one of the rare places in Depression-era New York where black and white partygoers could meet as equals.

New York in the interwar years was a place of de facto segregation. There were no signs declaring open apartheid as there were in southern states, but there were only a few neighborhoods where black citizens could freely live, and the city's restaurants, bars, and public spaces had for years been an unpredictable patchwork of acceptance and exclusion. Jessie Redmon Fauset, the literary editor of the *The Crisis* under W. E. B. Du Bois, wrote in her fiction and journalism of the humiliation of getting caught in those cracks. She described the exhaustion of trying to make a well-meaning white friend understand that her choice of restaurant for their lunch date wasn't an option, and at the friend's indignation, insist that she'd rather eat somewhere shabby and anonymous than go through the work of putting up a fight in public to be served. Or her anger at witnessing a white man tussle with a black woman for a subway seat, a man who would never dream of sitting if a white woman was standing, but whose chivalry sorted women into categories and judged by race first.[28]

In the years between the end of World War I and the start of the Depression, around 1.5 million African Americans had moved from the South to the industrialized northern cities. Immigrants from the Caribbean had also flocked to American cities, New York in particular, in the same period, and they made up a quarter of Harlem's black population by 1930. The Depression slowed the movement until 1940, when the needs of the war industries spurred a second migration, drawing more than three times as many people north in the ensuing three decades. As early as the end of World War II, African Americans had become a predominantly urban population, and that shift would fundamentally reshape the political and cultural life of America's cities.

The Harlem Renaissance in the 1920s had turned the streets of upper Manhattan into a mecca for African American artists, writers, musicians, performers, and, in short order, hangers-on and tourists. Its ritzy image was boosted by journalists and photographers, black and white, who were enthralled by the style of the locals and the wild innovations of jazz. On 133rd Street between Lenox and Seventh Avenues, the three landmark nightclubs, Small's Paradise, Connie's Inn, and the Cotton Club, were all racially segregated—the last of these, the biggest and ritziest of them all, was also the strictest about keeping its white clientele separate from its black performers and servers, a gap enforced by the white gangsters who owned the place. But there were dozens of other speakeasies off the main drag, where prices were lower for drink and drugs, crowds were more mixed, and the music and dancing kept going long after the cabarets closed at 3 a.m. Many white visitors who wrote about "venturing" north of 125th Street to visit the jazz clubs treated the neighborhood as an exotic playground, without caring to know anything about the people who lived and worked there after the sun came up. Even those, like the photographer and bon vivant Carl Van Vechten, who tried to become a part of the neighborhood, and to boost the reputation of Harlem artists among wealthy white patrons, still saw it as foreign to the rest of the city, a place that needed to be interpreted before it could be understood by outsiders.

Few Harlem Renaissance characters embodied uptown glamour quite like A'Lelia Walker, who in her wealth, independence, and penchant for hospitality was a forerunner to the Live-Aloner—albeit one who had been married three times, and took glamorous living to an extreme. Walker's mother was Sarah Breedlove, better known as Madam C. J. Walker, the country's first black female millionaire, who made her fortune selling cosmetics and hair-straightening products. When her mother died in 1919, A'Lelia was ready to embrace the role of heiress, hostess, and patron of the arts. She lavished her mother's money on clothes, parties, and the finest and most expensive furniture, buying into the Harlem vogue with vigor and flair. A wall inside her two conjoined townhouses on 136th Street was adorned with poetry by Langston Hughes, who called her the "queen of the night" and "the joy-goddess of Harlem's 1920s."[29] Her parties were legendary, at her townhouse and at her mother's Hudson Valley estate: royalty and heads of state from Europe and Africa were invited to mingle with the artists, poets, and civil rights leaders who were driving the Harlem Renaissance. One possibly apocryphal tale claimed that one of her parties involved a carnivalesque inversion of racial hierarchies, with the white guests (including Van Vechten) made to eat in the kitchen and serve champagne to the black attendees, who were draped in the robes of kings and queens.[30]

When the crash hit, it flattened the Walker family business. A'Lelia's priceless art collection, and soon enough her country estate, went on the auction block, and her patronage of poets and writers evaporated—she died not long afterward, in the summer of

1931, still partying as though the Depression had never happened. At the same time, many of the white publishing houses like Alfred A. Knopf, which had supported the Renaissance and the authors who defined it (mostly thanks to Alfred's wife, Blanche), drew in their belts and left many of their authors out in the cold.[31] During the Depression Harlem struggled, hit harder by unemployment than any other part of the city, and offered scant public support.

In 1932 the African American commercial artist Elmer Simms Campbell, a friend of band leader Cab Calloway, produced a map of the nightclubs of Harlem. Published first in *Manhattan Magazine* and then in the newly launched *Esquire*, it celebrated the energy of the various nightspots while also making clear that there was too much going on to crowd into one map, and that establishments opened and closed too quickly to be documented. It also made clear that while outsiders might be able to find a good time, they would need help to find the best of what was on offer. The witty map took a deliberately sunny-side-up view of the neighborhood's spirit and ignored the routine, relentless discrimination that meant rents were higher and wages and living standards lower than anywhere else in New York. Even the "nice new police station" on the map, where black and white officers play cards together, looks like a friendly place.

Shortly after Campbell's map was published, the repeal of Prohibition meant that the ease of getting liquor at the Mob-ruled nightclubs was no longer the draw for white tourists that it had been, and the influx of partying outsiders to the neighborhood began to slow. When Marjorie Hillis offered her white readers advice on visiting Harlem in *New York, Fair or No Fair*, she suggested that they take an escort, "not because it's dangerous, but because it will be dull." For tourists, after all, the attraction was "the dance halls and night clubs," and in daylight the neighborhood didn't reveal much from the outside, or to outsiders. "It looks like any other not-very-smart section of the city, but with more black faces than white," Marjorie wrote dismissively, in what was a typical attitude for white observers—the sense that Harlem was closed to them, and not worth the discomfort of exploring.[32]

For the women of Harlem who were not heiresses, however, the dance halls and nightclubs were just a small part of the larger cultural revolution that offered the possibility of a new, proud, and creative kind of life. They came from Philadelphia, Chicago, Washington, and all over the South, as well as the Caribbean and Europe; some had parents who had come north in the Great Migration some years before; some had migrated from no farther than midtown. Women like Zora Neale Hurston and Nella Larsen were writing and publishing poetry and stories that sought to represent the experiences of black women in the modern city as well as in the rural communities that their authors were leaving behind. Jessie Redmon Fauset was editing, hosting literary salons, and nurturing new writers. Playwright Regina Anderson Andrews, who had fought to become the first African American supervising librarian in the New York Public Library, at the 135th Street branch, hosted regular artistic gatherings with her roommates at 580 St. Nicholas Avenue—when Zora Neale Hurston first arrived in Harlem, she crashed on their couch. At the World's Fair, Harlem artist Augusta Savage created a monumental sculpture, "The Harp," that was one of the few examples of African American art recognized as part of "the World of Tomorrow" there, outside the brief flowering of "Negro Week," held in the summer of 1940. Savage, Andrews, and Fauset would be among the ten black women honored at the fair for their contributions to culture and the arts.[33]

Novelist and journalist Ann Petry first came to live in Harlem in 1938, by which time much of the energy of the Renaissance and its key players had dispersed—Hurston, by this time, was carrying out anthropological research in Florida under the auspices of the WPA. With her husband away serving in World War II, Petry wrote a weekly society column for one of Harlem's newer, left-wing newspapers, the *People's Voice*, and was the paper's women's editor in the early 1940s. In 1946, Petry published an immensely popular novel, *The Street*, in which she imagined the reality of life alone for a black single mother in Harlem. Her heroine, Lutie Johnson, tries to live according to the inspirational self-help principles of Benjamin Franklin, but the pressures of racism and the predations of men threaten her independence at every turn.

As the daughter of a well-to-do family in suburban Connecticut, Petry had been visiting Harlem regularly for years to see shows and plays, and was a regular guest at the Emma Ransom House, the women's residence at the YWCA in Harlem. One of the few convenient and respectable options for young African American women coming to the city in search of work, the Emma Ransom House could either be a permanent home, for five to eight dollars a week, or a temporary one, for around a dollar a night. Like its more glamorous counterpart, the Barbizon, the residence offered a place to stay and a social life, with optional maid and laundry services, a beauty parlor, space for social gatherings, and "beau parlors" where women could entertain male guests (under supervision, and only until curfew). But the YWCA also offered more practical services, including a trade school to train prospective nurses and secretaries, and an employment office to help job seekers. The veteran civil rights activist Dorothy Height, who worked at the YWCA in the late 1930s, recalled in her autobiography the pressure on the Emma Ransom House at the time of the World's Fair, due to the "thousands of Negro girls" who were drawn by the promise of jobs. The staff had to convert one of their club rooms into an emergency dormitory, and did everything they could to make sure the girls weren't turned away—even those who couldn't afford the fifty cents a night for a bed in the makeshift dorm.[34]

It was no wonder that the World's Fair jobs, and the YWCA beds, were so highly coveted. Young black women who came alone to New York in search of work during the Live-Alone era faced considerably fewer opportunities, and greater risks, than their white counterparts. Most found themselves shunted into domestic service, where legal protections were scarce and opportunities for advancement were few. But change was on the horizon, spurred by the national crisis of World War II, and the passing of laws prohibiting racial discrimination in the defense industry, which opened up factory jobs. Work outside the home was about to become the patriotic duty of all American women, many of whom were going to find themselves Live-Aloners for the first time. But Marjorie Hillis, this time, wanted no part of their struggle.

ROSIE AND
MRS. ROULSTON

Live-Aloner No More

High Lindens, also known by the less bucolic, more cigar-chomping name of the John P. Kane mansion, is an elegant house on the north shore of Long Island, outside the well-heeled town of Huntington, and just a life preserver toss from the Huntington Yacht Club, once part of its grounds. Dating back to the 1830s, it is one of the oldest mansions on what would become known as the island's Gold Coast. Originally a two-story, flat-roofed house with a colonnade along the front, its design was fully in keeping with the airy openness of Italian mansions that Edith Wharton celebrated in her book *The Decoration of Houses*. It was extended over the years until in 1917 it could be advertised for sale in *Country Life* magazine as a blend of tradition and modernity, appealing "to gentlefolk seeking a delightful country place of charm and pleasing atmosphere." In addition to the seven-bedroom main house, the twenty-two-acre grounds encompassed three cottages, a greenhouse, and a bungalow perched on one thousand feet of private shoreline.[1]

The gentleman who fell for its charms was Thomas H. Roulston, head of a chain of more than seven hundred grocery stores that bore his name, tentacling out from their Brooklyn base across Queens, Staten Island, and Long Island. Thomas's father lit out from County Tyrone in Ireland in the late nineteenth century in search of work and opportunity, and found it with a grocer in Red Hook, Brooklyn, whose store he eventually bought out. He hung up his own name, first on that store, and then across his adopted city. The principles guiding Roulston & Sons would still suit a thriving Brooklyn grocery store a century later: local produce sourced from Long Island farms, its own bakery, exclusive Roulston coffee roasted on-site, and "famous" eggs.[2]

When Thomas senior died in 1918, his eldest son, Thomas Henry, known as Harry, inherited the business, employing his bachelor brother as his second-in-command. High Lindens was Harry's reward, and a marker of his new status as the family patriarch—but he and his family would get to enjoy it together for only a summer or two, before his wife Florence died in 1920. Thomas's spinster aunt Charlotte moved in to help the widower keep his house and care for his children, and in due course both children, Elizabeth and Henry, grew up and married. They stayed close to home, and Henry went to work in the family firm, the third generation of Roulston men to do so.

When he met Marjorie Hillis at a Christmas party in 1938, Harry Roulston was a wealthy widower in his early sixties, self-made, active, and devoted to his family. As a talented salesman, it's possible he reminded Marjorie of her beloved father, and like Reverend Hillis, Roulston was clearly a man who relished a challenge.

His grocery stores would have been a familiar feature of Marjorie's Brooklyn childhood, but she didn't meet their owner until she was already famous as the Live-Alone guru. Undaunted, he took her on vacation to Nova Scotia, and at some point managed to convince her that even though they were mature people long past the age of foolishness, romance still might have the power to win out over even the most elegant breakfast in bed. Or perhaps he argued that the solitary delights she celebrated in *Live Alone* could be all the more delightful when shared.

On August 1, 1939, at her sister's home in Pennsylvania, the staunch Live-Aloner got married. The forty-nine-year-old bride wore a gown of "pale smoke blue" in marquisette, a gauzy mesh fabric lightweight enough for the summer heat. She wore a hat with an ostrich feather perched on her tightly curled iron-gray hair, and carried a bouquet of rosebuds and orange blossoms. Her sister, Nathalie, was her matron of honor, and the best man was Henry, her adult stepson—coincidentally also married to a woman named Marjorie. The event offered the press an irresistible combination of society wedding and minor sociological scandal. In the loyal *Brooklyn Daily Eagle*, under the headline "Goodby [*sic*] to All That," the paper's anonymous "Trend" columnist had an exuberant time with the Live-Alone guru's capitulation to matrimony. "Literati, cognoscenti, illuminati, intelligentsia and sweet old Aunt Matty just beamed," Trend rattled off, in the convoluted "corkscrew" English popular with smart magazines of the day.[3] Several other New York newspapers covered the wedding, no doubt as a diverting distraction from the worsening news in Europe.

To the more cynical of these observers, Marjorie Hillis was exposing herself as a fraud by getting married. In June, when she

announced her engagement, the *Chicago Tribune* ran her photograph under the headline "Didn't Like It." From her "bachelor-girl
apartment," she told reporters that she was "prepared to endure a
fair amount of jocularity," wrote the *Herald Tribune*, but considered the trade-off worthwhile.[4] The *New York Times*, finding the
bride-to-be's phone busy, speculated that she had taken it off the
hook to avoid facing the indignation of her single fans, who surely
considered her engagement a "gross betrayal"—although it didn't
manage to find any fans who would say as much in print.

On the occasion of the wedding announcement and several
times afterward, Marjorie struggled to convey the nuances of
her theory and her actions to skeptical journalists. "At first with
patience and then with resignation, our bride of the week tried to
explain when her engagement was announced last month that she
didn't say in her book she preferred single blessedness," "Trend"
reported. "She did say, though, that Mr. Right would have to be
strict Grade A." If he was, then the essence of the Live-Alone
message could survive even Marjorie's coupled state. She was still
arguing that women should cultivate the highest standards for
themselves, choose their lifestyles according to their own desires,
and never marry a lower "grade" of man out of social pressure and
simple fear. Seen in this light, her wedding did not repudiate, but
reinforced her quietly radical rethinking of what happiness could
look like for women, and how it might be achieved.

But the jokes were just too easy. "Duck and twist as she may,
the fact remains that Marjo is now masticating some of her very
persuasive and well-paid words without condiments," quipped
columnist Alice Hughes.[5] Before long Marjorie resigned herself
good-humoredly to the humiliation. Three weeks after her wedding, she "broke down and confessed," according to one journalist, to an audience of fifteen hundred of her husband's employees

that like them, she secretly enjoyed having Mr. Roulston as her "boss." At the same event, the firm's annual dinner in the Hotel Astor, the boss took the opportunity to frame his marriage as a successful business venture, holding it up as evidence of his skills as a salesman. The "former champion of single blessedness" looked on, reportedly all smiles.[6]

At first, Marjorie's married life didn't look all that different from her Live-Alone life. She honored the commitments she'd made before her wedding, which included chairing the Brooklyn division of the women's committees for the World's Fair's "Women's Month," in May 1940, and receiving an award for her contributions to literature from the Brooklyn Women's Club. But beyond those obligations, she vowed to "renounce" her public persona, giving up her newspaper column and her lectures, although she reserved the right to write "when she felt the urge."[7] She moved with Roulston back to Brooklyn, no longer on the water where she could hear the ships, but to a leafy block of First Street, steps from Prospect Park. There, she embraced the role of an "old-fashioned housewife," but firmly dismissed reporters who suggested she might write a sequel to *Live Alone* on the pleasures of matrimony.

Whatever else it may have done for her, marriage effectively silenced Marjorie Hillis. In January 1940 she wrote from Brooklyn to thank Laurance Chambers for his Christmas gift, and confessed that she was still "in a non-writing mood," which she hoped wouldn't "prove to be a permanent part of matrimony." Chambers wrote back to express his anxiety that the mood would be temporary and short-lived.[8] It wouldn't prove entirely that, but Marjorie turned her attention inward, to her new life and her past. She published nothing during her marriage but a guide to the birds on her country estate.

What, after all, could she say? A woman was expected to like her married life—and in the era of the companionate marriage, in which a husband was supposed to be a friend, a confidante, and a supporter, there was nothing radical in the idea of "live together and like it." Yet there was still something unconventional in marrying as Marjorie did, in continued quiet and profound resistance to the expectations of society. She married late in life, after children were no longer a possibility, and after her husband's children were grown, though she relished her role as step-grandparent. She married after her own financial stability was guaranteed, although the change took her from comfortable to wealthy. She married, in the end, for the simplest of reasons—because she liked him.

Rosie the Riveter

On August 3, 1939, the newlywed couple sailed on the *Normandie* for their European honeymoon. When they returned less than a month later, it was in darkness and anxiety. Their liner had been forced to take precautions including a zigzag route, radio silence, and blackouts of the main cabin lights at night. No explanation was given to the passengers except the occasional mutter of "Hitler," and nobody knew until they arrived whether or not war had started in Europe. The 1,417 passengers—including Hollywood stars Constance Bennett and James Stewart—cheered and danced for joy upon learning that a precarious peace still held. It would last in Europe for just three more days, until September 1, when Germany invaded Poland. Despite this looming threat, reports of the ship's tense return to New York also demonstrated that the marriage of Marjorie Hillis was still news—one took the trouble to quote Thomas Roulston declaring that his wife would write "no more books."[9]

As alarming as their crossing on the *Normandie* must have been, the Roulstons were cushioned by wealth and privilege from the escalating threat of the war, and it remained distant for them, as for many similarly fortunate Americans. Indeed, at first the war was good news, at least for the domestic economy, as the massive expansion of industry absorbed many thousands of long-unemployed men. As early as 1940 the factories began to open their doors to women, too, to meet the upsurge in demand and heed President Roosevelt's call for the United States to become the "arsenal of democracy." In New York, women began driving taxis and operating elevators, as well as flocking to assembly line work at the Brooklyn Navy Yard and other local factories. After the bombing of Pearl Harbor in December 1941, women's participation in the war effort was no longer optional. As men deployed overseas, their wives—of all races and classes—found themselves breadwinners and heads of households in unprecedented numbers. Five million women moved into the workforce between 1940 and 1944, including into the heavy industries that had never admitted them before.[10]

Once war became inevitable, married women's labor was no longer judged to be harmful to family life, but was reframed as their patriotic duty. This took away—or at least muted—the question of choice that had always been so problematic in discussions of women working. During the Depression even single women had faced public vitriol for "taking" jobs from men—even though most jobs were gender-segregated, and men were hardly clamoring for positions in the low-paid stenography pool. But it was also widely accepted that single women were more likely to have to work, having no one else to support them—and economic necessity was something everyone had to respect. For married women, however, especially those with young children, the decision to work outside the home still carried a stigma of selfishness and neglect. Even during the war, many women struggled to weigh their family's needs and their own desires against their country's call, and women's magazines frequently reassured them that staying home and raising children was war work of a different kind.

In the early 1940s, the war's impact was unavoidable. Marjorie herself had barely settled into her new life of traditional domesticity, than women across the country found themselves facing the opposite prospect. While she turned away from the world, to wealth and marriage and building her new home with her husband, millions of women were turning to hardship, work, and self-reliance for the first time. Thousands of young women rushed into marriage before their sweethearts shipped out overseas, so that they began married life in the curious position of de facto Live-Aloners. But they could no longer draw strength from the independent and glamorous stories contained in Marjorie Hillis's books: it was not a time for bed jackets, orchids, or tea parties. Marjorie was no longer in step with the culture, nor pointing the way—she ducked out, and it surged on without her.

Instead, the woman Americans looked to was a symbol: Rosie the Riveter, in her head scarf and overalls, embodying strength, beauty, and can-do spirit. "Rosie" was a composite, based on the experiences of a handful of women who worked in different industrial jobs, and her name soon became a synonym for any young woman who had rolled up her sleeves and joined the factory workforce. She first entered popular culture in early 1943, in a catchy song by Redd Evans and John Jacob Loeb, recorded by the Four Vagabonds, a pioneering African American a cappella group, who studded the performance with a distinctive rolling-*r* sound to mimic Rosie's drill. The song, which enjoyed wide radio play, celebrated both Rosie's patriotism and the novelty of her labor in its chorus: "She's making history / Working for victory." But any fears the song might stir up in celebrating Rosie's power—perched on the body of a powerful weapon, riveting gun in hand, doing her work as well as any man—are allayed by the reassurance that she has a boyfriend serving in the Marines. Presented as the effort to protect her Charlie, Rosie's potentially liberating work is brought back under domestic control. Her long hours on the assembly line serve her man as much as her country.[11]

The most famous painter in America, Norman Rockwell, was inspired by press reports of women's industrial work to create his own homage. On Memorial Day 1943, the cover of the *Saturday Evening Post* featured a Rosie who was anything but frail, and who was yoked to the national cause rather than to any individual boyfriend. Despite her rouged cheeks, red hair, and bright lipstick, Rosie's femininity is muscled out by her overalls, goggles, massive rivet gun, and bulging biceps (Rockwell's model, a nineteen-year-old local telephone operator named Mary Doyle, was so shocked at how her slim frame had been expanded in the painting that Rockwell called her to apologize).[12] Rosie's commitment to the war effort is made explicit in the rippling backdrop of the Stars and Stripes, and the copy of *Mein Kampf* she's trampling underfoot. Her twisted pose, crossed feet, the upward perspective, and the position of her hand deliberately evoke Michelangelo's depiction of the prophet Isaiah in the Sistine Chapel—with a half-eaten ham sandwich shoved into the prophet's empty fingers.

The religious connection (underscored by the *Kansas City Star*, which ran a side-by-side comparison on June 6, shortly after the Rockwell painting appeared) transmuted Rosie, with her dirt-streaked face and serene, superior gaze, into a figure of effortless, superhuman power—but today, hers is not the image that comes to mind when we hear the name Rosie the Riveter. Instead, we see a glamorous cartoon version, featuring Rosie in spotted head scarf, overalls, and raised fist, under the heading "We Can Do It!" That version, however, was seen only by a handful of Americans during the war, if they happened to work in the Pittsburgh factory where she appeared briefly on a poster designed to boost morale. It wasn't until the 1980s, when feminist activists seized on her image, that she began to supplant Rockwell's painting as the iconic female war worker. Although both versions feature a woman in work clothes pictured alone, only Rockwell's radiates a sense of solitude—perhaps surprising given that factory work was necessarily cooperative, and most other propaganda showed women working in teams. Rockwell's Rosie has the air of a wartime Live-Aloner, maintaining her self-reliance even in the midst of the collective national effort, stomping Hitler with no hint of Charlie or any boyfriend in her thoughts.

Rosie's influence continued through the later war years, but it was rare that she appeared as butch and nonchalant as Norman Rockwell painted her. Wartime movies that placed women in factory roles made sure that the stars looked feminine and delicate, and that the plots continued to revolve around romantic entanglements. The movie *Rosie the Riveter*, released in 1944, is a musical comedy starring platinum-blonde B-movie comedienne Jane Frazee. Essentially a bedroom farce, the plot revolves around a shortage of lodging space near a California defense plant, which requires workers Rosalind "Rosie" Warren and her friend Vera to share their space with two men who work a different shift. Rosie falls in love with one of her rotating roommates and breaks off her existing engagement, while spending the rest of her spare time trying to reunite her landlady's daughter with her estranged husband.

The lightness with which the fictional *Rosie the Riveter* treated women's work and its impact on their relationships is in stark contrast with the story of Rose Will Monroe, one of several women who had a claim on "the real Rosie." Tough enough to suit Rockwell's vision, Kentucky-born Monroe worked as a riveter in an aircraft factory in Ypsilanti, Michigan, where she assembled B-24 and B-49 bombers. A film crew visited her factory in 1944 to shoot footage for propaganda films, and Rose was duly discovered by their star, the popular actor Walter Pidgeon, going on to make several promotional films with him. She was no glamorous starlet but an approachable, curly-haired brunette who displayed skill and confidence at her manual job. Recently widowed and with two young children, Monroe had no choice but to provide for her family, but she was also ambitious and good at her work—a tomboy, according to her daughter, who knew the skills of her father's carpentry trade. Whether from practical need, personal desire, or some combination of the two, Rose Monroe did not retreat into her home after her industrial job disappeared at the end of the war. She took a series of jobs that were still rare for women—driving taxis and school buses—and eventually started her own luxury-home construction business, proudly self-named: Rose Builders. She had originally hoped that the aircraft factory where she worked would train her to fly, but they refused because she was a single mother. Years after the war, she earned her pilot's license from a local aeronautics club, where she was the only female member, and then taught her daughter to fly, too.[13]

In *Life* magazine on August 9, 1943, the pioneering photojournalist Margaret Bourke-White created a vivid picture of the working lives of the women at a Gary, Indiana, steel mill. The cover image and photo spread portrayed a variety of women, from teenagers to middle-aged mothers, with all the grit but little of the glamour of the Rosie ideal. Some were married with children, others fresh out of school, and several had relatives or husbands working elsewhere in the plant. Despite the powerful propaganda image of the husband off fighting overseas, less than 10 percent of women war workers were in fact in this situation. Many were carrying on as before, albeit in industrial environments that were new to them. The magazine noted that the women in the Gary factory were not treated as "freaks or novelties" by the men, yet the magazine took care to insist that their presence was still exceptional, a "revolutionary adjustment" of the natural domestic order, and that once the "crisis" had passed, they would go home.

The expressions on the women's faces convey a range of emotion, from pride to boredom to lurking fear, and for most it's apparent that hard work is nothing new to them—unlike the curiosity of the press. According to the accompanying article, it is a diverse group: "They are black and white, Polish and Croat, Mexican and Scottish." Where the photograph is a portrait, the captions name the women, their jobs, and an identifying detail or two, and avoid making any comment on their physical appearance. One jarring exception is the photograph of one Mrs. Rosalie Ivy, pictured at work in her overalls and described as "a husky Negro laborer." Her race overwrites her femininity, underscoring that she is a "laborer" before she is a woman, and that hard physical work is, for her, no revolution.[14]

The opening up of access to industrial work during World War II was nonetheless transformative for African American women like Rosalie Ivy. Unlike white women, they did not require a propaganda push to entice them out of their homes—simple necessity had always done that, and 90 percent of those who were working at the end of the war had been working at its outset. But the new opportunities in industry gave black women options, often for the first time in their lives. By the end of the war the proportion of them employed in domestic service—those dead-end, unavoidable jobs to which they had long been relegated—had dropped by 15 percent.[15] "My sister always said that Hitler was the one that got us out of the white folks' kitchen," recalled Fanny Christina "Tina" Hill, a Texan who went to work at North American Aircraft in Los Angeles at the age of twenty-four, and used it as her ticket into a comfortable middle-class life. Unusually, after leaving the factory at the end of the war to have a baby, Tina returned, and worked there for the rest of her life.[16] Even though black women workers were still barred from many of the higher-paying riveting and welding jobs in factories, there was palpable pride in doing work of national importance.

The access of women like Rosalie Ivy and Tina Hill to factory work was the result of tenacious activism on the part of black unions and civil rights leaders, using tactics more usually associated with the 1960s movement: boycotts, marches, and rallies. The irony of the U.S. government going to war to defend freedom and democracy abroad while vicious Jim Crow laws ruled at home struck many African Americans as grotesque. Yet at the same time they recognized that military service, ever since the Revolution, had offered a way for black Americans to prove their loyalty to the state and win incremental victories in the fight for racial equality. Was there a way for black Americans to fight Hitler—even in a segregated military—and win their own rights in the process? In early 1942 a young man from Wichita came up with an answer. He wrote a letter to the editor of the prominent black newspaper the *Pittsburgh Courier* suggesting that the common slogan of "V for Victory" was not enough for black Americans, who should insist on a "double V"—victory from without and within, abroad and at home. The newspaper seized eagerly on the concept, creating posters, buttons, and songs to promote it, and push the government to make good on its democratic promise.

Harnessing the power of the Double V campaign, NAACP head Walter White and others planned a march on Washington for 1941, refusing appeals from First Lady Eleanor Roosevelt and then the president to call it off. They only relented when Roosevelt signed Executive Order No. 8802, banning discrimination in the defense industry on the basis of "race, creed, color, or national origin." The military itself would not be desegregated until 1948, under President Truman, but the antidiscrimination legislation was an important victory, laying the groundwork for the postwar civil rights activism that would gradually transform American society.

The civil rights leaders spearheading the Double V campaign recognized the importance of publicly celebrating the contributions of women. At the annual Negro Freedom Rallies organized throughout the war in Madison Square Garden, a "Miss Negro Victory Worker" was crowned; in June 1944, *The Crisis* reported that the winner would be presented to the "huge Garden crowd" and receive a merit certificate and a war bond. Dancer and anthropologist Pearl Primus performed in front of a crowd that was indeed huge: twenty thousand people watched her crown the African American equivalent of Rosie the Riveter, the symbol of black women's strength, dedication, and patriotism. By staging the rallies downtown, rather than in Harlem, the organizers made it clear that the work of Double V and the contributions of black workers were central to New York's and the nation's war effort.

As Farah Jasmine Griffin has detailed, Pearl Primus was herself symbolic of the conflicting constraints and opportunities of black life during World War II. A Caribbean immigrant and a brilliant student, when she graduated from Hunter College in 1940 with a degree in biology, Primus found that no lab would hire her. She took a series of jobs that shuttled her between Kitty Foyle and Rosie the Riveter— switchboard operator, riveter, clerk, shipyard welder. The frustration of trying to build a scientific career led her to switch paths, and she returned to dance, which she'd studied as a student but hadn't considered a worthwhile career. But coupled with her interest in and study of anthropology, as well as the progressive political circles she moved in, she began to discover that her art could become something more than decorative. After she was invited to become a regular performer at the integrated downtown nightclub Café Society, she began to find ways to meld the African dance traditions she had studied overseas with a political sensibility born of her experiences and observations of a still unjust and unequal America.[17]

Despite the anti-discrimination orders, many black women were held back in menial jobs, and it took luck and grit for them to fight their way through to higher-status, higher-paying jobs. Yet for many of them, the mere fact of working in the factories side by side with white women, for a common cause, was empowering. Griffen writes that the war represented a remarkable "flowering of opportunity" for all American women, not merely in the literal provision of a paycheck but in the expansion of their understanding of their place in the world and their capabilities.[18] For many, it was the arrival of choice, that great privilege, for the first time.

Selling the Women's War Effort

For most women during the war, living alone—often by necessity and wracked by anxiety for absent loved ones—was hardly a glamorous project. It was a hardship to be endured, rather than a freedom to be enjoyed. The authorities guiding Americans in how to live well were no longer the self-appointed success gurus of the 1930s. Instead, the can-do spirit of self-help was co-opted by the government, through the messaging of the new Office of War Information. Operating from June 1942 until the end of the war, the official mandate of the OWI, under Executive Order 9182, was to use the press, radio, and movies to create and disseminate information that would "facilitate the development of an informed and intelligent understanding, at home and abroad, of the status and progress of the war effort and of the war policies, activities, and aims of the Government."

In practice, that meant selling America to itself and to the world. Abroad, the OWI hoped to showcase the wealth, peace, and superiority of American life under democracy, and at home, to ensure that its citizens—especially women—understood their role in that project. It sent regular bulletins to the editors of magazines and newspapers to suggest ways they should handle war-related topics, and attempted to coordinate these messages in print and on air, so that each medium would reinforce the message. It made and distributed short films, including those that celebrated women's factory work, and collaborated with the newly formed War Advertising Council on a series of public service messages. This forerunner to the Ad Council created campaigns promoting war bonds, victory gardens, and above all, women's work—pushing the message that female employment was a patriotic responsibility. The Ad Council touts this program as "the most successful advertising recruitment campaign in American history," bringing some two million women into the workforce, and breaking down cultural prejudices against women's labor. The campaign rhetorically collapsed the boundaries between soldiers and civilians, home front and war zone, by insisting that "in this war, every civilian is at the front."[19]

The huge increase in women working meant that the government was paying attention to the practicalities of that life for the first time: the thorny subject of what we now call work-life balance. Despite the dearly held notion that women were physically incapable of hard labor, the real obstacles to factory jobs for women during wartime proved to be logistical: how would they get to work, and who would watch the children while they were away? Official efforts to provide child care to the country's female labor force were slow, haphazard, and dogged by lingering prejudice against mothers leaving their children to go to work. At first, the government pushed the message that mothers who stayed home with their young children were performing "an essential patriotic service," and should not go out to work. Alarming newspaper stories about the fate of latchkey children, meanwhile, reinforced the idea that absent mothers would damage their children and, by extension, the fabric of the society they were at war to defend.

But the country was in desperate need of labor, and couldn't afford to exclude mothers for long. Women with children made it work, relying on family and neighbors: carpooling, swapping favors, and pitching in together. It wasn't until 1943 that any kind of systematic, federally funded child care system was in place, patched together from Depression-era programs and local efforts, and it was far from adequate. By 1944, only a fraction of an estimated two million required child care slots were available, and those were often in understaffed and poorly run facilities. But when stories surfaced of children sleeping in cars in factory parking lots while their mothers worked the night shift, blame settled on the women, not the government. What child care there was available was permitted strictly for the duration of the war—the only way that Congress would agree to fund this essential tool of women's liberation.[20]

Although women working was a widespread new reality during World War II, the official messages associated with it anticipate the powerful domestic push of the postwar years. Women who worked outside the home were not let off the hook of high domestic standards, but were expected to understand their housework as part and parcel of their wartime labor. A 1944 advertisement in *Good Housekeeping* for Swift's beef trumpets not one or two but seven wartime "jobs" for women, beginning with "Wife!"—"a loving and lovable person, doing a fine job of home-making"—and followed by other roles mixing the domestic and the public: "Mother!" and "Cook!" then "Purchasing Agent!" "Salvage Expert!" "War Worker!" and "War Bond Buyer!"[21] In this list, the woman's actual paid work is far down the list, and it is her role as a household manager and thrifty consumer that makes up the bulk of her responsibility. A woman might be forgiven for wanting to enlist in the military for a little peace.

The advertising industry was still a fledgling business in the early 1940s, and had struggled to survive the Depression. The war proved to be its salvation, sowing the seeds of the postwar *Mad Men* boom era. Thanks to the OWI's positioning of women as consumers for the common good, and their buying decisions as part of the job of "purchasing agent," there was no end to the potential manipulation of their formerly private lives as housewives into some semblance of a public role (without, of course, any wages). In an ironic reversal of the Live-Alone era—now that a great many more women *did* find themselves, at least temporarily, living without husbands—single women seemed to disappear from public view. Instead, women's roles as wives and mothers were emphasized all the more, and it was clear that there was no space in either household budgets or popular culture for a woman's individual desires. Everything she did, bought, and thought was for the war effort.

Just to be sure, a series of national programs set out to absorb any extra money or time that a wartime Live-Aloner might suddenly possess as a result of her well-paid job or absent husband. She was encouraged to buy war bonds, plant a victory garden, and maintain vigilance around the tasks of rationing and recycling, which were turned into quasi-military operations. A *Life* magazine headline summed up the expected attitude: "Think War, Buy Little, Maintain Our Ideals."[22] The strenuousness with which American advertisers, the OWI, and the War Advertising Council worked to convince the domestic population to "think war" reflects the ironic reality that the fighting itself still lay at a physical distance. In contrast to the other Allied countries that were enduring physical bombardment, the United States home front was a relative haven of peace and security, for those who were not forced into detention camps. Many of its citizens were better off, materially, than they had been during the Depression, despite rationing, and the industrial boom that would fuel postwar prosperity was well under way.

The Domestic Turn

The years of her marriage turned Marjorie Hillis Roulston's focus inward. She made an attempt at an autobiography, *Before and After*, using her wedding to frame the story of how she had arrived at her comfortable perch. She had not, however, been married long enough to take a measured view of her new state, and appears to have written her own story under an extremely flattering honeymoon glow, starting out each chapter with a description of the beauty of the birds or flowers at High Lindens, and occasionally digressing into rhapsodies over the perfection of her husband. She might be forgiven this rosy view of married life, given how convinced she had been for half her life that she would never get to enjoy it, but the readers' reports on the manuscript were savage. "I don't remember ever reading an autobiography by a more serenely complacent and well satisfied person," wrote one, going on to say that she had "better look out: the Greeks had a word for it."

The draft offered idyllic accounts of summers spent with her maternal grandparents in Marengo, Illinois, which resonated with Bobbs-Merrill's Indiana-based readers: "circuses, the Opry House, Wild West shows, band concerts on Saturday night, the barn, the big house, the big yard—how many of us Midwestern children can match those summers." Her stories of Brooklyn were hardly less magical, as she described the pride she and her siblings felt hearing their beloved father preach, and how they looked forward to Sunday dinners, fried chicken and all the fixin's, and lots of company. Her school days, she did admit, were "slightly clouded" by her bad clothes, "but gilded by [her brother] Dick and Dick's friends who rallied round her bravely for dances and other parties."

A second reader concurred, agreeing that while the story of Marjorie's *Live Alone* success was entertaining, there weren't enough juicy anecdotes about the well-known names, like Dorothy Parker, who appeared in the story. And it was particularly disappointing that the real story readers wanted—of her unlikely romance—was missing. Despite all these flaws, both readers agreed that with substantial revision, the book might still hold enough appeal to Marjorie's fans to be worth publishing.[23] But for whatever reason, she abandoned the project, dropping the personal examinations in favor of bird-watching, and volunteering with the local branch of the Red Cross to help the war effort.

In January 1944, as if cruelly bearing out the threat of hubris that first reader had warned about, the Roulston household experienced a sudden tragedy. Harry's son, Henry, collapsed at his Long Island home and died, aged just thirty-seven, leaving behind his wife, Marjorie, and two children, thirteen-year-old Heather and eleven-year-old Tom. Henry had been a senior executive in the family business, and had been expected to take it over—now, Harry and his younger brother William had to keep things going rather than ease into retirement. The grief of Henry's death was no doubt intensified by the war, which seemed no closer to ending.

The following summer, however, brought peace—under the cloud of the atomic bomb. Shock and relief were intermingled, so perhaps in an effort to give their families happier news, the next generation of Hillises rushed to the altar. Like thousands of young women across the country who had served in the women's auxiliary forces, Marjorie's young nieces quickly swapped their uniforms for wedding gowns. First, two of Dick's four daughters, his youngest, Ann, aged nineteen, in 1945, and his eldest, Elizabeth, twenty-seven, in 1946, and then Nathalie's daughter Polly, twenty, in 1947.

Then suddenly, in the late summer of 1949, five years after the death of his son, and just days after his and Marjorie's tenth wedding anniversary, seventy-five-year-old Thomas Roulston suffered a fatal heart attack at High Lindens. Like her mother twenty years before, Marjorie found herself in the exhausting position of collecting other people's outpourings of shock and sympathy. Her Brooklyn-bred husband's funeral was held at her father's old seat, Plymouth Church, in the afternoon of Saturday, August 20, and he was buried in Green-Wood Cemetery. By coincidence, his obituaries shared column space with an account of the funeral of Margaret Mitchell, the author of that other 1936 bestseller *Gone with the Wind*, who was killed in a car accident the same week in August. Roulston's hometown *Daily Eagle* glowed with patriotic pride in describing him as "a typical American success story" as it traced his immigrant roots and his hard work in building up his father's single grocery store into a citywide chain. As an employer and an active member of various charities and community organizations, his story made him, the paper reiterated, "typical of what is possible under the American system."[24]

8

STARTING ALL OVER

To illustrate how her life changed after she married, Marjorie Hillis Roulston told two stories. In the first, before her wedding, she's in the midst of a lecture tour in the Midwest when her travel arrangements suddenly change, and she's forced to take a train after midnight. With nothing for it but to walk to the station in the dark, with the night clerk of the hotel carrying her bags, she then finds the train delayed by several hours. The hotel clerk hightails it, leaving the touring author to spend several hours alone in a musty waiting room, with only "a trio of drunks" for company. It's not pleasant, but nothing "crucial" occurs, as she puts it. It's just one of those things that an independent woman learns to take in stride.

The second story takes place after she has married Roulston and moved out to his palatial Long Island home. She tells him she needs to drive into Brooklyn for some errands, and the protective husband asks about her plans down to the last detail. He then proceeds to write out correspondingly lengthy instructions for the chauffeur, which makes his wife burst out laughing—does he think she'll get lost in the neighborhood where she grew up? He explains that he trusts her sense of direction, but wants to protect her from having to cross busy Fulton Street by herself. He has plotted out the route perfectly, so that the car will be waiting on the right side of the street for each errand, and Marjorie won't have to risk stepping into traffic. The former bachelor girl is amused—and decides to be flattered, not offended, by this assumption of helplessness. Thus begins the long unlearning of everything Marjorie Hillis taught herself the hard way: "efficiency, looking out for myself, earning my own martinis." Instead she finds herself, in marriage, "wrapped comfortably in cotton wool." She comes to enjoy this coddling, and eventually to depend on it. "At the end of ten pretty perfect years, I thought I *was* a fragile creature," she admits.[1]

Among the friends to write to Marjorie expressing their shock and sorrow was her friend and former boss at *Vogue*, Edna Woolman Chase. Still at the helm of the magazine, where she would remain until 1954, Chase soon invited her old colleague back to contribute an article called "Who Is the Older Woman?"[2] Betraying no trace of grief or specific advice to widows, this article, which appeared in October 1950, instead celebrated the ascendency of older women. It anticipated what would become the dominant theme of Marjorie's late career, that women in their fifties and beyond had just as much right to the independence, glamour, and pleasure that younger women enjoyed. She would insist, too, that they had plenty to contribute to society, through their expertise and experience, longevity, and wealth—even after they were no longer the center of male attention.

The former editor began her article by poking fun at her own youthful self, recalling the captions she would write, thirty-odd years ago when she was in her twenties, "on the rare occasions when we published clothes for the doddering old dear." She would "pityingly" describe how the cut of a dress or "the soft fold of white chiffon at the neckline" might flatter an older wearer. But today, a woman in her forties could wear whatever she liked: "You can find her in her garden in slacks, on the tennis court in shorts, and on the beach in something almost as abbreviated as her daughter's bathing costume."

The new prominence of older women, Marjorie continued, extended beyond fashion to culture. Older heroines in plays could have a romantic life—she gave the example of *The Wisteria Trees*, an adaptation of Chekhov's *The Cherry Orchard* that had enjoyed a hit run on Broadway through most of 1950, starring the fifty-year-old Helen Hayes in the lead role. What was more, these older characters were allowed to be sexually active—their romance did not have to end "with them sitting cozily before the fire." In magazine stories—nearly all mass-market magazines at the time published fiction, often by highly respected authors—the female heroines were no longer exclusively younger than twenty-two. By contrast, in modern fiction, "our best heroines have daughters, if not granddaughters." Those former leading ladies, the "sweet young things," were no longer taken so seriously—or, alternatively, taken much too seriously, and presented as "Social Problems." This was a prescient observation—the publication of J. D. Salinger's *The Catcher in the Rye* was a few months off, which would inspire an outcry at the behavior and attitudes of modern American youth.[3]

Older women in 1950, Marjorie wrote, could look around and find plenty of real-life inspiration in actresses like Irene Dunne and Gloria Swanson, and public figures like the Duchess of Windsor, Eleanor Roosevelt, and Clare Boothe Luce. It's striking—and a little chilling—that the two politicians she singles out for admiration would shortly find themselves embattled against the encroaching power of Joseph McCarthy. Margaret Chase Smith, the long-serving Republican senator from Maine, had just criticized McCarthy and the actions of the House Un-American Activities Committee in a speech in which she passionately defended the right of Americans to voice their opposition to the government without being accused of Communist sympathies, declaring, "I don't want to see the Republican Party ride to political victory on the Four Horsemen of Calumny—Fear, Ignorance, Bigotry and Smear." The last of those horsemen was about to trample Marjorie's other political heroine, California representative Helen Gahagan Douglas, whose political career would soon be ended by a bruising run for Senate against Richard Nixon, in which he accused her of being "pink right down to her underwear."[4]

Nobody could accuse *Vogue* magazine of Communist sympathies, however, and the rest of Marjorie's article was an unabashed celebration of older women's economic power. An older woman didn't have to be a politician to have an impact on society—as long as she had money, she mattered. Stereotypes about impoverished widows notwithstanding, Marjorie wrote that older women controlled "a startling proportion of the wealth in the country" and that it was for them, not their daughters or nieces, that "the expensive resort hotels refurbish, the cruise ships polish their decks, the restaurateurs concoct new menus, the jewelers assemble diamonds and emeralds, and the furriers buy mink and ermine." Coming full circle, the mature woman now influenced fashion, rather than having to rely on the few items *Vogue* deemed appropriate for her. Her independent way of thinking was influencing designers to emphasize subtle, flattering lines and a versatility that allowed her individuality to shine. Her power, ultimately, lay in numbers—there were more older women, more visible in society, than ever before, Marjorie claimed. The world was "teeming with gray-haired wives and widows, looking younger than ever under their becoming well-groomed haloes."

While she was composing this optimistic assessment of the fortunes of the older woman, sixty-year-old Marjorie was busy upending the life she had settled into as a married woman. Once her late husband was buried and she had made it through the initial, exhausting grieving period, she put both High Lindens and the Brooklyn house up for sale, explaining later her belief that "a house one has shared with a person one cared about is far lonelier than a house one has never shared with anyone at all."[5] Just as she had after losing her parents, when she fled Bronxville for Tudor City, she turned her back on the suburbs and began to hunt for a new apartment in the city. This process took long enough, she told one newspaper, that by the time it was over, she found she was back to "some semblance of normal living."[6]

By now a very wealthy widow, Mrs. Roulston no longer needed an economical pad within walking distance of the office. She headed instead to the Upper East Side, to a gracious apartment building on the corner of Park Avenue and Sixty-Third Street, and set about revising the old Live-Alone plan to suit her new circumstances. This meant replacing her married routines with new ones—in particular, she found herself dreading five o'clock, the hour when her husband used to arrive home and the couple shared a predinner cocktail. So she took action, inviting friends over at this time "every night for a while," until the role of solo hostess had begun to crowd out the memory of domestic intimacy. She also reconsidered who was on the guest list, feeling that she no longer fit in with the couples she had been friends with during her marriage. Instead, she revived older friendships from her Live-Aloner days. The "complete readjustment" to her new life could be a thrill, even if she was now more blunt about its shortcomings: "I don't mean that it will ever be a life as full as that you had when you were married," she confessed to an interviewer, "but it can be both stimulating and interesting."[7]

By the end of January 1951, just a year and a half after Roulston's death, Marjorie was ready to share her revised Live-Alone message with a new audience. The cover of her new book *You Can Start All Over* promised to reveal "how to live alone <u>again</u> and like it," and was addressed to widows, divorcées, and aging Live-Aloners. Once again drawing on her own experiences, the book's celebration of independence was tempered now by the knowledge of what it felt like to give it up. Her bereavement allowed Marjorie to write with a new empathy for her readers, and she shared more of her own emotions, more directly than before, dropping the glamorous facade to admit to loneliness, depression, and fear. She admitted that starting over for the third time—after her parents' deaths, her marriage, and now her widowhood—was harder than ever before. But her old optimistic spirit glimmered through. As the book progressed, its narrator grew noticeably more confident that her new life could prove to be "full of interest and color," just as it could be for anyone else, "with a little spunk and determination."[8]

You Can Start All Over was specifically aimed at those older women Marjorie had recently praised in *Vogue*, and not at young widows or divorcées raising young children—even though the war and its aftermath had created plenty of both. She acknowledged that a totally fresh start would be difficult and unwise for those women, whose experiences she had never shared, so instead, she wrote for those who weren't likely to marry again. This approach allowed her to speak with authority, but also to avoid becoming entangled in the widespread divorce panic that had been swirling since the late 1940s. World War II had seen young American couples rushing to the altar in droves before men shipped out for overseas service, and now thousands of those hasty marriages were coming just as hastily unstitched. The skyrocketing divorce rate inspired a rash of moralizing critiques, and much fearful discussion of the possibility that marriage as an institution was in terminal decline. Marjorie referred at the beginning of her book to the "thousands of words" that were "being turned out every week" on the evils of divorce—but she didn't back away from her conviction that divorce and widowhood were similar experiences requiring similar recovery efforts. (She did acknowledge that a divorcée, unlike a widow, probably didn't feel that losing a husband was "the most completely devastating loss one can experience.") It would have been easy to reframe the book to focus exclusively on widows of all ages, and to capitalize on the public sympathy for women who had lost husbands in the war. Yet her pragmatism prevented her. Both widows and divorcées needed time to grieve, after which they owed it to themselves to let go of the past and rediscover themselves—or in the latter's case, to "really wash that man right out of your hair and send yourself on a new way."[9]

Although she continued to champion women's independence, the older and wiser Marjorie Hillis Roulston sounded more conservative in this new book than ever before. With the experience of marriage behind her, she now declared confidently that a happy marriage ought to be the ultimate goal of a woman's life—perhaps

thinking back on her mother's advice from forty years ago with
more sympathy. The loss of a husband, she wrote, meant the loss
of a woman's "most vital job" and sense of purpose in life. But
she had not become pious in her old age. She advised women in
mourning to avoid both alcohol and regret—the former because its
comforts were short-lived and could backfire embarassingly, and
the latter simply because it was a "futile and wasteful emotion."[10]

One of the major challenges a widow or divorcée had to face was
the scrutiny and judgment of other people, and their expectations
of how long it ought to take a woman to "get over" her loss. Marjorie counseled that the best approach was to take this attention
with a shrug, accepting that some people would criticize no matter
what. "If you show spunk, a very good quality to muster as soon as
you can, they will say you are flippant (as they will of this book),"
she admitted.[11] This was especially true for divorcées, who bore the
added burden of representing, to some, the larger social decline.
Yet displaying too much obvious sadness, for too long, could make
you look and feel weak.

Marjorie returned to the no-win question of mourning behavior in the syndicated newspaper column "Everybody's Etiquette."
For several years from the late 1940s, this column invited experts
and celebrities to respond to a wide range of social dilemmas,
including actress Barbara Stanwyck on "How Not to Be a Door-
mat," and swimming star Esther Williams on what to wear to the
beach. Confronted with the question, "How long do you think a
widow should follow mourning convention?" Marjorie responded
that a widow needed her friends and should feel free to go out and
enjoy herself. While it might be in "better taste" to avoid nightclubs and large parties, she deemed movies, plays, and concerts
perfectly appropriate, as long as the widow could keep her emo-

tions in check and show interest in subjects other than her own grief. However, she warned that not everyone would be so supportive, and that some people would still negatively judge a widow "unless she remains a figure of sorrow far longer than is wise for her health or kind to those around her." She added pointedly that those people would criticize her "more sharply than they would a man in the same position."[12]

Keeping busy was essential for the newly single Live-Aloner to keep regret and loneliness at bay. Marjorie encouraged her reader to focus her energies on her home, her friends, one consuming interest, and a mixture of hobbies—in that order. And she ought to surround herself with friends who were similarly active, as women with jobs or a larger purpose tended to have "held up" better than the ladies of leisure, who often "have frankly slipped." For the woman on the lookout for a new activity, Marjorie suggested collecting, politics, finance, photography, genealogy, travel, crafts, or translating books into Braille—some absorbing passion that would engage her brain and distract from her solitude: "We suspect that the first enterprising lady after Eve who lost her mate, or didn't want one, went in for How to Know the Wild Flowers of her era, or collecting recipes for preparing dinosaur."[13] One unqualified advantage to newfound singleness, after all, was no longer having to pretend to share a husband's tedious passions for, say, horse shows or classical concerts.

Marjorie was firm in her belief that it was better to find a rewarding hobby than a second husband. Marriage was a long process of adaptation, in her view, and even if it was pleasurable to do it once, she didn't advise trying to repeat the experiment. "There is no more compensating job in the world when you do it for the right man, but there is a limit to the number of times you can do a complete remodeling job on anything, yourself included." She admits that young widows might have more energy for such "remodeling," and that young divorcées could also be optimistic about their romantic prospects—perhaps thinking of her sister Nathalie's successful second marriage. Nevertheless, she admitted to feeling surprise that the latter would be so hopeful, "on the principle of the burned child dreading the fire."[14]

Besides, for mature Live-Aloners, the available men were hardly the prizes they thought they were. Marjorie observed tartly that as their ranks thinned "along with the hair on their heads," men came to value themselves ever more highly.[15] Along with this elevated sense of self-worth, they developed a fear of being "hunted," which held them back from the honest friendships that she believed women would probably prefer. She warned readers about the men "whose intentions are what used to be called Dishonorable"—who might feel freer to pursue a widowed or divorced woman than someone who had never been married. "Before you were married you had (we assume) what they considered an Asset, though it was also an Obstacle in their eyes," she coyly explained. "Now, you haven't it, but its very absence has become an Asset—again, in their eyes. It relieves them of responsibility."[16] It's tempting to speculate about what kind of encounters might have made the widowed Marjorie Hillis so disparaging of men and their motives, especially given that in her previous books they barely figured at all, except as dinner dates and convenient handymen.

The question of money had always lain at the heart of the Live-Aloner's independence—and in considering the prospects for an older woman who previously enjoyed a husband's financial protection, Marjorie pulled no punches. "For sheer and prolonged terror, there are few things that happen in this more-or-less civilized hemisphere that are worse than the experience of a woman who has been well taken care of for years and who suddenly finds herself without enough money to live on."[17] She therefore devoted a considerable chunk of the book to encouraging women to work to support themselves. With a sideswipe at contemporary articles worrying over the fate of "mere chits of 35," she made it clear that she considered women well over fifty to have plenty to contribute both socially and economically. Listing all the jobs her own friends had taken up, from real estate to advertising to secretarial work, she acknowledged that some had exchanged "glamour" for money, but emphasized that all had held on to their independence. Despite claiming to hate statistics, she referred to the 1947 census to back up her argument, which revealed that four million women ages forty-five to sixty-five were holding jobs.

In addition to money and independence, a job also kept a woman engaged in the world. After her retirement, therefore, she had to work even harder to stay young and keep up with a changing society. While Marjorie allowed her to give up on cutting-edge fashion and sleep in as late as she liked, the retired Live-Aloner had a responsibility not to give up any further. She should take care to maintain her figure, get a modern haircut, and steer clear of "those surplice 'mama' dresses." She ought to read the current bestsellers, keep up with culture, and talk to the grandchildren about their lives (not difficult given that "most normal young people are Complete Egocentrics").[18] To make sure that her home didn't become "so much as a shade musty" she ought to renovate, Dorothy Draper-style, with fresh paint and creative flair, perhaps sawing an old table in half or turning a vase into a lamp. At all costs, she must avoid moving in with younger relatives, no matter how sensible it might seem—it went against the natural order of things: "The point of view of each generation is completely differ-ent from that of the one preceding or following it, and ought to be."[19] There was no sense or pleasure, in Marjorie's view, in trying to reorder one's life to fit into someone else's lifestyle.

The new table lamp or the part-time job were just part of the larger goal of *You Can Start All Over*, which was to "recapture that feeling that you are a very special person"—in other words, to steal back a little of that egocentricity from the younger generation. Once upon a time, like them, "you believed that no one else in the world was quite like you—and you were right." A single woman living alone at seventy has just as much right to her place in the world as she had at twenty.

Most reviews of *You Can Start All Over* were positive, if nostalgic for the original *Live Alone*, and responded to the sprightliness and sense of the advice. But a review in the *Washington Post* hinted that the world of the 1950s would prove much colder to the Live-Aloner than the world of fifteen years before, and that there would be "no nightgowns named for her new book (as there were for her first provocative volume)." The reviewer complained: "The net result of this slightly weary persiflage is something less than stimulating," and added that "somehow it reminds the reader of a woman talking to herself in her mirror; a lone individual living in a relative vac-uum." Complaining that the book hardly mentioned children and grandchildren, the reviewer implied that a woman's solitude was bleak and narcissistic, that without an extended family, she was cut off from the world, communicating only with herself. Nothing could be further from the picture of confident social usefulness that Marjorie Hillis advocated and embodied, but already the lone female was becoming a figure of fear and scorn.

The same reviewer went on to note, as Marjorie had in *Vogue*, that older women were living longer than men and controlled a significant portion of the nation's wealth—but he didn't see that as liberating. Instead of encouragement to put on a negligee, mix a cocktail, and curl up with *The New Yorker*, he argued that women needed "a good solid, factual chapter on the economics of widowhood," which would cover budgets, investments, insurance, taxes, "and warnings against the pitfalls which on the average defraud a widow of her capital in seven years." And for good measure, this revised and dreary textbook ought to include "more about health, diet and recreation." The review's blend of judgment and condescension anticipated the way that the upcoming decade would treat single women, as pariahs and figures of threat to the all-consuming cult of the nuclear family.[20]

The Live-Aloner in the Nuclear Bunker

The moment when Marjorie Hillis packed up and sold her two large houses to move back, alone, to Manhattan was perhaps the lowest point for the status of the Live-Aloner in the entire twentieth century. Her simple assertion that "there is a thrill in making a life of your own" would sound more rebellious than ever in the paranoid, fenced-in '50s.[21] During the years of Depression and war, when American society was in flux, and cultural certainties looked much more like contingencies, it had been possible to transform the "extra woman" into a figure of strength and defiance. But she crumbled in the nuclear era, under the relentless assault on gender nonconformity and any ambition that might reach beyond the front door of the home.

Just as Marjorie Hillis returned to the world of advice giving, her indefatigable peer Dorothy Dix left it. In December of 1951 newspapers reported Dix's death, at age ninety—although she had claimed to be ten years younger. Her syndicated columns—"Of Men and Women" and "Dorothy Dix Says"—appeared right up until the end, so that the advice contained in "I Can Give You No Hope That Your Skirt-Chaser Husband Will Reform" overlapped with her obituaries.[22] In fact, the column was in other hands by this point—Dix herself had had to give it up after a stroke two years earlier—but it was only at her death that the syndicate announced this fact, and that they would retire the name, rather than continuing it under other authors, "Dear Abby"-style. With her passing, a link to an older version of advice giving was broken: the style that Marjorie Hillis shared, in which authority was derived from feminine common sense and life experience, rather than scientific theories and experimentation. Nobody would have called Dix a modern woman, but her pragmatic approach gave her insight that would be lost as the 1950s wore on—like her conviction that teenage weddings were unwise, and that men and women really ought to get to know each other before they married. Before long, Americans were marrying younger than ever before, and the "old maid" came to seem not just unfortunate, but pathological.

The 1950s were not inevitable. American men and women had worked together to fight World War II in unprecedented solidarity. When men went overseas, they left their sisters and sweethearts to take their places in the workforce, from offices and shops where they were already comfortable, to light and heavy industry, which were for the most part entirely new arenas. Those wartime upheavals came on the heels of a Depression that had also shaken up traditional gender roles. By 1945, women had access to jobs, education, divorce, and birth control in unprecedented numbers—and to many observers, it looked as though "traditional" marriage and family life were doomed.

The war years had also drawn black and white Americans of both genders together in the collective national effort. While this proximity hardly generated mass white support for the ongoing civil rights struggle, the "Double V" campaign exposed to many complacent whites the disconnect between the doctrine of liberty the country was spreading overseas, and the injustices of Jim Crow at home. One version of American freedom in the face of the Communist threat, therefore, might have embraced greater racial and sexual equality, a national commitment to giving all citizens an equal chance at education, work, upward mobility, and success. According to historian Elaine Tyler May, "Nothing on the surface of postwar America explains the rush of young Americans into marriage, parenthood and traditional gender roles."[23]

The 1950s were also not normal—even though "normal" was the defining virtue of the decade.[24] The decade did not simply represent the return of "traditional" modes of living after the upheavals of the war, but something both old and new: half-buried Victorian family structures were resurrected in the fresh clothing of modern psychology. Men and women were hurried and prodded into earlier and earlier marriage not because it was "traditional"—it hadn't been, for decades—but because cutting-edge science told them that the only way to be happy was to conform to rigid gender roles. Popular culture, meanwhile, held up a narrow slice of the population—a white family made up of a male breadwinner and a female homemaker, and two or more children, in a suburban neighborhood—and pretended it was the whole pie. What made this suburban cliché so pervasive was the very fact that it was new. Just as journalists have been obsessed with the attitudes, beliefs, and failings of "millennials" for at least the past decade, so in the '50s they wrote endless disquisitions on suburbanites and their discontents. Along the way, they turned "career woman" into an insult and made it clear that an unmarried woman was about as trustworthy and welcome in the community as a stray Soviet missile.

The rate of marriage in the United States between 1920 and 1940 forms a neat U shape, dipping to all-time lows during the Depression, then steadily climbing back up. And it kept on climbing. At first, such a spike was unremarkable—weddings and births always rise after a war—but the post-World War II spike lasted so long that it started to look like the new normal.[25] Thanks to the flurry of late-1940s divorces, marriage in the 1950s appeared deceptively stable. The baby boom lasted until 1957, twelve years after the end of the war, with an average 123 births per 1,000 women, compared with 79.5 per 1,000 in 1940 (and just under 60 per 1,000 today, the lowest rate since the government began keeping track in 1909).[26] Despite the new availability of contraceptives, which had been gradually decriminalized and normalized since the mid-1930s, couples were having more children, sooner, and closer together. At the same time, the average age of marriage fell, so far and so fast that by 1960 fully half of all American women were teenagers when they made their vows. The generation that came of age during and after World War II was "the most marrying generation on record"—despite having more options *not* to be so than ever before.[27]

If they were white, those couples had the opportunity to live better than they ever had before, in suburbs that looked like the way of the future. Under the New Deal, generous subsidies were awarded to developers who—openly or covertly—built segregated communities, in the belief that neighborhoods were more stable and prosperous if they were separated by race and class. So-called white flight from cities after the war was both push and pull—

whites who wanted to escape ethnically diverse and economically starved cities received government help to buy their homes. Less than 2 percent of the $120 billion paid out in such subsidies by 1960 went to minorities.[28]

The novel suburban family quickly became normal. Young and white, these families were almost always supported by a male breadwinner who commuted to a city office. Less than 10 percent of wives worked, and children and teenagers rarely lifted a finger, as they would have on the farm or in the family store in a previous generation. Instead, they watched television. A rarity in the late 1940s, by 1960, 87 percent of American households had a television—but this family, and this family only, saw itself reflected in the little curved screen.

Although it was prosperous, the postwar period was hardly peaceful—or postwar. At the beginning of 1951, in an article promoting the forthcoming *You Can Start All Over*, Marjorie Hillis declared that "the live-alone ladies" could be of particular use to "Uncle Sam" in "the emergency days confronting the nation." The emergency was the Korean War, ongoing since the previous summer, and Marjorie predicted that it would require a mobilization of women even greater than World War II. She suggested that older women could volunteer to organize play groups for children, so that their young mothers would be free to carry out war production work, and that for wives with husbands overseas, war work would give them something useful to do, so they wouldn't have to "sit at home and just be scared."[29]

Useful war work or not, everyone was scared. The memory of Hiroshima and the nuclear brinksmanship of the Cold War era made the specter of total annihilation all too vivid—and the illusory security of domesticity all the more tempting. Just a decade before, Marjorie could gaily exhort her Live-Aloner to "be a Communist" as though it were just another hobby, equivalent to stamp collecting. By the 1950s, to "be something!" was to stand out, and to stand out was risky—any kind of nonconformity was tainted with a pink blush, deepening to red, that could get a person fired or arrested or worse.

Suspicion landed particularly heavily on women who chose not to marry. The House Un-American Activities Committee warned in 1950 that teachers at girls' schools and women's colleges were "often frustrated" and likely to be "loyal disciples of Russia." Even where she was not suspected of Communist sympathies, the self-directed career woman replaced the seductress as the scariest version of the "femme fatale" out there. In the 1950s, according to film historian Peter Biskind, the scarlet letter "A" came to stand for "ambition," not "adultery."[30]

The Job of Marriage

At the end of World War II, many women showed up for work to find their final paycheck and a pink slip waiting. By 1947 three million women had lost their jobs, sparking off union-led battles at several workplaces, including at the Ford plant in Highland Park, New Jersey, where 150 women successfully picketed the employment office to protest their firing on the grounds of sex discrimination.[31] But in general, women found the public utterly unsympathetic to their cause. Less than 20 percent of Americans of either sex in the late 1940s believed married women had any right to a job, or that they deserved a chance to compete fairly with men for work. The steep decline in women's wages made work even less appealing for those who could afford to choose. At the same time, the wages of white American men skyrocketed, making marriage the best shot most women had at a share of the country's postwar prosperity.

That prosperity was sharply limited by race. The aspirational male breadwinner–female homemaker model was out of reach even for most African American college graduates, who earned significantly less than a white man who had only finished high school. The majority of black middle-class families in 1960 therefore had two incomes and 64 percent of black mothers held jobs, compared with 27 percent of white middle-class women and 35 percent of white working-class women. Economic necessity was not the only force driving black women into the workforce, however— in fact, middle-class black women were the most likely to work, in spite of the fact that they had even less access than white women to jobs carrying any prestige, creativity, or autonomy.[32] They were not immune to the doctrine of the happy homemaker being pushed all around them, but they were less likely than their white counterparts to view their roles as students and workers as temporary and limited to the period before they could begin their "real" lives as wives and mothers. African American women who went to college did not see it as a husband-hunting ground, but as part of the route to a job and a role in the community—a 1956 study of these students found that all but a tiny handful of them intended and expected to forge some kind of career. The same young women believed that there were other claims on their time beyond wage work and family care: They saw themselves as active participants in their religious and political communities. They were less likely to let their husbands decide whether or not they could work, and saw no conflict between their identity as mothers and their roles in the wider world. As such, they have been called the "true pioneers of modern family patterns."[33]

What is most surprising is that despite the sneers and the smears directed at "career women," across the spectrum of race and class, women's participation in the labor force rose steadily during the domestic decade. By the late 1950s, fully a third of women—married and single—held jobs. But what did that really mean? They were doing jobs men did not want to do: hordes of secretaries and stenographers, young and on the hunt for a husband, like the characters depicted in Rona Jaffe's bestselling 1958 novel *The Best of Everything*. Or they might be older and working out of necessity, but not in a role that brought them power, prestige, wealth, or the freedom to do as they pleased. In October 1956, *Look* magazine approvingly noted that women had "gracefully conceded" the upper rungs of the career ladder to men, even as its front cover blared "The American Woman: She's Winning the Battle of the Sexes."[34] According to the widely quoted psychologists Ferdinand Lundberg and Marynia F. Farnham, authors of the virulently antifeminist 1947 book *Modern Woman: The Lost Sex*, any career—which they defined as "work plus prestige"—was "antifeminine to its core" and "an assault on men's self-respect."[35]

It was not for lack of an education. During the 1950s more girls completed high school and a higher percentage went to college than ever before. Yet their presence on campus was overwhelmed by men given new access to college by the GI Bill—from an almost fifty-fifty share in 1920, women made up only a third of undergraduates by the mid-1950s, and their needs and interests lost ground to those of their male peers. Further study moved out of reach: in 1920, women had earned 20 percent of all PhDs, but between 1950 and 1955, that proportion fell to a low of just 9 percent. In professional fields, their options had been shrinking for a while—almost 90 percent of school districts nationwide had bans on hiring already-married women, and almost as many required women to quit if they got married. These work restrictions combined with increasing cultural pressure to marry caused serious labor shortages in the traditionally female fields of teaching, nursing, and social work by the mid-1950s. The crisis was such that President Eisenhower urged Congress to pass an equal pay law, claiming in his January 1956 State of the Union Address that "equal pay for equal work without discrimination because of sex is a matter of simple justice."[36] There was, however, no move by the Republican government to act on the president's sense of justice, nor did Eisenhower or anyone address the entrenched discrimination in hiring. Newspaper job ads were separated into "Help Wanted: Male" and "Help Wanted: Female" until the late 1960s.

In her 1957 advice book *The Modern Book of Marriage*, author Lena Levine urged women who worked to make sure that their husbands knew that the job was always secondary to the home. She approvingly discussed the "bright new trend" of young women dropping out of college in order to support their husbands' study, earning them a "PhT," for "Putting husband Through."[37] Women were repeatedly told that being married to a successful man was a career in itself; as advice author Emily Mudd put it, this "career" would require "the qualities of a diplomat, a businesswoman, a good cook, a trained nurse, a schoolteacher, a politician, and a glamour girl."[38] Like the wartime housewife, the 1950s homemaker also held seven jobs—but now, not a single one earned her any money or independence. In 1953, Dorothy Carnegie, the wife of success-guru Dale Carnegie, chimed in with her own book that was decidedly of its time, *How to Help Your Husband Get Ahead*, which promised to teach wives how to boost their husbands "up the ladder of success."[39] Winning friends and influencing people was for men; the only person a woman had to win and influence was her husband.

Sex and the American Housewife

The gender extremism of the 1950s held that a woman could only be truly happy and fulfilled performing the fundamentally biological role of mother. She was also supposed to be sexually active, desirable, and desiring—this was the aspect of suburban femininity that was supposed to make her modern, and distinguish her from her prudish Victorian ancestors. *Time* magazine's 1960 cover story on "The Suburban Wife—an American Phenomenon" was typical of press coverage that raised the June Cleaver cliché to the status of a national icon. Although the modern stereotype of a housewife and stay-at-home mom leans more toward the frumpy and frazzled, the 1950s version was as glamorous as any '30s career girl had been—far more so, as the once-aspirational independent woman was now seen as a miserable, unattractive spinster.

But for all that she was supposed to find fulfillment in the private sphere of the home, the 1950s housewife was in no way a private figure. Journalists and politicians kept dragging her out from behind her lace curtains to hold her up to the world as a symbol of enviable American freedom. Her proxy political role reached its apogee in 1959 in the "kitchen debate" between Vice President Richard Nixon and Nikita Khrushchev. As part of an effort to promote understanding between the two nations, exhibitions in New York and Moscow showcased the lifestyles and attitudes of the Cold War adversaries. In Moscow, touring the kitchen of a "typical" suburban house constructed as part of the American National Exhibition, the two leaders jockeyed for dominance in a conversation about the availability of new kitchen technologies, like dishwashers. Nixon pointed out the appliance as an example of how America was working to make life easier for housewives, to which Khrushchev countered that the Soviet Union did not share the "capitalist attitude toward women." Nixon suggested that the housewife's freedom to choose which washing machine to buy could stand in for the "right to choose" enjoyed as a cornerstone of American democracy—a phrase that had not yet become synonymous with reproductive choice. The implication was that the housewife could choose to stay home, unlike the Soviet working woman, whose obligation to work supposedly made her ugly and unfeminine.[40]

Three years later, in December 1962, the *Saturday Evening Post* presented a cover story in praise of "the typical American woman," underscoring her role as housewife. Based on the results of Gallup polls (and thus promoting the polling organization— the article was written by George Gallup), the typical woman was revealed to be in her mid-thirties, with two or more children, a full-time homemaker with a high school education and, although this wasn't explicitly stated, white. She knew that she possessed all the rights of a man, but chose, freely, not to exercise them, understanding that men were naturally suited to business or politics just as she was naturally suited to cooking, cleaning, and ferrying her children from playdates to dance lessons. Gallup wrote that he was ignoring "the extremes" who lived at the margins of typical femininity: "old maids," divorcées, childless women, and working mothers. These "unusual" women did exist in American society, the pollster grudgingly admitted, but they were curiosities, of interest only to sociologists. Mainstream society was not "geared" to them.

Yet there were visible currents of unrest, even in this celebratory article, which was already on the defensive against other media portrayals of the housewife that stereotyped her as "lonely, bored, lazy, sexually inept, frigid, superficial, harried, militant, overworked." Despite having the comfort of knowing "precisely why they're here on earth"—to be a good mother and a good wife—fully half of the "single girls" quoted, and a third of the married ones, complained about the inferior status of women.[41] No matter how natural or typical her existence, somehow the apogee of American womanhood couldn't just be quiet and submit happily to her so-called freedom.

Perhaps when she peeked out from behind the curtains she had noticed that her "choice" to submit to male authority—and even her choice of dishwasher—was an illusion. Her husband's authority was enshrined in law in big and small ways, restricting her freedom and overwriting her identity. She was dependent on him financially, and although he was required to provide "necessaries" for her and their children, it was up to him to determine what was necessary and what was a luxury. She had no right to any of the money he earned while she was keeping his house and raising his children. After they walked down the aisle, women in many states were still legally required to take their husband's name, despite the efforts of the Lucy Stoners, and could not rent or buy a home alone. If a woman wanted to open a business by herself, she had to submit a petition attesting to her good character. An employer could fire her if she became pregnant, or not hire her at all based on her plans for a family, and job advertisements freely included attractiveness in the list of desirable attributes for a secretary or an office "gal Friday."

The most intimate aspects of a woman's life were the most tightly regulated. She could not say no to sex with her husband.

No state acknowledged, much less outlawed, marital rape until decades later, and it wasn't until the 1990s that it was made illegal nationwide. The use of contraceptives was restricted in many states until the mid-1960s, even for married couples, and their use was a misdemeanor in Massachusetts until 1963. A middle-class girl who was unlucky enough to get pregnant out of wedlock was expected to hide away until the birth and give the baby up for adoption immediately. Abortion, of course, was illegal, although common enough to cause injury and death to thousands of women. Amid these restrictions, double standards, and violations, women in the 1950s were expected to exude sexual pleasure and availability, and discuss intimacy more openly than ever before.

The Freudian Mystique

Marjorie Hillis had little interest in either sex or psychology, despite bolstering her theories, in *Live Alone and Like It* and its sequels, with "case studies"—a term that carries the veneer of clinical practice. She never probed the depths of Miss C.'s happiness or Mrs. M.'s disappointment, but relied on straightforward emotional language that was easily correlated to circumstances. Even in *Work Ends at Nightfall*, her most emotionally sophisticated book, the characters feel regret, envy, loneliness, satisfaction, or joy, but they are never at the mercy of subconscious desires or repressed urges. Marjorie paid no attention to sex as distinct from a relationship, and wrote about it only in coy or roundabout ways, focusing more on heartbreak than therapeutic orgasm. It was one more way in which her books no longer sounded modern.

Postwar America has been called "the era of the expert," in thrall to mostly male authority, from baby care guru Dr. Spock to positive-thinking popularizer Norman Vincent Peale.[42] But more than any other guru in the 1940s and 1950s, America was in the grip of Sigmund Freud. According to one historian of psychoanalysis, Freud's appeal connected with a collection of distinctly American traits: "our love for all things modern, ambivalent feelings about sex, pronounced streak of individualism, and entitlement to happiness."[43]

Freud's work had first been translated into English at the beginning of the twentieth century, and the Viennese doctor's only visit to America was in 1909. During the 1920s his theories of sexuality and human development entered highbrow and progressive circles, carrying the glitter of illicit knowledge. Yet he did not fully enter the American mainstream until after World War II, when his ideas migrated from the realm of science into popular culture. In a paranoid era obsessed with hidden threats and lurking evils, novelists and filmmakers like Alfred Hitchcock seized on the idea that characters could be driven to act by secret psychosexual urges. Trickling down from academies and institutes to magazines and therapists' couches, Freudian theories about the role of sex and sexual difference in human happiness were inescapable. Many Freudians held that marriage and children offered women the pinnacle of happiness, and argued that any resistance to this model was evidence of neurosis, hysteria, sexual repression, penis envy, or some complex or other—terms that had entered the national vernacular recently enough to still sound reassuringly scientific. Even though Freud's writing never reached a wide readership, and few Americans underwent analysis according to his precise methods, the ability to discuss Oedipal desire and feminine hysteria over highballs became a sign of sophistication. As feminist leader Betty Friedan would later put it, Freud's antifeminist convictions settled over the country in this period "like fine volcanic ash."[44] In this climate, feminism, living alone, or any other rejection of the prevailing ideology was treated as a pathology.

In the Live-Alone heyday of the late 1930s, not far from the home base of Marjorie's Indianapolis publisher, another man who would have an outsized influence on 1950s attitudes to sex and relationships was just getting started. Alfred Kinsey, a straitlaced professor of zoology at Indiana University, rocked the small academic world of Bloomington in 1938 with the announcement that he would be teaching a new course in the fall semester on human sexuality.[45] Up to that point, Kinsey's research had focused on the minute variations that could be observed within a particular species of wasp—which led him to the conclusion that members of an apparently identical group were vastly more diverse than a casual glance might reveal. This began to fuel his theory that human sexual behavior, similarly, might be more fluid and variable than society sanctioned. At the time, most sexual behavior outside the heterosexual marriage bed was not only impossible to discuss publicly, but was actually illegal. Sodomy was outlawed in every state before 1962, punishable by imprisonment or hard labor, and in numerous states those laws also extended to ban oral sex. Even within marriage, sexual behavior was tightly regulated, so a college course that shared with undergraduates the basics of their biology in a frank and scientific way was revolutionary. The class was restricted to seniors and married students, leading to a rash of fake wedding rings and a flurry of early-September weddings. On the first day, Kinsey gave the class a new definition of "sexual dysfunction" that inverted the moralistic nonsense they'd grown up with. Abstinence and celibacy, far from being admirable, were, in Kinsey's view, the only true forms of dysfunction.

Kinsey immediately faced pressure from the conservative faculty to shut down the class. But the professor, who had been traumatized by his inexperience and discomfort on his wedding night as a twenty-seven-year-old virgin, was determined that students deserved and could handle the truth about their bodies, detached from moral terrors. By the second year of the class, Kinsey found himself counseling troubled students during his office hours, and he and his wife Clara began to invite them instead to their home, where they could ask for advice on sex and relationships over cups of tea. The professor even began to lend out his car, with its capacious backseat, to amorous young couples who had nowhere else to go. Along the way, he became curious about the varieties of experience among the students, and started to take their sexual histories in conferences after class. In a nonjudgmental and straightforward way, he asked them questions that would have been unthinkable anywhere else: about masturbation, premarital sex, homosexuality, and the presence or absence of desire. Eventually, the protests against Kinsey and his course gained enough strength that even the university's supportive president was forced to act. Given an ultimatum between giving up the course and giving up his academic post, Kinsey left the university and began to widen his net of inquiry beyond students to men in prison, men in Chicago's underground gay scene, and as many groups as possible, always with a goal of diversity in age, race, and social status. The questions that Kinsey first asked his students in his Bloomington living room became the basis of a groundbreaking research project into human sexuality that would span the next decade and more. When the results of his studies were published as books, *Sexual Behavior in the Human Male* (1948) and *Sexual Behavior in the Human Female* (1953), they were enduring bestsellers, and no modern-minded American could ignore them.[46]

Kinsey's books might have offered some readers a prurient thrill, but for many they were a lifeline, offering the reassurance that normality "was merely a statistical concept."[47] In the midst of a culture that insisted on a healthy sex life as a prerequisite for marital happiness, but refused to discuss what that really meant, the studies were revelatory for both men and women. A new wave of self-help was already emerging in the late 1940s and '50s to spread sexual knowledge to an eager audience, and was bolstered by Kinsey's findings. The days when the family "marriage manual" was shamefully stuffed under the mattress were over, along with the idea that it was women's fate merely to endure, never enjoy, a man's attentions. But the idea that sex was frightening and filthy was deeply ingrained, as the title of one of the most popular new sex guides, published in 1947 by a British doctor named Eustace Chesser, suggests. *Love Without Fear: How to Achieve Sex Happiness in Marriage* advocated birth control and attacked the "absurd, and sometimes hysterical, campaign against masturbation."[48] It also operated as a practical workbook, including lists, question-and-answer sections, and "score cards" for husbands and wives to improve their sex lives—all evidence that attitudes toward sex within marriage had profoundly changed. Sold under the tagline of "The Modern Manual for the Modern Husband and Wife," the book could not have been more emphatic in its insistence that it was a harbinger of a more enlightened era.

Can This Marriage Be Saved?

During the 1930s, American popular culture had largely concurred with Marjorie Hillis's forgiving vision of divorce, which saw it as arising out of a dispute between equals, and offering a relatively harmless way out of a bad situation. Norma Shearer's

Oscar-winning role in the pre-code drama *The Divorcee* set the pattern, which Katharine Hepburn, Rosalind Russell, and Irene Dunne would refine. Shearer's character, Jerry, a "quintessential New Woman" believes in marital equality to the extent that when she discovers that her husband has cheated on her, she immediately cheats back, telling him she has "settled their accounts." The marital breakdown is averted when Jerry, inspired by a self-sacrificing married friend, decides to give up her other man and recommit to her husband. No lasting damage has been done by anyone's bad behavior, and infidelity is easy to fix.[49]

Twenty years on, such a plot would be unthinkable without some serious, possibly tragic punishment coming down on the cheating woman. Sex-advice writer Eustace Chesser labeled "female promiscuity" a profound threat to family life, and a perversion championed only by "misguided feminists."[50] Like most of his peers, he insisted that divorce was a mistake and those who undertook it always regretted it—therefore, it had to be avoided at all costs. The experts who lined up in magazines and self-help books insisted that no marital problem was too severe to be overcome. Paul Popenoe's popular column "Can This Marriage Be Saved?" in *Ladies' Home Journal* was only one plank in the platform of the man they called "Mr. Marriage," since he had first established his pioneering American Institute of Family Relations in in 1930.

A horticulturalist by training, Popenoe's background hardly sounds relevant to becoming the nation's leading marriage guidance counselor, any more than Kinsey's study of wasps made him a likely human-sexuality expert. But in fact there was a grim logic to it, as Popenoe proved all too eager to transfer what he'd learned about selectively breeding plants to human beings. A committed eugenicist, Popenoe had advocated sterilizing the "unfit," and "believed with an evangelical fervour" in preserving marriage between couples of the "better type"—white, middle class, and able-bodied.[51] Historian Kristin Celello charts the "phenomenal growth" of marriage counseling from a handful of isolated clinics in the early 1930s to cultural ubiquity in the 1950s. She demonstrates that over the same period, the idea that a successful marriage took sustained effort became ingrained in American culture—a typical *Ladies' Home Journal* column, "Making Marriage Work," debuted in 1947. Despite the racist basis of Popenoe's theories, the idea of marriage as work also proved popular in media aimed at African American women, and *Ebony* and *Jet* magazines ran similar columns, often citing the same experts. These columns rarely gave couples advice on navigating concrete, external challenges—like finances and families—that were likely to cause real problems. Instead, they focused on the psychological "adjustment" necessary for a happy marriage—an adjustment that fell disproportionately on women.[52]

The notion that women had to change themselves in marriage to accommodate a man's more rigid habits and beliefs was widespread—even Marjorie Hillis made it clear that her own adjustment to marriage took so much work that she never wanted to repeat it. Self-help for single women in the 1940s and '50s therefore focused on the changes that they could make to themselves in order to attract a mate. Celello describes another *Ladies' Home Journal* column, beginning in 1954, titled "How to Be Marriageable," which focused on twenty-nine-year-old "Marcia," a schoolteacher who moved to Los Angeles in the hope of finding a man. Marcia gave readers first-person accounts of her sessions in the Marriage Readiness course at Popenoe's American Institute of Family Relations, and by lowering her expectations and changing her appearance, she eventually landed her "Dick." But as Celello shows, the real story of this project was fraught—it took a long search for AIFR to find a student for whom the Marriage Readiness course actually worked, and Marcia kept her participation a secret from her new husband.[53]

Marcia's subterfuge was small potatoes compared with the kind of tricks that 1950s self-help books encouraged women to try, in order to achieve the all-consuming goal of marriage. At the very least, a girl had to pretend to be whoever the man wanted her to be, suppressing her own personality in order to "please and flatter a man into proposing."[54] She had to be sexually alluring, but not sexually available, doing everything she could to guarantee that a flirtation got a ring on her finger, rather than a notch on his bedpost.

Reading these advice guides gives an exhausting sense of the effort it took for women to win the dubious, high-stakes game of marriage, and it's hard not to feel how futile it all was, aimed at at a form of family life that made so many of them so unhappy. Men, too—the founding of *Playboy* magazine in 1953 presented a glamorized image of bachelor life that made marriage look less appealing than ever, for all its cultural ubiquity. Through it all, despite the efforts of the magazines, the experts, the sex manuals, and the advertisers, Americans kept getting divorced—one in four marriages, or nearly four hundred thousand per year, broke apart during the 1950s, more than twice as many as during the previous divorce-panic era of the 1920s. Maybe Marjorie Hillis was right— marriage wasn't the only way to be happy, and there was life after the death of the union.

Life's a Banquet

Given the vilification of unmarried women and feminists during the 1950s, it's surprising that one of the most popular heroines of the decade was a defiant throwback to the Live-Alone era, and proof that Marjorie's vision maintained a powerful appeal, even if it had now moved to the realm of fantasy. *Auntie Mame* leaped like a flame from page to stage to cinema beginning in 1955, when Patrick Dennis's loosely autobiographical novel arrived on the best-seller list, where it remained for more than two years, selling one thousand copies a day at its peak. Dennis's heroine, based on his freethinking aunt, was a bon vivant and artist whose medium was other people's lives. Immortalized in the stage adaptation and 1958 film by Rosalind Russell, Mame became an unlikely icon, offering audiences a thrill that was a blend of nostalgia, fantasy, and the hope that there might be a way to live happily and well outside the boundaries of the white picket fence. Her story showed that non-conformity and living alone could still be desirable options—at least if the trappings were sufficiently glamorous and the heroine safely upper class.

The film opens in 1928 with the reading of a will, leaving orphaned, nine-year-old Patrick to the care of his father's sister, Mame, on the condition he not be brought up to be anything like her. The boy is duly delivered to his aunt's apartment at 3 Beekman Place, on the eastern edge of midtown Manhattan, just below Dorothy Draper's transformed row houses on Sutton Place, and a little above Marjorie Hillis's Tudor City. The model for Mame, Patrick Dennis's aunt Marion Tanner, lived in less refined and more reliably bohemian Greenwich Village, where she turned her townhouse into "a haven and salon for struggling artists, writers, freethinkers [and] radicals."[55] In the film, Mame's elegant domain is likewise a place of restless creativity, where the decor changes at regular intervals, cocktail parties are constant, and the bedrooms are full of their owner's abandoned artistic passions—when they aren't occupied by her worse-for-wear friends. Patrick is plunged into a world of curiosity and ideas; instructed to fill a notebook with words he doesn't understand, he comes back with a list that encapsulates Mame's world, including "stinko," "blotto," "Cubism," and "Karl Marx."

Riding a seemingly endless economic upswing, 1950s audiences could laugh at the clichés when the Wall Street crash crashes Mame's party: the stockbroker who calls to say goodbye just before he jumps out the window, and the wealthy characters' faith that their bank is safe, two minutes before it, too, goes under. After failing to make it as an actress, Mame tries to claw back her social status with a whirl through the typical single-girl employment options of the 1930s, including switchboard operator and Macy's salesgirl—in which role she meets her savior, a Southern oil tycoon who doesn't have to worry about the Depression, as his oil "just keeps on gushin'!" He marries Mame, restores her wealth, and they set off on a round-the-world trip, which is cut short only when he accidentally falls off the Matterhorn while taking a photograph of his bride.

Back in New York, a Live-Aloner once more, Mame redecorates her house and reconnects with her old friends—just as Marjorie Hillis advised—and is inspired to write her memoirs. But soon a more urgent project interrupts, when the adult Patrick brings home his fiancée to meet his aunt. Patrick has been turned into a straitlaced bore by his years at boarding school and college, and his girl, Gloria, is a nasal, dimwitted snob—despite her resemblance to Grace Kelly, whose televised wedding two years earlier had been a high point of the marriage-obsessed decade. When Mame visits Gloria's parents in Connecticut, they confide their fear that the parcel of land next door will be sold to one "Abraham Epstein"— who Mame, of course, identifies as a famous cellist. Exacting her revenge on the couple and their desire to keep their property "restricted," she buys the land and establishes it as a home for refugee Jewish children. Mame's machinations to stop Patrick's wedding work out just as neatly. When she assembles a "family dinner," introducing Gloria and her parents to all the offbeat bohemian characters who previously attended her cocktail parties, it is an opportunity to remind her angry nephew that these people raised him, even if they don't look like a conventional family. By the time the film ends, Patrick has married Mame's former assistant, and Mame is poised to take their young son with her to India—her curiosity and open-mindedness passed on as a gift for the next generation.

When Rosalind Russell took on the role of Mame Dennis, it had been more than fifteen years since her last iconic outing, as the bold, smart, glamorous "girl reporter" Hildy Johnson in Howard Hawks's *His Girl Friday*, trading machine-gun-fast banter with Cary Grant. At the end of the film, when Hildy decides to leave her dull fiancé and return to both her ex-husband and the grubby turmoil of the newspaper business, there's no question that this is the only possible choice she could make and be happy.

The fate of the fast-talking dames of the screwball era looked uncertain in the 1950s. Those spiky, mysterious, and coolly independent stars like Russell and Marlene Dietrich, Bette Davis, Joan Crawford, and Katharine Hepburn were supplanted by busty yet childlike Marilyn Monroe, Debbie Reynolds, and Brigitte Bardot. In magazine profiles these young actresses were encouraged to talk endlessly about men, romance, and babies, rather than their careers or their art.

The same year that the novel *Auntie Mame* appeared, Katharine Hepburn had her own solo vehicle in David Lean's *Summertime*, playing Jane Hudson, an enthusiastic Midwestern spinster who travels to Venice for the trip of a lifetime. Swooning along with the audience at the gold-bathed buildings and picturesque bridges, Jane finds her plucky independent veneer cracked by the city's beauty, exposing her own loneliness and envy of the romantic couples she sees everywhere. When she catches the eye of a handsome, untrustworthy antiques dealer, sitting alone in St. Peter's Square, Jane lets her feelings rule her better judgment, at least for the length of a short affair. He's a better souvenir than Venetian glass, he tells her. But in the end, Jane's emotional and sexual awakening proves more tragic than triumphant.

Auntie Mame was not immune to romance, but she held on fiercely to her independence—even more so than the characters Russell and Hepburn played in the 1930s, who in the end were tamed back into marriage plots. Mame was an anomaly, both self-reliant and ultimately victorious. For Russell, who was fifty-one when she played Mame, the role was transformative, and she identified strongly enough with the character to title her memoir after the start of her character's immortal line: "Life's a banquet, and most poor suckers are starving to death." Ironically, she lost the best-actress Oscar in 1958 to Susan Hayward playing an innocent woman sentenced to death for murder, in a drama whose title—*I Want to Live!*—sounds like a watered-down version of Mame's other signature call to arms: "Live, live, live!

Russell's performance as Auntie Mame, and the film as a whole, are masterpieces of camp, and it's no coincidence that the film owes its spirit and visual style to gay men who spent their lives negotiating the limits of freedom within an atmosphere of extreme homophobia. Russell's outlandish outfits were the creation of Orry-Kelly, the visionary designer who won a string of Oscars for the iconic costumes he designed for Ingrid Bergman in *Casablanca* and Marilyn Monroe in *Some Like It Hot*. Born Orry George Kelly in small-town Australia, the designer moved to New York in his late teens, and according to his own account lived for almost a decade with a young English immigrant, Archibald Leach—before they both migrated to Hollywood and Leach became Cary Grant.[56] Unlike other Hollywood talents, on and off screen, Orry-Kelly refused to enter a marriage of convenience, and lived as openly as it was possible to do as a gay man at the time, protected by powerful friends and his undeniable talent. Author Patrick Dennis, meanwhile, was the pseudonym of Edward Everett Tanner III, a respectably married man of letters who was also a fixture of the Greenwich Village gay underground in the 1950s. The experiences of these men, trying to live freely somewhere between the closet and the open air, infused the various incarnations of *Auntie Mame* with a knowing bravado. The film's witty mockery of everyone who comes at the world straight, without culture or curiosity, are integral to its charm and subversive impact.

Gender Trouble

In February 1953, a woman in a fur coat landed at Idlewild Airport, arriving into a crowd of reporters with press cards tucked into their hat brims, thrusting microphones at her as she smiled and waved and descended the steps to walk across the tarmac. At the podium set up for a press conference, she answered questions graciously, adopting the mannerisms and somewhat fixed smile of a minor European royal or past-her-prime screen siren, and replied yes, she felt fine, and yes, she was looking forward to her new life. Christine was not her given name—she had named herself after her surgeon, a Danish pioneer named Dr. Christian Hamburger. Born George Jorgensen in the Bronx in 1926 and drafted into the army in 1945 after high school, Christine began researching gender reassignment surgery and taking estrogen, before traveling to Denmark, where she applied for special government permission to undergo surgery. On her return to America, Christine welcomed the spotlight and used it to control how her story was told and interpreted. She set the terms with a letter to her parents, published in a *Daily News* feature headlined "Ex-G.I. Becomes Blonde Beauty"—"Nature made a mistake, which I have had corrected, and I am now your daughter."[57]

The contradictions of Christine Jorgensen make her a fascinating case study for the limits of femininity in the 1950s. The press treated her as a curiosity, but seemed reassured by her embrace of conventional feminine fashion and beauty. Jorgensen reveled in her femininity, performing on stage in Las Vegas and at Café Society in New York in a ballerina's tutu. But when she and her male partner applied for a marriage license, they were refused, on the grounds that Christine's birth certificate listed her as a man. Marriage between two men, even when one of them wore red lipstick and high heels, was not only illegal: it was unthinkable. The media fascination with Christine Jorgensen and the relative acceptance of her sex change may have been due to the fact that she did little to challenge the notion of extreme and fixed differences between the sexes. She went from army boy to nightclub singer, swinging all the way through the pendulum. Far more threatening was the suggestion that there might be space in the middle where men and women could happily live: hence the hysterical denunciations of "sissy" men and single career women.

Experts in the 1950s diagnosed the career woman with a range of neuroses, but usually returned to the idea that she was trying to be a man, and that the impossibility of this unnatural task would eventually send her mad. If she tried to have both a family and a career, she would soon discover that the latter was ruinous to her home, children, and sexual satisfaction. In 1956, *Life* magazine called the career woman "that fatal error that feminism propagated." A few years later, *Redbook* opined that "Few women would want to thumb their noses at husbands, children and community and go off on their own." (The rarity of the independent woman was frequently held up as evidence that she was unnatural—even though it was likely these relentless accusations of unnaturalness were what made her seem rare.) The magazine continued, "Those who do [go off alone] may be talented individuals, but they rarely are successful women."[58]

There had been nothing in Marjorie Hillis's prescriptions for the Live-Aloner that suggested she had to be either a nun or a hermit, shunning community for isolation. On the contrary, true happiness was impossible without engagement with the world and a purpose in life that took her out of the house. But by the early 1960s, that vision of self-sufficiency was a vanished dream. The same year that *Redbook* drew a distinction between "individuals" and "women," Betty Friedan wrote an article for *Good Housekeeping* magazine pointedly asking, "Are Women People?"

The book Friedan went on to publish in 1963, *The Feminine*

Mystique, is often credited with being the book that ignited second-wave feminism and the women's movement of the late 1960s and '70s. Its impact reverberated forward in time, although the book itself looked backward, setting out to explain to readers what on earth had happened in the fifteen years since the end of the war to land them where they were now: educated women sitting alone in big houses tricked out with the latest appliances, feeling trapped, alone, and desperate.

Friedan is often criticized for her narrow focus on the plight of upper-middle-class white women, and it's true that her lens is limited. In part, that limitation exists because much of her source material—magazines, newspapers, advertising, psychological studies—was concerned with this same narrow group of women, and particularly worried about their plight. But these women were also the ones who had seen their options shrink most dramatically. Well educated in the years before "career woman" became a dirty word, and alive to the possibilities of self-reliance, they knew that things had once been different.

The Feminine Mystique was accordingly steeped in nostalgia for the Live-Alone era, to which it looks back for clues as to what might help women regain a sense of self and fulfillment. A sophisticated synthesis of popular culture and sociological and psychiatric thought from the previous three decades, the book demonstrated how the career woman became a pariah, and how deep and strange and sudden was the postwar retrenchment into domesticity. It began as a survey Friedan conducted in 1957 of the classmates who had graduated with her from Smith College in 1942, asking what had changed for them over the past fifteen years. From there, it examined more broadly what had changed in the lives and expectations of women, and what they were now being told—by journalists, psychologists, and experts—about who they were and what they needed to be happy. "The feminine mystique" was her memorable name for the "image to which we were trying to conform" and for the gap between that image and the individual identities that women were struggling to hold on to.

In the pages of *The Feminine Mystique*, Betty Friedan presented herself as primarily a housewife, a married mother of three just like her readers—albeit one who published freelance articles for major national magazines. Like them, she claimed to be struggling to understand how she had arrived at this place of suburban isolation, restlessness, and dissatisfaction, which she dubbed "the problem that has no name." Her book, however, was no memoir. As a recent biography of Friedan revealed, in contrast to the mythology she herself created, the author had a long history of involvement in the labor movement and left-wing politics. In the early 1950s, when she lived in the racially integrated Queens development of Parkway Village, she had been closely engaged with her community and wrote regularly for union newspapers. Even after moving farther from the city, she remained active in education and mentoring initiatives in her neighborhood. However, she knew from painful personal experience how important it was to distance herself from this activist past, no matter how innocuous it might have been, as any accusations of Communist sympathies would sink her message.[59]

Friedan is therefore careful not to present her book as a political tract, but instead leads the reader along with her as she sifts through the evidence and makes her discoveries, like "a reporter on the trail of a story." Looking over her shoulder at back issues of *Ladies' Home Journal*, *McCall's*, *Good Housekeeping*, and *Woman's Home Companion* from the 1930s and '40s, we see for ourselves how these mass-market magazines used to feature heroines who were much more mature than the "childlike, kittenish" housewives in the modern stories. These heroines were "happily, proudly, adventurously, attractively career women," Friedan writes, yet their careers did not make them unloving or unlovable—on the contrary, men were drawn to their independence of character. She highlights one *Ladies' Home Journal* story from February 1949 as the swan song for these spirited women. "Sarah and the Seaplane" is about a young woman who secretly takes flying lessons, and at the climax of the story feels the thrill of a solo flight. Winning the love of the handsome flying instructor is a bonus, but not the central point. "No, she was not Henry's girl. She was Sarah. And that was sufficient." Leafing through these magazine archives, Friedan voices a powerful sense of loss: "It is like remembering a long-forgotten dream, to recapture the memory of what a career meant to women before 'career woman' became a dirty word in America."[60]

Just after Sarah takes flight, Friedan spots the first of the "innumerable paeans" to housewifery as a multifaceted "career" that should be able to fulfill a woman's every ambition. As Friedan reads further into the magazines of the 1950s, she no longer finds any heroines who have any discernible "commitment to any work, art, profession or mission in the world," other than being a wife and mother. "I helped create this image," Friedan admits, recalling a profile she wrote in 1949 of the Pulitzer Prize-winning poet Edna St. Vincent Millay, which focused on the poet's cooking. She interviews a female magazine editor who recalls working with female writers in the 1930s and '40s, until the men who had been at war and "dreaming about home, and a cosy domestic life" returned home and wrote this fantasy into being. The editor

describes talking to a group of college students who were shad-
owing the magazine's staff—as Sylvia Plath had done, as a *Glamour* guest editor in 1952. When she asked them about their career
plans, not a single girl raised her hand. "When I remember how I
worked to learn this job and loved it," the editor says, wistfully, to
Friedan. "Were we all crazy then?"[61]

The power of Friedan's book lay in her recognition that by the
early 1960s, the women she was speaking to, both in and through
the book, were genuinely confused by their unhappiness, and asking in all seriousness, "am I crazy?" The suburban housewife was
used to being labeled, patronizingly, as "bored," but really she was
paralyzed by the mixed messages the era was sending. Once upon
a time, domesticity had simply been a woman's lot in life, but now
it had been transformed into her privilege and her pleasure. If it
didn't fulfill her entirely, she was a failure as a woman. It was not
that she was crazy, but that she was being held in her place by
crazy, incompatible ideas: that on the one hand, as a woman, she
was "naturally" passive, maternal, and domestic; but at the same
time, she had to work relentlessly to fit herself to this mold, and
quash her own unhappiness in the process. Unfolding her thesis slowly and dramatically, Friedan revealed this woman to herself: "The chains that bind her in her trap are chains made up
of mistaken ideas and misinterpreted facts, of incomplete truths
and unreal choices. They are not easily seen and not easily shaken
off."[62] Writing about the wake-up call of *The Feminine Mystique*,
one early reader recalled that it would have been much easier to
fight back against overt misogyny, but the mystique "was like
being enveloped in a big cloud of cotton candy, sweet and sticky.
You couldn't punch your way out."[63]

Betty Friedan was far from the first person to recognize that there was something wrong with American housewives. Indeed, as Stephanie Coontz demonstrates in her study of the book's impact and legacy, Friedan's publisher, W. W. Norton, worried before its release that the book would "have to fight its way out of a thicket."[64] Friedan herself admitted that "by 1962 the plight of the trapped American housewife had become a national parlor game."[65] Magazines regularly featured mothers who felt trapped and unsatisfied, and the question of "what women want" was widely discussed. But before Friedan, most experts tackling this issue never questioned the fundamental assumption that women could derive all their meaning from family life—instead, they asked why women undervalued their own domestic roles, and what could be done to boost their self-esteem. There were plenty of scapegoats to go around: higher education was making women dissatisfied and failing to prepare them for marriage and motherhood. The American gospel of success was still driving some poor women to seek careers. Their kitchen appliances were not yet efficient enough, and housework was still hard work. Or they were sexually maladjusted, and just needed a dose of psychiatric therapy. In July 1960, a male writer in *Harper's Bazaar* suggested—with the defense of humor—that the problem might be solved by taking away women's right to vote.[66] These objections attacked women for their ingratitude, their privilege, or their refusal to accept that anatomy was destiny. Friedan's revolutionary contribution was to show that something was wrong with society, not with women.

The Feminine Mystique has been called "the first modern self-help book for women," as an acknowledgment of the way that women read and responded to it, flooding Friedan with letters about the shock of recognition they felt when they read it, and expressing their profound relief that they were not alone.[67] Coontz describes how reading through the archive of these letters, and talking to women who read the book as young wives and mothers, tempered her own skepticism about the book's weaknesses—its sweeping historical generalizations, its class and race blinders, its refusal to acknowledge earlier feminist thinkers who had paved the way for the book's thesis. Those readers repeatedly said that the book "transformed their lives, even that it actually 'saved' their lives, or at least their sanity." Even if they did not see themselves reflected in the women Friedan described, readers responded as though someone had reached through the window and hauled them out of a building they didn't even notice was on fire.

Yet despite its powerful afterlife, and Friedan's later role as one of the founders of NOW and a figurehead of the mass movement for "women's lib," *The Feminine Mystique* was not a call to arms. It did not advocate that women rise up en masse and walk out on their families to find themselves, alone. It did not blame men for contributing to women's unhappiness. Instead it took a pragmatic, rather than revolutionary approach, suggesting that the reader start with a thorough and honest reckoning of her own situation. Only then could she know what she needed to change. Friedan counseled unhappy women to begin with themselves, and to find happiness much as Marjorie Hillis had once advised: by figuring out what they valued and what interested them, and pursuing it with determination. She proposed a "GI Bill for Women" that would subsidize tuition, books, even household help, for women who had raised children and wanted to go back to school. It was only later that readers of the book, and Friedan herself, would come to acknowledge that women's problems were large and systemic, and that it would take more to solve them than a part-time job and a husband who listened.

The book's success brought fame to Friedan and a powerful platform for more advocacy, but it did not in itself carry any program for political action. Nevertheless, in the federal government and among civil rights organizations, there was a growing recognition that discrimination against women was a serious injustice. At the end of 1961, President John F. Kennedy created the Presidential Commission on the Status of Women to investigate the issue, which two years later issued a report laying bare just how widespread the problem was. Published in 1965 as a book, edited by the anthropologist Margaret Mead, it became a bestseller. In 1963, the Equal Pay Act outlawed sex discrimination in hiring, and the following year, as part of the maneuvering to pass the landmark Civil Rights Act, sex was added at the last minute to the list of categories, along with race, color, religion, or national origin, upon which basis it was now illegal to discriminate. The law was largely ignored, however, for most of the rest of the 1960s, during which time the press regularly joked about the Playboy Club being forced to hire men as "bunnies" on the basis of equal rights.[68] But despite the slow pace of legal change, the question of women's rights to work and to live as they pleased had returned in full force to the mainstream of American culture. The moment was ripe for the return of the defiant single girl.

Sex and the Single Girl

In *Live Alone and Like It* and in her column, Marjorie Hillis raised and then sidestepped the question of sex and the single girl. "If you are hoping that we are going to tell you to go as far as you like, so that the responsibility won't be on your shoulders, you are in for a disappointment," she wrote. "This is every woman's own special problem, which nobody else can settle."[69] Her tone was forthright, and her message was clear—the reader wasn't going to get any dispensation from the author as higher moral power. No matter whether it was buying a lamp or bedding a lover, you, the Live-Aloner, were the one who had to live with it. So why on earth would you surrender your decision to someone else?

By the early 1960s, however, in the wake of Kinsey, Freud, and the Pill, the emphasis had changed—what mattered was the sex itself, not the responsibility of choosing how far to go and with whom. In 1962 a book appeared that would irrevocably yoke together sex, youth, and singleness with a marketing campaign, controversy, and runaway sales figures that recalled the *Live Alone* frenzy a quarter-century before. Its title, *Sex and the Single Girl*, like the similarly alliterative *Live Alone and Like It*, was meant to catch your attention, and then stick in your head like an advertising jingle. We can overestimate the shock value of the word "sex," given how popular books about sex had been throughout the supposedly straitlaced '50s. It was the coupling, so to speak, of sex *and the single girl* that made the book notorious.

The book's author, Helen Gurley Brown, was like Marjorie Hillis a late bloomer. Forty and married when she rocketed to fame, she believed that it was high time somebody admitted out loud that unmarried women were having sex, and that many of them were surviving, enjoying the experience, and even turning it to their professional advantage. Three years later she would become editor in chief of *Cosmopolitan* magazine, and transform it into the bible of sexually liberated young women. There was no looking back.

That *Sex and the Single Girl* and *The Feminine Mystique* appeared within a few months of each other, in that order, can create whiplash—they seem to be writing for entirely different audiences, cultures, and eras. Gurley Brown's funny, brassy, chatty style is worlds away from Friedan's polished, erudite prose. Yet a closer look reveals their connections, their immersion in the marriage culture of the period, and their tentative efforts to find a way out. Both writers suggest that women can find a route to happiness with their own individual rebellion against conformity, but neither advocates an overthrow of the system. Indeed, they derive authority from their skill at maneuvering within it. Friedan let her readers know that she was married only when it was directly relevant, but Gurley Brown announced it in the first line of the book, as a victory, explaining her late start as the years she needed to become "emotionally ready" for her Hollywood-producer husband. Keen to emphasize that her book wasn't a land-your-man manual, however, she waved off marriage as "insurance for the *worst* years of your life," adding that "During your best years you don't need a husband."[70]

Helen Gurley Brown's attitude to single life was full of contradictions. She declared that "the single woman, far from being a creature to be pitied and patronized, is emerging as the newest glamour girl of our times" and that the dire statistics around marriage published in magazines "give me a royal pain." However, there was a caveat to this declaration of independence—you might not need a husband but "You do need a man of course every step of the way." What follows in the first few chapters of the book is an oppressive catalogue of all the men out there, how to find them and how to get them to notice you. Men's preferences and desires set the stage, and the single girl must wait for her cue. Her attractiveness and worth exist in the eyes of a man, when "He pictures her alone in her apartment, smooth legs sheathed in pink silk Capri pants, lying tantalizingly among dozens of satin cushions, trying to read but not very successfully, for *he* is in that room—filling her thoughts, her dreams, her life."[71]

In order to turn herself into this male fantasy figure of "single bliss," Gurley Brown was beyond blunt: "You have to work like a son of a bitch."[72] The following chapters are, indeed, exhausting to read and contemplate, as the author instructs the single girl to mentally round up all the men in her life, from the "Eligibles" to the "Don Juans" to the "Homosexuals," and extending to her boss, uncle, clergyman, dentist, and the husbands of her friends. The goal might be to try to become "The Girl" to one of them, but the real purpose of making the list was to counteract any feeling of despair from those terrifying statistics: "over four million more single women than men at the last count."[73] But this counted only marriageable men, Gurley Brown reassured her readers. There were more than enough relatives, tradesmen, and weirdos out there to make any girl feel she lived in a man's world.

If even after making her extensive lists, the single girl still felt herself insufficiently surrounded by men, it was her job to go out and insert herself into their spaces and their lives. This might mean changing jobs, if at the current office, "you never even *see* somebody you could be happily ensconced in a bomb shelter with."[74] Activities like sports should be pursued in accordance with how much men enjoy them, though Gurley Brown does admit that there's a "compensatory thrill" to whizzing down a ski slope. Lest women get carried away pursuing their own pleasure, however, they're reminded that skiing, skating, or tennis will also keep them thin and give them an opportunity to wear a cute outfit.[75] If the ice rink didn't do it, there were political clubs, singles mixers, Alcoholics Anonymous, work trips, and vacations—all of which were hunting grounds where a woman could position herself as appealing prey: "Girls with something to do and places to go are better game than placid creatures who are kind of underfoot."[76] In familiar self-help style, Gurley Brown wove in the stories of her friends, under pseudonyms, to provide "case studies" where her own experience was lacking. She was careful to warn against going on the prowl at one likely haunt, however, no matter how many men were there—in bars, men were apt to judge a woman as lonely, or "an itsy witsy bit frantic."[77]

Making oneself over into prey, or "man bait," took work, but luckily men were easy to distract with shiny objects. A girl wearing unusual jewelry, reading a controversial book, lying on a "mad" beach towel, riding a Vespa, or driving a bright pink car could be guaranteed at least some attention. However, "You don't have to be Auntie Mame and electrify everybody with your high-voltage personality," Gurley Brown sniffed—it was tiresome to make yourself the center of every story. A single girl could stand out only so far, and only as a way of ultimately fitting in.

When Gurley Brown got around to discussing sex, she betrayed the influence of the scientific experts of the 1950s, in their gender essentialism, faith in psychiatry, and Freudian theories about sexual development. A sexy woman was one who enjoyed sex, which meant that she accepted herself "as a woman . . . with all the functions of a woman." The author explained that this meant "You like to make love, have babies, nurse them and mother them (or think you would)."[78] She cites Alfred Kinsey and the early twentieth-century sexologist Havelock Ellis as authorities to back up her somewhat hazy theories about men who were attracted to certain body types because they reminded them—or didn't—of their mothers. For a woman who *wasn't* sexy, meaning she didn't enjoy sex, there were two options—either to "be an actress" and fake it, or get "*qualified* help" to sort out her psychological barriers (calling up one of the most diehard Freudian clichés of the era, she claims that "Manhaters may secretly envy men's penises").[79]

The real shock of the book for its first readers lay in chapter 12, "The Affair: From Beginning to End." Earlier on, Gurley Brown listed the pros and cons of an affair with a married man, concluding that it was better to "keep them as pets," but this section went into far more detail about when, why, and how to have a sexual relationship.[80] Like Betty Friedan, Gurley Brown took aim at the false messages being peddled by the majority of magazines—"other than *Playboy*"—that any woman who had an affair had to marry the man, leave town, or die. On the contrary, she says, "Nice, single girls *do* have affairs," and might or might not suffer for them—but that depended on the man and the circumstances, not on the sex.[81] She advised against pursuing an affair if it was only out of physical desire ("the urge to merge"), or in pursuit of security or approval, but purely moral considerations were out the window. Imagining a reader's question as to whether the man should think she is a virgin, her response was simple: "I can't imagine why, if you aren't. Is *he*?"[82] She even, briefly, acknowledged the existence of same-sex relationships, although she told lesbians she had no particular advice to share: "It's *your* business and I think it's a shame you have to be so surreptitious about your choice of a way of life."[83]

Helen Gurley Brown's frank discussion of unmarried sexuality, and the consequent notoriety of her book, woke other self-help authors up to this new market and new reality. Even Eustace Chesser, the 1940s author who had demystified sex for married couples, published a sequel—or perhaps prequel—*Unmarried Love*, in 1965, "somewhat to his dismay." By the end of the decade, the single woman "accepted sexual freedom as her due," marking the beginning of the era in which sex became a part of individual experience, rather than being understood and discussed strictly in the context of marriage.[84]

Was there a way for the single girl to be happy when she wasn't in bed? In the second half of her book Gurley Brown channeled her inner Marjorie Hillis, offering advice about living alone, decorating, eating, and entertaining. "Roommates are for sorority girls," she decreed early on. "You need an apartment alone even if it's over a garage."[85] Many of her principles could be straight out of *Live Alone and Like It*, that a single woman's apartment deserved just as much money and attention paid to it as a family home, that it shouldn't cost too much money, and it made sense to avoid a lengthy commute—either to one's job, or to the man one was dating. But here again, the central importance of men was underscored in a way that was quite alien to Marjorie. A woman ought to make her apartment sexy and welcoming to a date, with pictures and posters, a television, hi-fi, and plenty of books, not to mention good towels and "an ash tray with two fresh cigarettes and matches handy in the john." It had to smell good and seem inviting—but the author drew the line at lingerie in plain view. "She wants her apartment to be sexy, not necessarily to encourage *rape*."[86]

When it came to entertaining, a single woman eventually had to return the favor of the parties to which she'd been invited—here again, Gurley Brown complained that magazines were out of touch with the lives and needs of single women, perhaps anticipating her makeover of *Cosmopolitan*. *Corned Beef and Caviar*-style, she offered up a trio of dinner menus and recipes, but emphasized that these were strictly for guests, involving elaborate preparation and expensive ingredients. Alone, the single woman ought to be feeding herself far more frugally. Gurley Brown was a self-professed "health nut" and a "skinny," and for all her emphasis on eating protein and a filling breakfast, it's clearly the skinny part that matters more than the health—if only on the basis of her terrifying two-day crash diet that consists of an egg and a glass of white wine for breakfast, two eggs and two glasses for lunch, and for dinner, a steak and the rest of the bottle. Don't plan on doing much else while you're on this kamikaze diet, though: "Sufficient nutrition is here, but you get fuzzy."[87]

After the success of *Sex and the Single Girl*, Gurley Brown capitalized on her notoriety with a sequel, *Sex and the Office*, published in 1965. Beginning with advice on how to manage the boss, the most important man in a working girl's life, the book went on to cover how to dress for the office, how to make the most of the lunch hour and navigate office politics, and how to "start sneaking up on the boys career-wise," which Gurley Brown advised would take more than brains and talent, requiring "a certain amount of listening, giggling, wriggling, smiling, winking, flirting and fainting" to get ahead.[88] She went on to lecture the reader that she needed to actually work at her job, and not simply expect to turn up and be decorative. "Forget the fact that working hard at a job seems kind of antique . . . something girls did only during the Great War or the Great Depression."[89] A job, Gurley Brown had already decreed in *Sex and the Single Girl*, offered an unmarried woman an identity, "something to *be*," where a married woman already was something: "somebody's wife." Furthermore, a career was "the greatest preparation for marriage," as it trained a woman in how to please men.[90]

The workplace, in Helen Gurley Brown's writing, was not a place for political action—although later in the 1960s it would be the site of fierce battles over women's rights, wages, and bodily autonomy. If you discovered that someone else made more than you, her advice was to "be philosophical," and accept that "every company has things completely screwed up in matching the rewards to the workers." She even claimed that "no-one knows why." The best thing for a woman to do, as Marjorie Hillis advised in *Orchids on Your Budget*, was to keep a tight rein on what she could control—her own budget. Having grown up poor in small-town Arkansas, Gurley Brown's money advice came from a place of steely determination and self-discipline. She advised negotiating the rent, taking on extra jobs, brushing your teeth with baking soda, and never, ever paying for your own cocktails. Like Hillis, though, she insulated the book against the specter of real poverty by couching this economy in the language of pleasure: "Scrimp on what isn't sexy or beautiful or really any fun, so you can afford what is."[91]

A single woman in the 1960s trying to use Helen Gurley Brown to lead her to happiness was liable to feel just as much paralyzing confusion as the housewives in Betty Friedan's book. Rife with contradictions about how to be happy and what a purposeful life could be, *Sex and the Single Girl* struggled to find a balance between an oppressive culture of "normality" and the safe limits of rebellion. In the final chapter, "The Rich, Full Life," Gurley Brown revived some of the more general principles of Marjorie Hillis's Live-Alone program, but without the conviction that made that earlier book so convincing. At the time of writing, forty-six-year-old Marjorie had not yet met the man she would marry, while forty-year-old Gurley Brown had married recently enough that her triumph and relief were still fresh. "We know the married state *is* the normal one in our culture," Gurley Brown wrote to her single sisters, "and anybody who deviates from 'normal' has a price to pay in nonacceptance and nonglorification."[92] This depressing state of affairs was something a single woman simply had to accept. Gurley Brown painted a picture of a world doing battle with the women who—by choice or accident, to use Marjorie's phrase—didn't fit its mold: "You see enough picture stories in national publications about couples and families to make you feel like the sole occupant of a life raft," she wrote. Couples were "blueberry-pie normal" and "as much at home in the world as an egg in custard," while single women were ignored or pathologized.

So how could they fight back? Was there any real hope for happiness? Friendships with other women were in no way a source of comfort and support, in Gurley Brown's ruthless world. "Don't run with the mouse packs," she advised—other single girls were competition, and en masse they would threaten and scare away men. But there was freedom in singleness—you could travel alone, live abroad, use your free time to expand your mind and your horizons. In particular, there was freedom in growing older. While Gurley Brown of course advised her readers to stay as healthy, youthful, slender, and beautiful as they could, for as long as they could, she nevertheless saw a glimmer of hope in the future, when "it helps to have other things going for you—a little money . . . a little travel, the ability to cook well and entertain."[93] Unlike the married women in their forties who, with their children grown up, found themselves suddenly at the end of what society deemed their useful lives, a single woman who had never done what society demanded suddenly might find herself happier, and more optimistic, than her blueberry-pie-normal sister.

Keep Going and Like It

In 1967, Marjorie Hillis Roulston published her final book, *Keep Going and Like It*, which promised to teach readers "How to be as glamorous in December as you were in May." On the back of the hardcover, decorated with bright pink and yellow cartoon flowers, was a portrait of the white-haired author, resplendent in a satin blouse with huge fur cuffs and dark silk skirt, leaning toward the camera with one eyebrow arched conspiratorially. The photograph marked a departure from thirty years before, when her books were illustrated with line-drawn figures that were more symbols than individuals. Here, the reader is reckoning with Marjorie Hillis herself: her life story, which is woven through the book, her beliefs, and the lessons she's learned. The advising "we" of the early books has disappeared; in her place is a confident, glamorous "I."

This image of the author—a mature dowager in her elegant Upper East Side apartment—sits incongruously with the pop-art design of the front cover, suggesting a mismatch between her message and the youth-obsessed culture of the late 1960s. But what emerges from the book is a strong sense that being young is not the same thing as being modern: in many ways, Marjorie sounds more modern than Helen Gurley Brown, in her continued commitment to the simple idea that women are people and ought to be able to determine their lives as such. Published when Marjorie Hillis was almost eighty, *Keep Going and Like It* opened with the assertion that age was no dictator of personality, any more than gender ought to be: "This little book is written in the belief that you can have as interesting, useful, and even gay life in the sixties and seventies and often the eighties as at any other time in your life."

Her final book combined the two modes of writing that Marjorie Hillis loved: the earnest advice for happiness, and the social satire that took nothing too seriously. The chapters, with titles like "Those Little Ailments" and "There Are Still a Few Odd Men," approached the new challenges of sixty-plus life with sympathy and seriousness, but were capped off with witty poems that either amplified the message of the chapter, or made fun of it.

Much of the book was a reiteration of the familiar Live-Alone principles for those who might have forgotten them, with plenty of advice about clothes and beauty. But it was also a backward glance, and a meditation on what had changed. In her mother's day, Marjorie recalled, women over sixty thought of themselves as "matrons and dowagers" and dressed accordingly. Today, however, "You see them on the tennis courts in shorts, in their gardens in slacks, and on the beach in bikinis" (though she considered this last trend, in most cases, a mistake, as "time has an unpleasant way of making some minor but unappetizing changes in most women's appearance"). But in general, most women could adapt modern fashions for themselves, with a "hint of understatement."[94] And while the gradual disappearance in formal dressing—gowns and white tie for the opera, for instance—might have made life a little less elegant, it certainly made wardrobes cheaper.

The "setting for sixty plus" was not much different from the "setting for a solo act" Marjorie had described years ago. If the reader hadn't taken her advice back then, by now it was high time to downsize from her cluttered and sprawling home to a more efficient place—no matter how painful the upheaval might be. "A good move means discarding every single thing that one isn't going to need and enjoy, and then calling up the nearest thrift shop or the Salvation Army, and closing one's mind to sentiment," she urged briskly.[95] Starting afresh with streamlined, modern furniture, "possibly Scandinavian," was a great way to present an equally fresh impression to the world. And it wasn't too late to start: "Creating a place in which one is comfortable, happy, and which expresses one's own personality is one of the great satisfactions of life."[96] A retirement home was a last resort for those in very poor health—in general, Marjo-rie considered it a mistake to spend time only with those of one's own age.

The attitude of the world to older women—and more impor-tantly, the attitude of older women to the world—had also changed profoundly. She no longer wanted to be revered as a wise elder, if she ever had: "veneration is the last thing any modern American woman wants," Marjorie insisted. "She wants to be alert and busy and popular." This last part was important, and a direct rebuke to another lesson of her mother's, imparted years before, that life was like a pebble thrown into a lake, with ripples that grew bigger and then inevitably, smaller. Now, she saw no need to stop being sociable and making new friends. "Nobody, but nobody, needs to be lonely."[97]

However, Marjorie had a particular warning for retired career women. Having been used to being Somebody, now, without a job, such a woman might think she's Nobody—"a depressing feeling that often results in a lessening of interest in clothes and groom-ing, and sometimes, unhappily, a tendency to take too much to drink." The remedy was simple, however, as it always was, with a little effort: to volunteer, or more appealingly, have fun, by taking part in the cultural life of one's city or town. "The answer if you feel lonely or neglected, is to get on the telephone, make the date, get the tickets, plan the bridge game, order the dinner, and involve yourself in the activities of the world." The "Song of the Sixties" set the tone:

> "We are the ladies whose age is unknown.
> Whose hair may be false, but whose cash is our own.
> We work hard to look like a ripe seventeen

But we play a big part in the smart current scene,
Through unceasing effort, we all get around
At an age when our grandmothers slept underground."[98]

In her later life Marjorie took great joy in being a grandmother to her stepchildren's children, but characteristically, her approach to this relationship rejected the cloying sentiment that often clung to it. She cautioned grandmothers against making grandchildren the center of their world, as well as against giving them advice, or becoming an obligation. Her advice was to make your own life instead: "The woman who does it so well that her grandson says, 'I have to call well in advance to get a date with my grandmother,' makes one feel that here is a woman who not only has popularity but deserves it."[99]

A few unmistakable signs of the changing times did creep into this Live-Alone swansong. Although Marjorie railed against the habit of sharing gory details about one's own and other people's ailments, she does advise readers to take advantage of the still-new Medicare provisions, enacted by President Johnson two years earlier, in 1965. And in the chapter "There Are Still a Few Odd Men," she no longer needs to be coy about the real subject of the discussion, which is "what we might as well refer to frankly as sex, since it is so called everywhere from pulpit to paperback."[100] The word appeared too frequently for this to be a direct gibe at *Sex and the Single Girl*, but it's hard to believe Marjorie would have missed the book's appearance—whether or not she read it. The book's final poem, "A Touch of Impropriety," celebrates the gap that exists between the young single women who made up Helen Gurley Brown's audience, and the Live-Alone survivors like herself. "There's a difference we acknowledge, / Twixt your age and girls in college. / They are sharply watched by all society." But she doesn't envy the younger women, who are under the constant pressure of this social surveillance. As Gurley Brown also hints, there's a freedom that derives from being old enough to escape the world's scrutiny. If she's careful with her money and her health, the older Live-Aloner may do in old age what she has done, if she's smart, all along: exactly what she likes, how she likes, and with whom she likes—men, mothers, and moralizers be damned.

FOUR YEARS AFTER she published *Keep Going and Like It*, Marjorie Hillis Roulston passed away at the age of eighty-two, just missing the debut of *Ms.* magazine, the passage of Title IX, and the *Roe v. Wade* decision. A brief obituary in *Time* magazine sniffed that she "glorified spinsterhood," while the *New York Times* praised her as a pillar of the community like her father, rather than as a feminist pioneer. But her smart and witty books—and the life on which they were based—lit a path through the middle of the twentieth century for women who didn't think they could "have it all," but understood that having anything at all depended on being able to make their own choices.

EPILOGUE

Six months after my father died and I first encountered Marjorie Hillis's stern, funny, sensible voice, I met someone by chance, in New York, in a bar—thus breaking one of the few rules both Marjorie Hillis and Helen Gurley Brown shared. It was June, and by October we were living together. I'd jumped from living with roommates into my first ever real relationship, hastened as these things always are in the city by my lease coming up for renewal. I felt a pang of regret that I never got the chance to create my own Live-Alone oasis, to decorate exactly as I pleased, and to serve my friends elegant suppers in my very best formal pajamas in front of the fireplace (we may as well be optimistic).

Doing things faster than we really thought was wise became a theme of our relationship. Three years after I moved in, on another cold sunny day in October, we stood under the Hell Gate Bridge in Astoria Park, on the Queens side of Marjorie Hillis's beloved East

River, and stumbled through a short wedding ceremony that we had cobbled together. I didn't write out my vows and can't remember now exactly what I promised. I do remember at the last minute that we decided we wanted a reading, just one, and handed a piece of paper to our friend Adrian, an artist with a booming voice and the partner of my best friend, Ali, who gave me that first copy of *Live Alone and Like It*. The reading wasn't about love or marriage but about the river behind us and the city beyond it. It was a passage from Marjorie Hillis's hymn to New York, about the way its energy lights a reciprocal spark in your mind, and how what looks like anonymity and loneliness can, with a quarter-turn to the light, look instead like friendliness and welcome and home.

Our wedding, the one we wrote ourselves and celebrate as our anniversary, was real but it wasn't official. We'd already undergone the legal procedure at City Hall back in May, at the end of the semester that meant the end of my visa. Over the summer we ran around trying to check everything off the elastic list of ways to prove that we were a real couple—opening a joint savings account, begging our friends to send us all the photographs they had of the two of us together, and choosing a handful of those with the most respectable jobs to sign affidavits swearing that we were in love. We got them notarized. I got screened for tuberculosis. Three days after our ceremony under the bridge, we went to the immigration office in Long Island City and tried to focus on a word-search game while around us, lawyers huddled with nervous couples. We were called in early, and the friendly agent with the Caribbean accent asked me apologetically, once again, if I was a prostitute or a terrorist, just in case I'd checked those boxes incorrectly on the form. I pushed more photos and more affidavits across his desk. We were in there just a couple of minutes before he told me he had approved my provisional green card, that I could expect it in the mail within a week. He said he knew we were a couple from the way we'd been sitting together in the waiting room.

When we got out past the metal detectors and security guards it was barely eleven and weakly sunny. The closest bar was a huge empty restaurant over a century old, all mahogany wood and stained glass lampshades, and we ordered gin martinis and sat at the bar. My hands were shaking too much not to spill my drink.

I tell this story because it is easy for many people, even me, to forget that marriage is always political, a rite of citizenship that is offered or withheld by the state. Because it's easy to forget that exercising the right to live your life as you choose is still a political act, and a brave act—far braver for some people than for others, of course. Because there are still many, many powerful people who are afraid to allow women happiness, independence, pleasure, and the right to be alone—all the rights that Marjorie Hillis claimed for her Live-Aloner, without thinking of them as such. So while we can admire her devotion to a well-cut dress, well-ordered home, and perfectly mixed Manhattan, we should remember that it isn't easy for any of us to create a life we really like, and harder still to do it in style.

ACKNOWLEDGMENTS

This book exists thanks to the curiosity, generosity, encourage-ment, and patience (so much patience!) of many people. Sev-eral world-class institutions in the United States supported me through years of research and writing. The New York Public Library gave me space to think and write, in the Frederick Lewis Allen Room and other research spaces, and access to its invaluable digital and human research resources. The Brooklyn Historical Society allowed me to piece together the life of the charismatic and controversial Newell Dwight Hillis, while the libraries of Columbia University, New York University, and the New-York Historical Soci-ety have offered me a quiet corner to work and daydream. Thanks to an Everett Helm Visiting Fellowship from the Lilly Library in Bloomington, Indiana, I was able to dig through the Bobbs-Merrill archive and read Marjorie Hillis's letters on her unfaded pale-blue personal stationery. The generous librarians and archivists at

Condé Nast let me leaf through old issues of *Vogue* dating all the way back to when the magazine published poetry, as well as the correspondence of Edna Woolman Chase. In 2014 the beautiful Wildacres retreat in Little Switzerland, North Carolina, offered a residency to this city girl and taught her once and for all that she very much does not like living alone in a cabin in the woods.

At Columbia, I was lucky enough to find wonderful mentors and teachers in the English department, especially Sarah Cole, Marianne Hirsch, and David Damrosch, while at the New-York Historical Society, my current professional home, I have been privileged to work with the remarkable historians on the advisory board of the Center for Women's History; thanks especially to Alice Kessler-Harris, Lara Vapnek, and Julia Golia for their generous welcome, teaching, and friendship. Laura Mogulescu, Jeanne Gutierrez, Lana Povitz, Sarah Litvin, Lindsay King, and especially Sarah Gordon have been inspirational colleagues and friends, and nothing we do would be possible without the mentorship of the inimitable Valerie Paley.

My unflappable agent, Kate Johnson, let me buttonhole her in the middle of Fifth Avenue to share my excitement about Marjorie Hillis, and guided me through several iterations of her story before it found its ideal home with Liveright. There, the astute and enthusiastic Katie Adams has been a dream editor, and I am grateful to her and the rest of the team, especially Bob Weil, Gina Iaquinta, and Cordelia Calvert, for guiding me through the new and often bewildering publishing process so cheerfully.

As a freelance writer I've depended on the support and collaboration of many wonderful editors. Thanks are due in particular to those who took a chance on small sections and early versions of Marjorie Hillis's story: Sasha Weiss, Miriam Markowitz, Sara Polsky, and Lily Rothman. I'm grateful to the people who helped me discover a world of literary and intellectual fellowship outside academia: At Housing Works Bookstore, one of the most important communities in New York, Laura Tanenbaum, Rachel Fershleiser, and Sam Sacks, a brilliant editor who helped me hone my nonacademic voice. Thanks to David Haglund and everyone at PEN America, for letting me be an overgrown intern and build a new career, and for the much more important work you do daily on behalf of writers around the world. Serving as a board member of the National Book Critics Circle was an honor and a genuine pleasure thanks to the fellowship of smart and dedicated critics, especially Kate Tuttle, Walton Muyumba, Tom Beer, Ron Charles, and Laurie Muchnick. And to everyone who helps make the New York literary community what it is—thanks for letting me be a part of it.

THIS BOOK BEGAN with a gift, from the unfailingly generous and thoughtful Ali MacGilp, who could not have known where it would lead. She has been a incredible source of support and love, along with her sisters, Helena and Mazz, since we were tree climbing tomboys together, and with Adrian, Flora, Dave, and the UCL and Camberwell family. Lucy Ellis and her family have always been there for me, and I'm so grateful for the unofficial second home they gave me as a teenager. When I moved to New York in 2003 I was smart enough to bring some of England's finest with me, for the long or short haul: Mark Dean and Grace Pickering, steadfast and hilarious allies; Mat Coakley; Esther Waters; and all too briefly, Max and Sophie Deveson. For them and everyone at King's, especially Katie, Helena, Jenny, Helen, and Kirsten, thank you for teaching me that any kind of living alone and liking it is only possible with a loyal crew.

My PhD years were immeasurably improved by a cohort of

brilliant women, at Columbia and NYU, among them Beth McArthur, Lauren Walsh, Lianne Habinek, Sharon Fulton, and Sara Landreth. Sarah Klock has been an inspiration and a dear friend since we met in Ann Douglas's Cold War Culture class at Columbia. Jack, Arlo, and Juniper—this might be the first book with your names in it, but it won't be the last. Susan Harlan, the exemplary Live-Aloner, has contributed more to this book than even she knows.

I met Tony Hightower six months after I "met" Marjorie Hillis, and right then I knew that I'd missed my shot at living stylishly alone. He makes everything else possible, and I'm grateful every day. Not least for bringing me to Astoria and to the Lady Pat, where Sam Meyer and Bari Dulberg have been better friends and upstairs neighbors than any sitcom could dream up, along with Scott Lydon and Kristy Tye (come back!), and the sharp, brilliant Michelle Dean (also come back!). Thanks our extended local family: Brittney, Dominique, and Vivien, Lexi and Connie at Astoria Bookshop, and Dennis and Liz at Astoria Coffee, where not-inconsiderable chunks of this book were written.

I owe more than I can say to my stylish, energetic, supportive, and brilliant mother, Andrea, to my ever-cheerful brother, Robert, my stepfather, Dave Jessup, and our funny, big-hearted, ever-expanding family. Much love to Bud, Eva, Jeanne, Andrew, and Rose for welcoming me so warmly into the family.

My father, Jeremy, for better or worse, shaped my image of a writer: late-night whisky, blown deadlines, and all. I wish he could be here to see this.

NOTES

INTRODUCTION

1. "Record Share of Americans Have Never Married," Pew Research Center, Washington D.C. (September 24, 2014), http://www.pewsocialtrends .org/2014/09/24/record-share-of-americans-have-never-married.
2. Ariela R. Dubler, "'Exceptions to the General Rule': Unmarried Women and the 'Constitution of the Family,'" *Theoretical Inquiries in Law* 4, no. 2 (2003): 809g.
3. Susan Ware, *American Women in the 1930s: Holding Their Own* (Boston: Twayne, 1982).
4. Tony Marcano, "Famed Riveter in War Effort, Rose Monroe Dies at 77," *New York Times*, June 2, 1997.
5. Jean Van Evera, *How to Be Happy While Single* (New York: J.B. Lippincott, 1949).
6. See, for example, Judith Butler, "Sex and Gender in Simone de Beauvoir's Second Sex," *Yale French Studies*, no. 72, in *Simone de Beauvoir: Witness to a Century*, ed. Helen V. Wengel (New Haven, CT: Yale University Press, 1987), 35–49.
7. Robert Coughlan, "Changing Roles in Modern Marriage," *Life* special issue, "The American Woman: Her Achievements and Troubles" (December 24, 1956), 116.
8. "Marlo Thomas on Difficulty of Being 'That Girl' in 1960s TV Biz: TCA"

Deadline (January 15, 2013), http://deadline.com/2013/01/marlo-thomas-on -difficulty-of-being-that-girl-in-1960s-tv-biz-tca-405197.

9. The term "eyewitnesses" was particularly misleading—Genovese was killed at 3 a.m. on a cold night outside her apartment complex, so although some neighbors (far fewer than thirty-eight) heard her screams, they couldn't have seen what was happening. Two people called the police, and Kitty's friend ran outside and held her as she lay dying. Numerous articles and books have revisited the case, especially since Jim Rasenberger's article, "Kitty, 40 Years Later," *New York Times*, February 8, 2004, exploded many of its myths.

CHAPTER 1: SOLITARY SPLENDOR

1. Marjorie Hillis, *Live Alone and Like It: A Guide for the Extra Woman* (New York: The Sun Dial Press/Bobbs-Merrill, 1936), xii.

2. Marjorie Hillis, *New York, Fair or No Fair* (Indianapolis: Bobbs-Merrill, 1939), 11.

3. Trend, "Goodby to All That," *Brooklyn Daily Eagle*, August 6, 1939.

4. Publicity memorandum, D.A. Cameron, n.d., Bobbs-Merrill Archive, Lilly Library, University of Indiana, Bloomington.

5. D. A. Cameron to Mr. Kendall, July 24, 1936, Bobbs-Merrill Archive.

6. D. A. Cameron to Miss Helen Robertson, Home Economics Editor, Cleveland *Plain Dealer*, August 19, 1936, Bobbs-Merrill Archive.

7. "Excerpts from Letters to Marjorie Hillis," n.d., Bobbs-Merrill Archive.

8. Margaret Fishback to Marjorie Hillis, n.d., quoted in "Excerpts from Letters to Marjorie Hillis," Bobbs-Merrill Archive.

9. Margaret Fishback, "Maiden's Prayer," *The New Yorker*, November 12, 1927, 48.

10. Kathleen Rooney, "It's Glorious, It's Grand!" *Poetry Foundation*, December 14, 2016, https://www.poetryfoundation.org/features/articles/detail/91790.

11. Dorothy Dix, "It's No Longer a Disgrace to Be an 'Old Maid,'" *Daily Boston Globe*, November 20, 1936, 43.

12. Dorothy Dix to Miss Mueller, June 16, 1937, Bobbs-Merrill Archive.

13. Quoted in Inga A. Filippo, "Biography of Dorothy Dix," Research Guide to the Dorothy Dix Special Collection, Felix G. Woodward Library, Austin Peay State University, 2005, http://library.apsu.edu/Dix/research/guide.htm.

14. "Dorothy Dix, Adviser to Lovelorn for Half a Century, Is Dead at 90," *Atlanta Constitution*, December 17, 1951.

15. Dorothy Coleman, "Impressions of Marjorie Hillis," *St. Louis Post-Dispatch*, November 1, 1936.

16. Review excerpts press release, n.d. [1936], Bobbs-Merrill Archive.

17. May Cameron, quoted in Traveler's Memo #2, August 3, 1936, Bobbs-Merrill Archive.

18. Press release, n.d. [September 1936], Bobbs-Merrill Archive.

19. Paz Van Matre, "Women Don't Need Husbands to Gain Individuality, Says Marjorie Hillis." *St. Louis Star-Times*, October 28, 1936.

20. Hillis, *Live Alone*, 30.

21. Coleman, "Impressions," *ibid*.

22. Hillis, *Live Alone*, 17.

23. Mrs. Charles M. Bregg, " 'Lives Alone and Likes It, Miss Hillis Says," *Pittsburgh Sun-Telegraph*, October 31, 1936.

24. Marjorie H. Roulston, *You Can Start All Over: A Guide for the Widow and Divorcee* (New York: Harper & Brothers, 1951), viii.

25. See, for example, Debby Applegate, *The Most Famous Man in America: A Biography of Henry Ward Beecher* (New York: Doubleday, 2006).

26. "Chat and Gossip about Brooklyn," *New York Herald*, April 21, 1899.

27. Unpublished memoir by Marjorie Hillis, n.d., Newell Dwight Hillis Papers, Othmer Library, Brooklyn Historical Society.

28. "Hillis and Ferguson Vie in Bitter Words," *New York Times*, October 15, 2015.

29. Nathalie's wedding appeared in the society pages: "Week in Society," *Brooklyn Life*, June 21, 1924; "Kennebunkport, Me., Scene of Kellogg-Hillis Wedding," *Brooklyn Daily Eagle*, June 15, 1924.

30. "Marjorie Hillis Author of Jane's Business," *Brooklyn Life* (December 20, 1924): 12.

31. "Simplicity Urged in Lecture on Juvenile Fashions," *Women's Wear Daily*, April 1, 1927.

32. "Dr. Hillis' Body Cremated; Kin Fulfils Wish," *Brooklyn Daily Eagle*, February 28, 1929.

33. Roderick Phillips, *Untying the Knot: A Short History of Divorce* (Cambridge: Cambridge University Press, 1991), 191.

34. Cited in Jill Elaine Hasday, *Family Law Reimagined* (Cambridge, MA: Harvard University Press, 2014), 129.

35. Annie Hillis, *The American Woman and her Home* (New York: Fleming H. Revell, 1911), 44.

36. *Ibid.*, 28.

37. Alice Cogan, "Your Caller Can Take in the Milk," *Brooklyn Daily Eagle*, July 30, 1936, 3.

38. Annie Hillis, *American Woman*, 37.

39. *Proceedings of the First National Conference on Race Betterment*, January 8–12, 1914 (Battle Creek, MI: Race Betterment Foundation, Gage Printing, 1914), 351, https://archive.org/stream/proceedingsoffir14nati#page/350/mode/2up.

40. *Austin American Statesman*, October 27, 1936.

41. Evelyn Burke, "Live Alone, but Be Careful How," *The Pittsburgh Press*, October 31, 1936, 6.

42. F. Scott Fitzgerald, "My Lost City," 1932 (unpublished in Fitzgerald's lifetime), in *Writing New York: A Literary Anthology*, ed. Philip Lopate (New York: Simon & Schuster, 2000), 569–79.

43. Roulston, *You Can Start All Over*, viii.

44. Ira Wolfert, "Lives Alone and Likes It," *Daily Boston Globe*, November 29, 1936, C2.

CHAPTER 2: "SOMETHING TO GET YOUR TEETH INTO"

1. Marjorie Hillis to D. L. Chambers, April 18, 1938, Bobbs-Merrill Archive.

2. Edna Woolman Chase and Ilka Chase, *Always in Vogue* (New York: Doubleday, 1954), 26.

3. *Ibid.*, 39.

4. "Dorothy Parker: The Art of Fiction No.13." Interview by Marion Capron. *The Paris Review*, Summer 1956.

5. Chase, *Always in Vogue*, 104.

6. Leo Wingshot, "Orchids on Your Budget," *Philadelphia Record*, undated clipping [1938], Bobbs-Merrill Archive. Delafield was the then highly popular English author of a series of novels poking fun at rural life.

7. Chase, *Always in Vogue*, 102.

8. Hillis, *Live Alone and Like It*, 94.

9. Catherine Keyser's engaging study *Playing Smart: New York Women Writers and Modern Magazine Culture* (New Brunswick: Rutgers University Press, 2010) explores the "smart" phenomenon in detail.

10. "Makes History and Love," *The Austin American Statesmen*, December 6, 1936, 1.

11. "King's Friend Asks Divorce; Simpson Not to Fight Action," *Daily Boston Globe*, October 15, 1936, 12.

12. Sheilah Graham, "Film Queens Now Reveal Their Ages," *Hartford Courant*, November 1, 1936, A1.

13. Martha Scotford, "Cipe Pineles," *American Institute of Graphic Arts*. www.aiga.org/medalist-cipepineles.

14. This brief analysis of American self-help history owes much to Barbara Ehrenreich's *Bright-Sided: How the Relentless Promotion of Positive Thinking Has Undermined America* (New York: Metropolitan Books, 2009).

15. Steven Watts, *Self-Help Messiah: Dale Carnegie and Success in Modern America* (New York: Other Press, 2013), 131.

16. Ron Charles, "How to Win Friends and Influence People: Why the Grand-daddy of Self-Help Endures," *Washington Post*, March 31, 2017.

17. Steven Starker, *Oracle at the Supermarket: The American Preoccupation with Self-Help Books* (New Brunswick, NJ: Transaction, 1989), 104.

18. After extensive promotion by Oprah Winfrey, *The Secret* became a hit, although it has since been criticized for the lack of evidence for its pseudoscientific claims, and the sleight of hand it performs: like most self-help authors, it's only Byrne herself who seems to have truly turned her teachings into material gain. But the most powerful critique of this kind of magical thinking philosophy exposes its basic cruelty—it can't help but imply that those who are suffering have brought sickness and misery on themselves, simply by not wanting badly enough to be healthy and happy.

19. Stephen Recken, "Fitting-In: The Redefinition of Success in the 1930s," *Journal of Popular Culture* 27, no. 3 (Winter 1993): 205–22.

20. J. B. Woodside, "She Was Padded to Fame," *Photoplay*, December 1917, in Janet Walker, "Margery Wilson," *Women Film Pioneers Project*, Center for Digital Research and Scholarship, ed. Jane Gaines, Radha Vatsal, and Monica Dall'Asta (New York: Columbia University Libraries, 2013), https://wfpp.cdrs.columbia.edu/pioneer/ccp-margery-wilson.

21. This was the era when actresses weren't generally known by their names but by a physical attribute—the powerhouse female star of the silent screen, Mary Pickford, started out as "the girl with the curls."

22. For more on women's changing roles in Hollywood in the pre- and post-Code era, see Susan Ware, *Holding Their Own: American Women in the 1930s* (New York: Twayne, 1982), 183–92.

23. Margery Wilson, *The Woman You Want to Be: Margery Wilson's Complete Book of Charm* (Philadelphia: Lippincott, 1942), 5.

24. Ibid., 15.

25. Ibid., 24.

26. Ibid., 139.

27. Ibid., 22, 25.

28. "Excerpts from Letters to Marjorie Hillis," Bobbs-Merrill Archive.

29. Wilson, *The Woman You Want to Be*, 14.

30. More information about Collins's strange career and politics can be found in Michael J. Tucker, *And Then They Loved Him: Seward Collins and the Chimera of American Fascism* (Peter Lang Publishing, 2005). Marion Meade describes his erotica obsession in *Dorothy Parker: What Fresh Hell is This?* (New York: Penguin, 1987), 144.

31. Anonymous (William Gropper, illustrator), *Wake Up Alone and Like It! A Handbook for Those with Cold Feet* (New York: The Macauley Company, 1936), 177–78.

32. Recken, "Fitting-In," 215.

33. Marjorie Hillis, "Material Things," *Brooklyn Daily Eagle*, December 4, 1936.

CHAPTER 3: (NOT) A QUESTION OF MONEY

1. Marjorie Hillis, *Orchids on Your Budget: Or, Live Smartly on What Have You* (Indianapolis: Bobbs-Merrill, 1937), 7.

2. Marjorie Hillis to D. L. Chambers, February 19, 1937, Bobbs-Merrill Archive.

3. Marjorie Hillis to D. L. Chambers, May 7, 1937, Bobbs-Merrill Archive.

4. Hillis, *Orchids on Your Budget*, 135.

5. Ibid., 145.

6. Ibid., 131.

7. Marjorie Hillis to Burford Lorimer, April 24, 1937, Bobbs-Merrill Archive.

8. Internal memo to D. L. Chambers, May 12, 1937, Bobbs-Merrill Archive.

9. Leola Allard to D. A. Cameron, June 1, 1937, Bobbs-Merrill Archive.

10. Marjorie Hillis to D. L. Chambers, May 26, 1937, Bobbs-Merrill Archive.

11. Marjorie Hillis to D. L. Chambers, June 10, 1937, Bobbs-Merrill Archive.

12. Review excerpts gathered by publicity department, n.d.; royalty reports, Bobbs-Merrill Archive.

13. Hillis, *Orchids on Your Budget*, 147–48.

14. Ibid., 63.

15. Ibid., 65.

16. Ibid., 66.

17. Ibid., 66.

18. This argument forms the basis of Matt's book *Keeping Up with the Joneses: Envy in American Consumer Society, 1890–1930* (Philadelphia: University of Pennsylvania Press, 2002).

19. Ethan Mordden, *The Guest List: How Manhattan Defined American Sophistication—From the Algonquin Round Table to Truman Capote's Ball* (New York: St. Martin's Prss, 2010), 5.

20. Hillis, *Orchids on Your Budget*, 8.

21. S. Lightstone, sales promotion manager, to D. A. Cameron, October 2, 1937, Bobbs-Merrill Archive.

22. Hillis, *Orchids on Your Budget*, 42.

23. Ibid., 48.

24. Ibid., 50.

25. Wharton herself admits that a short book about an entire culture has its limits, and warns at the outset that hers is based on "desultory" observation and "rash assumption." However, she says, the recent war's upheaval of social norms has made it possible to get a more profound look into people's lives. Wharton, *French Ways and Their Meaning* (New York: D. Appleton, 1919), v.

26. Hillis, *Orchids on Your Budget*, 49.

27. Ibid., 90.

28. Ibid., 82.

29. Ibid., 172.

30. Patricia Wainwood's article on the "Recession of 1937–38" provides a brief overview, Federal Reserve history, last modified November 22, 2013, http://www.federalreservehistory.org/Events/DetailView/27. The impact of this uniquely rapid downturn and recovery was examined less than twenty years later by Kenneth D. Roose in *The Economics of Recession and Revival: An Interpretation of 1937–38* (New Haven, CT: Yale University Press, 1954).

CHAPTER 4: SETTING FOR A SOLO ACT

1. Marjorie Hillis, "Bandbox by the River," *Vogue*, November 1936, 88.

2. Unpublished memoir by Marjorie Hillis, Brooklyn Historical Society.

3. This and a wealth of other astonishing facts about Draper are to be found in the lively biography written by her protégée. Packed with details, quotes, and photographs, the book unfortunately lacks any supporting notes. Carle-

ton Varney, *The Draper Touch: The High Life and High Style of Dorothy Draper* (New York: Shannongrove Press, 1988), 126.

4. Mitchell Owens, "Living Large: The Brash, Bodacious Hotels of Dorothy," *Journal of Decorative and Propaganda Arts* 25, "The American Hotel" (2005): 254–87.

5. Chase and Chase, *Always in Vogue*, 15.

6. Dorothy Draper, *Decorating Is Fun!: How to Be Your Own Decorator* (New York: Literary Guild of America, 1939), 12–13.

7. Dorothy Draper, *Decorating Is Fun!* (New York: Literary Guild of America, 1939), pp. 4–5.

8. Varney, *Draper Touch*, 126.

9. Quoted in Kristina Wilson, *Livable Modernism: Interior Decorating and Design during the Great Depression* (New Haven, CT: Yale University Press, Yale University Art Gallery, 2004), 41. Modernity, however, was not the only choice. As Wilson explains, modern designs in the 1930s competed with an equally influential Colonial Revival, which looked to the early American past for comfort and continuity into the troubled modern age. It was a prevalent style of architecture as well as interior design, and its influence went beyond furniture and design—the "living history" museum Colonial Williamsburg opened in 1935 and was an immediate success. To counteract the emotional pull of this backward-glancing style, promoters of modernism emphasized the simplicity, efficiency, and affordability of modernist furniture.

10. "Macy's Shows Furniture in 10 Decorated Rooms," *New York Herald Tribune*, November 5, 1936, 28.

11. Dorothy Draper, *Entertaining Is Fun!: How to Be a Popular Hostess* (New York: Doubleday Doran, 1941), 3.

12. Marjorie Hillis and Bertina Foltz, *Corned Beef and Caviar for the Live-Aloner* (New York: Bobbs-Merrill, 1938), 88.

13. Review excerpts gathered by publicity department, n.d., Bobbs-Merrill Archive.

14. D. L. Chambers to Marjorie Hillis, October 7, 1937, Bobbs-Merrill Archive.

15. Review excerpts, Bobbs-Merrill Archive.

16. The gendered division in food is explored by Jessamyn Neuhaus in her book *Manly Meals and Mom's Home Cooking: Cookbooks and Gender in Modern America* (Baltimore: Johns Hopkins University Press, 2003).

17. Hillis and Foltz, *Corned Beef and Caviar*, 115–52.

18. Review excerpts, Bobbs-Merrill Archive.

19. Laurie Colwin, "Alone in the Kitchen with an Eggplant" in *Alone in the Kitchen with an Eggplant: Confessions of Cooking for One and Dining Alone*, ed. Jenni Ferrari-Adler (New York: Riverhead, 2007), 21.

20. "Working Girls Must Eat," Colby College, *The Colby Alumnus* 29, no. 7 (May 1940): 244. http://digitalcommons.colby.edu/alumnus/244.

21. Hillis and Foltz, *Corned Beef and Caviar*, 15.

22. Laura Shapiro, *Something from the Oven: Reinventing Dinner in 1950s America* (New York: Penguin, 2005), 97.

23. Alice Kessler-Harris, *Women Have Always Worked: A Historical Overview* (New York: Feminist Press, 1981), 80–90.

24. Quoted in Sherrie A. Inness, *Dinner Roles: American Women and Culinary Culture* (Iowa City: University of Iowa Press, 2001), 74.

25. Hillis, *Orchids on Your Budget*, 96.

26. Marion Rombauer Becker, biography of Irma Rombauer, *Harvard Square Library*. Abridged from *Little Acorn: The Story Behind the Joy of Cooking 1931–1966* (Indianapolis: Bobbs-Merrill, 1966). http://www.harvard squarelibrary.org/biographies/irma-rombauer.

27. For a fuller history of Irma Rombauer's creation of *The Joy of Cooking*, see Anne Mendelson, *Stand Facing the Stove* (New York: Simon and Schuster, 1996).

28. Mendelson, *Stand Facing the Stove*, 167.

29. Inness, *Dinner Roles*, 21.

30. Hillis, *Live Alone*, 104.

31. Dorothy Coleman, "Impressions of Marjorie Hillis," *St. Louis Post-Dispatch*, November 1, 1936.

32. Rosie Schaap, *Drinking with Men* (New York: Riverhead, 2013), 3.

33. Marjorie Hillis, "How Many Martinis?" *Boston Globe*, December 1, 1936.

34. Lois Long, "That Was New York—And Those Were Tables for Two," *The New Yorker*, February 17, 1940.

35. The complex history of the Hays Code has been explored in a number of venues. A good overview can be found in Leonard L. Leff and Jerold L. Simmons, *The Dame in the Kimono: Hollywood, Censorship, and the Production Code* (Louisville: University Press of Kentucky, 2001).

36. Brooklyn girl born plain Mary Jane, who became a vaudeville actress, playwright, and Broadway star. When she made it to Hollywood in 1933, West was just shy of her fortieth birthday (not that she shared the fact) and her swagger and sense of humor, in a body she was proud to flaunt, made her irresistible to audiences. Her 1933 movies, *She Done Him Wrong* and *She's No Angel*—both

costarring Cary Grant—were defiant smash hits for Paramount, and even their titles seemed intended to poke Hays like a sleeping bear. Mae West's heroines were intelligent schemers: single women who eyed men as prizes, patsies, and easy to manipulate with the most obvious feminine charms.

37. Hillis, "How Many Martinis?"
38 Virginia Elliott, *Quiet Drinking* (New York: Harcourt, Brace & Co, 1933), 3.
39. Ibid., 97.
40. Hillis, *Live Alone*, 108.
41. Alma Whitaker, *Bacchus Behave!* (New York: Frederick A. Stokes Company, 1933), 2.
42. Ibid., 110.

CHAPTER 5: WORK ENDS AT NIGHTFALL

1. Reader report by "Betsy," Bobbs-Merrill Archive.
2. "Miss Hillis and Seven Women," *Los Angeles Times*, October 9, 1938.
3. "Turns with a Bookworm," *New York Herald Tribune*, September 18, 1938.
4. Michael E. Parrish, *Anxious Decades: America in Prosperity and Depression 1920–1941*, rev. ed. (New York: W. W. Norton, 1994), 391.
5. Marjorie Hillis, *Work Ends at Nightfall* (Indianapolis: Bobbs-Merrill, 1938), 23.
6. Ibid., 45.
7. Hillis, *You Can Start All Over*, x.
8. Hillis, *Work Ends*, 28.
9. Patricia Lindsay, "Beauty and You: Successful Author Convinced That Careful Grooming Is Essential to Careerists," *Baltimore Sun*, October 25, 1938.
10. Hillis, *Work Ends*, 68.
11. Ibid., 87.
12. Ibid., 27.
13. Ibid., 25.
14. Reader report by "Betsy," Bobbs-Merrill Archive.
15. Hillis, *Work Ends*, 50.
16. Ibid., 49.
17. Hillis, *You Can Start All Over*, ix.
18. For a fuller discussion of this history and its impact on women, see Alice Kessler-Harris, *Women Have Always Worked: A Historical Overview* (New York: Feminist Press, 1981) and *Out to Work* (New York: Oxford University Press, 1982).

19. Hillis, *Orchids on Your Budget*, 70–73.

20. Ibid., 69.

21. Bregg, "Lives Alone and Likes It," *Pittsburgh Sun-Telegraph*, October 31, 1936.

22. Eleanor Roosevelt, "What Ten Million Women Want," *Home Magazine* 5 (March 1932), 19. Via The Eleanor Roosevelt Papers Project, https://www2.gwu.edu/~erpapers/documents/articles/whattenmillionwomenwant.cfm.

23. A much fuller picture of Perkins's life and career may be found in Kirstin Downey's thorough biography *The Woman behind the New Deal* (New York: Anchor Books, 2009).

24. The classic discussion of the Lucy Stone League may be found in Una Stannard, *Mrs. Man* (San Francisco, CA: Germain Books, 1977), 188–218.

25. See, for example, Stephanie Coontz, *A Strange Stirring: The Feminine Mystique and American Women at the Dawn of the 1960s* (New York: Basic Books, 2011). Her first chapter, "The Unliberated 1960s," is a reminder of how restricted women's legal identities were for much of the twentieth century.

26. Clifton Fademan, "Books: Kit Morley and His Philadelphians," *The New Yorker*, October 28, 1939, 77.

27. Christopher Morley, *Kitty Foyle* (New York: Grosset & Dunlap, 1939), 43.

28. Ibid., 189.

29. Ibid., 270.

30. Ibid., 261.

31. Ibid., 284.

32. Ibid., 141.

33. Ibid., 307.

34. Ibid., 65.

35. Ibid., 299.

36. Ibid., 303.

37. Julie Berebitsky, *Sex and the Office: A History of Gender, Power, and Desire* (New Haven: Yale University Press, 2012), 4.

38. Ibid., 334.

CHAPTER 6: MAD ABOUT NEW YORK

1. Ibid., 191.

2. Reader's report, n.d., Bobbs-Merrill archive.

3. Marjorie Hillis, *New York, Fair or No Fair: A Guide for the Woman Vacationist* (New York: Bobbs-Merrill, 1939), 11.

4. Ibid., 112.

5. Ibid., 199.

6. Ibid., 32.

7. "Women: Junior League," *Time*, October 29, 1928.

8. Sylvia Plath, *The Bell Jar* (New York: Harper Collins, 2013. Fiftieth Anniversary Edition. First published 1963), 4.

9. Morley, *Kitty Foyle*, 243.

10. Hillis, *New York, Fair or No Fair*, 23

11. Ibid., 72

12. Paul Freedman, *Ten Restaurants that Changed America* (New York: Liveright, 2016), 91.

13. Hillis, *New York, Fair or No Fair*, 41.

14. Ibid., 16.

15. Ibid., 152.

16. Ibid., 141.

17. "World's Fair Ceremony Hails Anne O'Hare McCormick as Woman of 1939," *New York Herald Tribune*, June 6, 1939.

18. Hillis, *New York, Fair or No Fair*, 59.

19. Ibid., 75.

20. Ibid., 77.

21. Ibid., 136.

22. "Liquor Flows Here at Its Usual Tempo," *New York Herald Tribune*, December 6, 1933.

23. "City Hails '34 in Legal Sips, Raises Glass to 'New Deal,'" *Baltimore Sun*, January 1, 1934.

24. For more on Nils T. Granlund and the new nightlife of the 1930s, see Burton W. Peretti, *Nightclub City: Politics and Amusement in Manhattan* (Philadelphia: University of Pennsylvania Press, 2013), 113–16.

25. The publicity-loving Peckham published two books about his exploits, from which these details are taken: *Gentlemen in Waiting* (1940) and the less restrained *Gentlemen for Rent* (1955).

26. Hillis, *New York, Fair or No Fair*, 96–97.

27. "Ted Peckham Faces Trial on Escort Bureau," *New York Herald Tribune*, May 4, 1939.

28. Jessie Redmon Fauset, "Some Notes on Color," *The World Tomorrow*, March 1922, 76–77, in Janet Witalec, *The Harlem Renaissance: A Gale Critical Companion*, vol. II (Detroit: Gale, 2003), 365–67.

29. Langston Hughes, *The Big Sea: An Autobiography* (New York: Alfred A. Knopf, 1940), 245.

30. For more on A'lelia Walker's parties and her role in Harlem society, see David Levering Lewis, *When Harlem Was in Vogue* (New York: Alfred A. Knopf, 1979; Oxford University Press paperback edition, 1989), 165–70.

31. The complexities of white artistic patronage of the Harlem Renaissance are explored in detail in Carla Kaplan, *Miss Anne in Harlem: The White Women of the Black Renaissance* (New York: Harper, 2013). The role of the Knopf publishing house, and Blanche Knopf in particular, is detailed in Laura Claridge's biography *The Lady with the Borzoi: Blanche Knopf, Literary Taste-maker Extraordinaire* (New York: Farrar, Straus & Giroux, 2016).

32. Hillis, *New York, Fair or No Fair*, 114.

33. Ethelene Whitmire, "Andrews, Regina" *American National Biography Online,* http://www.anb.org/articles/20/20-01927.html.

34. Dorothy Height, *Open Wide the Freedom Gates: A Memoir* (New York: Public-Affairs, 2003), 80

CHAPTER 7: ROSIE AND MRS. ROULSTON

1. Robert Hughes, "High Lindens," *Huntington History.* https://huntington history.com/2011/03/02/high-lindens.

2. "Thomas H. Roulston Rites Will Be Held Tomorrow," *Brooklyn Daily Eagle,* August 19, 1949.

3. "Trend: Goodby to All That," *Brooklyn Daily Eagle,* August 6, 1939. This style of writing was roundly mocked in *The Philadelphia Story*, the plot of which turns on a magazine's efforts to get access to a society wedding.

4. "Marjorie Hillis to Be Bride of T. H. Roulston," *New York Herald Tribune,* June 24, 1939.

5. *Washington Post,* August 11, 1939.

6. " 'Live Alone' Advocate Admits Being Mrs. Roulston is Better," *Brooklyn Daily Eagle,* September 25, 1939.

7. "Marjorie Hillis to Be Bride of T. H. Roulston," *New York Herald Tribune,* June 24, 1939.

8. D.L. Chambers to Marjorie Hillis, January 22, 1940, Bobbs-Merrill Archive.

9. "Miss Hillis Wed: Wrote 'Live Alone and Like It,' " *New York Herald Tribune,* August 29, 1939.

10. Kessler-Harris, *Out to Work*, 273.

11. Ibid., 276.

12. See Marcy Kennedy Knight, "Rosie the Riveter," *Saturday Evening Post*, July/August 2013, http://www.saturdayeveningpost.com/2013/07/01/art-entertainment/norman-rockwell-art-entertainment/rosie-the-riveter.html; "The Rosie the Riveter Story," Norman Rockwell Museum of Vermont, http://www.normanrockwellvt.com/rosie_riveter_story.htm.

13. Tony Marcano, "Famed Riveter in War Effort, Rose Monroe Dies at 77," *New York Times*, June 2, 1997.

14. Ben Cosgrove, "Women of Steel: LIFE with Female Factory Workers in WWII," *Time*, July 15, 2014.

15. Kessler-Harris, *Out to Work*, 279.

16. Sherna Berger Gluck, *Rosie the Riveter Revisited: Women, the War, and Social Change* (New York: Plume, 1988), 23.

17. Farah Jasmine Griffin, *Harlem Nocturne: Women Artists and Progressive Politics During World War II* (New York: Civitas, 2013), 36.

18. Ibid., 7.

19. "Women in War Jobs," The Ad Council, http://www.adcouncil.org/Our-Campaigns/The-Classics/Women-in-War-Jobs.

20. Sonya Michel, "The History of Child Care in the US," *Social Welfare History Project* (2011). http://socialwelfare.library.vcu.edu/programs/child-care-the-american-history.

21. Quoted in Caroline Cornell, "The Housewife's Battle On the Home Front: Women in World War II Advertisements," *The Forum: Journal of History* 2, no. 1 (2010), 28.

22. *Life*, September 28, 1942, 32.

23. "Before and After," internal reader's report, n.d., Bobbs-Merrill Archive.

24. Thomas H. Roulston obituary, *Brooklyn Daily Eagle*, August 19, 1949.

CHAPTER 8: STARTING ALL OVER

1. Hillis, *You Can Start All Over*, xiii.

2. Marjorie Hillis, "People and Ideas: Who Is the Older Woman?" *Vogue*, October 1950, 169.

3. The novel was published July 16, 1951, by Little, Brown.

4. The race became notorious in California politics for its low tactics. See Colleen M. O'Connor, "'Pink Right Down to Her Underwear': The 1950 Senate

Campaign of Richard Nixon against Helen Gahagan Douglas Reached an Unequaled Low," *Los Angeles Times*, April 9, 1990.

5. Hillis, *You Can Start All Over*, 29.

6. Gaile Dugas, "'Live Alone, Like It' Author Learns to Overcome Grief," *Austin American Statesman*, April 17, 1951.

7. Ibid.

8. Hillis, *You Can Start All Over*, 3.

9. Ibid., 19.

10. Ibid., 9.

11. Ibid., 11.

12. Marjorie Hillis, "Everybody's Etiquette: A Word to Widows," *New York Herald Tribune*, March 30, 1952.

13. Hillis, *You Can Start All Over*, 53.

14. Ibid., 105.

15. Ibid., 61.

16. Ibid., 62.

17. Ibid., 72.

18. Ibid., 138.

19. Ibid.,120.

20. "Widow Talks to Herself in Mirror," *Washington Post*, February 25, 1951. The review is signed only S. N., leaving the reviewer's gender unclear, but given the tone and the time, it seems safe to assume it's a man.

21. Hillis, *You Can Start All Over*, 16.

22. "Dorothy Dix Says," *Daily Boston Globe*, December 16, 1951, A18.

23. Elaine Tyler May, *Homeward Bound: American Families in the Cold War Era* (New York: Basic Books, 1988), 6.

24. One recent cultural study of the 1950s focuses explicitly on the era's celebration of normality: Anna G. Creadick, *Perfectly Average: The Pursuit of Normality in Postwar America* (Amherst: University of Massachusetts Press, 2010).

25. Coontz, *Strange Stirring*, 51.

26. Madison Park, "U.S. Fertility Rate Falls to Lowest on Record," CNN.com, August 11, 2016.

27. May, *Homeward Bound*, 28.

28. This history is analyzed in detail in David Kushner, *Levittown: Two Families, One Tycoon, and the Fight for Civil Rights in America's Legendary Suburb* (New York: Walker & Company, 2009).

29. Cynthia Lowry, "Challenge to Women," *Baltimore Sun*, January 7, 1951.

30. Cited in Coontz, *Strange Stirring*, 67.

31. See Ruth Milkman, "Redefining 'Women's Work': The Sexual Division of Labor in the Auto Industry during World War II," in *On Gender, Labor, and Inequality* (Champaign: University of Illinois Press, 2016), 47–78.

32. Coontz, *Strange Stirring*, 123.

33. Ibid., 126.

34. *Look*, October 16, 1956.

35. Coontz, *Strange Stirring*, 61.

36. Cynthia Harrison, *On Account of Sex: The Politics of Women's Issues, 1945–1968* (Berkeley: University of California Press, 1988), 49.

37. Coontz, *Strange Stirring*, 109.

38. Quoted in Starker, *Oracle at the Supermarket*, 77.

39. Ibid., 80.

40. May, *Homeward Bound*, 24–28. Revealingly, the only woman who is visible in William Safire's famous photograph of the kitchen summit, he describes as "my boss's wife, Jinx Falkenburg." Jinx was famous in her own right—before she married the publicist Tex McCrary in 1945, she was one of the most photographed women in the world—an actress, swimmer, and tennis star who regularly graced magazine covers and billboards in the late 1930s. After their marriage "Jinx and Tex" became the celebrity hosts of a series of radio and television interview and talk shows. William Safire, "A Picture Story," *New York Times*, July 27, 1984.

41. George Gallup and Evan Hill, "The American Woman," *Saturday Evening Post*, December 22, 1962, 15–33.

42. May, *Homeward Bound*, 26.

43. Lawrence R. Samuel, *Shrink: A Cultural History of Psychoanalysis in America* (Lincoln: University of Nebraska Press, 2013), xi.

44. Betty Friedan, *The Feminine Mystique*, 50th anniversary edition (New York: Penguin, 2010), 5. First published 1963.

45. See James H. Jones, *Alfred C. Kinsey: A Life* (New York: W. W. Norton, 1997), for a fuller account of his fascinating story.

46. History of Kinsey's research via the Kinsey Institute, Indiana University, kinseyinstitute.org.

47. Starker, *Oracle at the Supermarket*, 90.

48. Quoted in Starker, *Oracle at the Supermarket*, 89.

49. Kristin Celello, *Making Marriage Work: A History of Marriage and Divorce in*

the Twentieth-Century United States (Chapel Hill: University of North Carolina Press, 2009), 13–15.

50. Starker, *Oracle at the Supermarket*, 90.

51. Rebecca Onion, "Lock up Your Wives," *Aeon*, September 8, 2014, https://aeon.co/essays/the-warped-world-of-marriage-advice-before-feminism.

52. Celello, *Making Marriage Work*, 7.

53. Ibid., 78.

54. Coontz, *Strange Stirring*, 15.

55. Albin Krebs, "Obituary: Marion Tanner, Known as Model for Mame," *New York Times*, October 31, 1985. For a while, Tanner took pride in the Mame comparisons, but her relationship with her nephew soured in later years, as her generosity turned her house into a makeshift homeless shelter. She claimed to be "much nicer" than the character, and despite the parallels, the teetotal vegetarian Tanner apparently did not approach life's banquet with quite the appetite of the fictional Mame.

56. Orry-Kelly's story is told in Gillian Armstrong's 2016 documentary *Women He's Undressed*.

57. "Ex-G.I. Becomes Blonde Bombshell," *New York Daily News*, December 1, 1951.

58. Quoted in Friedan, *Feminine Mystique*, 14.

59. Coontz, *Strange Stirring*, 139–42.

60. Friedan, *Feminine Mystique*, 27.

61. Ibid., 37.

62. Ibid., 19.

63. Quoted in Coontz, *Strange Stirring*, 74.

64. Ibid., 144.

65. Friedan, *Feminine Mystique*, 15.

66. Coontz, *Strange Stirring*, 27.

67. Wendy Simonds, *Women and Self-Help Culture: Reading between the Lines* (New Brunswick, NJ: Rutgers University Press, 1992).

68. Coontz, *Strange Stirring*, 151.

69. Hillis, *Live Alone*, 93.

70. Helen Gurley Brown, *Sex and the Single Girl*, reprint edition with a new introduction by Helen Gurley Brown (New York: Barnes & Noble, 2003), 4. First published 1962.

71. Ibid., 6.

72. Ibid., 8.

73. Ibid., 15.

74. Ibid., 35. This line reads like a joke, but as Elaine Tyler May shows, the prospect of sharing a nuclear bunker was taken quite seriously in discussions of marital compatibility in the 1950s. She cites one couple featured in *Life* magazine that honeymooned in a backyard shelter, surrounded by an abundance of donated tinned food, smiling blissfully at their good fortune; May, *Homeward Bound*, introduction ix–xi.

75. Ibid., 45.

76. Ibid., 54.

77. Ibid., 48.

78. Ibid., 65.

79. Ibid., 71.

80. Ibid., 24. An "affair" at the time wasn't necessarily extramarital; as Marjorie Hillis and Helen Gurley Brown both use the term, it merely means some kind of romantic liaison, although by the 1960s, the implication was that it was also sexual.

81. Ibid., 224.

82. Ibid., 231.

83. Ibid., 234.

84. Starker, *Oracle at the Supermarket*, 90.

85. Gurley Brown, *Sex and the Single Girl*, 10.

86. Ibid., 134.

87. Ibid., 179.

88. Helen Gurley Brown, *Sex and the Office* (New York: Bernard Geis, 1964), 3.

89. Ibid., 6.

90. Gurley Brown, *Sex and the Single Girl*, 103.

91. Ibid., 117.

92. Ibid., 253.

93. Ibid., 263.

94. Marjorie Hillis, *Keep Going and Like It: A Guide to the Sixties and Onward and Upward* (New York: Doubleday, 1967), 53.

95. Ibid., 79.

96. Ibid., 81.

97. Ibid., 13.

98. Ibid., 15.

99. Ibid., 91.

100. Ibid., 104.

BIBLIOGRAPHY

Works Cited and Consulted

ARCHIVES

Bobbs-Merrill Archive, Lilly Library, Indiana University, Bloomington, IN.
Newell Dwight Hillis Papers, Brooklyn Historical Society, Brooklyn, NY.
Condé Nast Library and *Vogue* archives, New York.

ARTICLES AND BOOKS

Applegate, Debby. *The Most Famous Man in America: The Biography of Henry Ward Beecher*. New York: Doubleday, 2006.

Arnold, Rebecca. *The American Look: Fashion, Sportswear and the Image of Women in 1930s and 1940s New York*. London: I. B. Tauris, 2009.

Bagge, Peter. *Woman Rebel: The Margaret Sanger Story*. Montreal: Drawn & Quarterly, 2013.

Barnet, Andrea. *All-Night Party: The Women of Bohemian Greenwich Village and Harlem, 1913–1930*. Chapel Hill, NC: Algonquin Books, 2004.

Berebitsky, Julie. *Sex and the Office: A History of Gender, Power, and Desire*. New Haven, CT: Yale University Press, 2012.

Bolick, Kate. *Spinster: Making a Life of One's Own*. New York: Crown, 2015.

Brown, Helen Gurley. *Sex and the Office*. New York: Bernard Geis, 1964.

———. *Sex and the Single Girl*. Reprinted with a new introduction by Helen Gurley Brown. New York: Barnes & Noble, 2003. First published 1962.

Butler, Judith. "Sex and Gender in Simone de Beauvoir's Second Sex." *Yale French Studies*, no. 72, "Simone de Beauvoir: Witness to a Century" (1986), 35–49.

Cameron, Ardis. *Unbuttoning America: A Biography of "Peyton Place."* Ithaca, NY: Cornell University Press, 2015.

Celello, Kristin. *Making Marriage Work: A History of Marriage and Divorce in the Twentieth-Century United States*. Chapel Hill: University of North Carolina Press, 2012.

Chase, Edna Woolman, and Ilka Chase. *Always in Vogue*. Garden City, NY: Doubleday, 1954.

Chesler, Ellen. *Woman of Valor: Margaret Sanger and the Birth Control Movement in America*. New York: Simon & Schuster, 2007.

Claridge, Laura. *Lady with the Borzoi: Blanche Knopf, Literary Tastemaker Extraordinaire*. New York: Farrar, Straus & Giroux, 2016.

Cobble, Dorothy Sue, Linda Gordon, and Astrid Henry. *Feminism Unfinished: A Short, Surprising History of American Women's Movements*. New York: Live-right, 2015.

Coontz, Stephanie. *A Strange Stirring: The Feminine Mystique and American Women at the Dawn of the 1960s*. New York: Basic Books, 2011.

Cott, Nancy F. *The Grounding of Modern Feminism*. New Haven, CT: Yale University Press, 1987.

———. *Public Vows: A History of Marriage and the Nation*. Cambridge, MA: Harvard University Press, 2002.

Creadick, Anna G. *Perfectly Average: The Pursuit of Normality in Postwar America*. Amherst: University of Massachusetts Press, 2010.

Davis, Rebecca L. *More Perfect Unions: The American Search for Marital Bliss*. Cambridge, MA: Harvard University Press, 2010.

Dennis, Patrick. *Auntie Mame: An Irreverent Escapade*. New York: Broadway Books, 2013.

DePaulo, Bella M. *Singled Out: How Singles Are Stereotyped, Stigmatized, and Ignored and Still Live Happily Ever After*. New York: St. Martin's Press, 2006.

Dickstein, Morris. *Dancing in the Dark: A Cultural History of the Great Depression*. New York: W. W. Norton, 2010.

Downey, Kirstin. *The Woman Behind the New Deal: The Life and Legacy of Frances Perkins: Social Security, Unemployment Insurance and the Minimum Wage*. New York: Anchor, 2010.

Draper, Dorothy, *Decorating Is Fun!: How to Be Your Own Decorator*. Garden City, NY: Doubleday Doran, 1939.

———. *Entertaining Is Fun!: How to Be a Popular Hostess.* Garden City, NY: Doubleday Doran, 1941.

Dubler, Ariela R. " 'Exceptions to the General Rule': Unmarried Women and the 'Constitution of the Family.' " *Theoretical Inquiries in Law* 4, no. 2 (2003): 797–816.

Ehrenreich, Barbara, and Sigrid Estrada. *Bright-Sided: How Positive Thinking Is Undermining America.* New York: Picador, 2010.

Eldridge, David. *American Culture in the 1930s.* Edinburgh: Edinburgh University Press, 2010.

Elliot, Virginia. *Quiet Drinking: A Book of Beer, Wines & Cocktails and What to Serve with Them.* New York: Harcourt, 1933.

Ferrari-Adler, Jenni. *Alone in the Kitchen with an Eggplant: Confessions of Cooking for One and Dining Alone.* New York: Penguin, 2007.

Freedman, Paul. *Ten Restaurants That Changed America.* New York: Liveright, 2016.

Freeland, David. *Automats, Taxi Dances, and Vaudeville: Excavating Manhattan's Lost Places of Leisure.* New York: New York University Press, 2009.

Friedan, Betty. *The Feminine Mystique.* 50th anniversary edition. New York: Penguin, 2010. First published 1963.

Gabler, Neal. *Winchell: Gossip, Power and the Culture of Celebrity.* New York: Vintage, 1995.

Gaines, Jane, Radha Vatsal, and Monica Dall'Asta, eds. *Women Film Pioneers Project.* Center for Digital Research and Scholarship. New York: Columbia University Libraries, 2013.

Gluck, Sherna Berger. *Rosie the Riveter Revisited: Women, the War, and Social Change.* New York: New American Library, 1988.

Harrison, Cynthia Ellen. *On Account of Sex: The Politics of Women's Issues, 1945–1968.* Berkeley: University of California Press, 1988.

Hasday, Jill Elaine. *Family Law Reimagined.* Cambridge, MA: Harvard University Press, 2014.

Hauser, Brooke. *Enter Helen: The Invention of Helen Gurley Brown and the Rise of the Modern Single Woman.* New York: Harper, 2016.

Hawes, Elizabeth. *New York, New York: How the Apartment House Transformed the Life and the City, 1869–1930.* New York: Henry Holt, 1994.

Hecht, Jennifer Michael. *The Happiness Myth: The Historical Antidote to What Isn't Working Today.* New York: HarperOne, 2008.

Hillis, Marjorie, *Live Alone and Like It: A Guide for the Extra Woman.* New York: Bobbs-Merrill, 1936.

———. *New York, Fair or No Fair: A Guide for the Woman Vacationist.* New York: Bobbs-Merrill, 1939.

———. "Newell Dwight Hillis." In *A Church in History: The Story of Plymouth's First*

Hundred Years under Beecher, Abbott, Hillis, Durkee, and Fifield, 87–118. Brooklyn, NY: Plymouth Church of the Pilgrims, 1949.

———. *Orchids on Your Budget: Or, Live Smartly on What Have You*. New York: Bobbs-Merrill, 1937.

———. *Work Ends at Nightfall*. New York: Bobbs-Merrill, 1938.

Hillis, Marjorie, and Bertina Foltz, *Corned Beef and Caviar for the Live-Aloner*. New York: Bobbs-Merrill, 1938.

Hillis Roulston, Marjorie. *Keep Going and Like It: A Guide to the Sixties and Onward and Upward*. New York: Doubleday, 1967.

———. *You Can Start All Over: A Guide for the Widow and Divorcee*. New York: Harper & Brothers, 1951.

Inness, Sherrie A., ed. *Delinquents and Debutantes: Twentieth-Century American Girls' Cultures*. New York: New York University Press, 1998.

———. *Dinner Roles: American Women and Culinary Culture*. Iowa City: University of Iowa Press, 2001.

Israel, Betsy. *Bachelor Girl: 100 Years of Breaking the Rules*. New York: Perennial, 2003.

Jurca, Catherine. *White Diaspora: The Suburb and the Twentieth-Century American Novel*. Princeton, NJ: Princeton University Press, 2001.

Kaplan, Carla. *Miss Anne in Harlem: The White Women of the Black Renaissance*. New York: HarperCollins, 2013.

Kessler-Harris, Alice. *Out to Work: A History of Wage-Earning Women in the United States*. New York: Oxford University Press, 1993.

———. *Women Have Always Worked: A Historical Overview*. New York: Feminist Press, 1981.

Keyser, Catherine. *Playing Smart: New York Women Writers and Modern Magazine Culture*. New Brunswick: Rutgers University Press, 2010.

Klinenberg, Eric. *Going Solo: The Extraordinary Rise and Surprising Appeal of Living Alone*. New York: Penguin Press, 2012.

Kushner, David. *Levittown: Two Families, One Tycoon, and the Fight for Civil Rights in America's Legendary Suburb*. New York: Walker Books, 2009.

Lamb-Shapiro, Jessica. *Promise Land: A Journey through America's Euphoric, Soul-Sucking, Emancipating, Hornswoggling, and Irrepressible Self-Help Culture*. New York: Simon & Schuster, 2014.

Leff, Leonard J., and Jerold L. Simmons. *The Dame in the Kimono: Hollywood, Censorship, and the Production Code*. Lexington: University of Kentucky, 2001.

Long, Kat. *The Forbidden Apple: A Century of Sex & Sin in New York City*. New York: Ig, 2009.

Lopate, Phillip. *Writing New York: A Literary Anthology*. New York: Library of America, 2008.

Maitland, Sara. *How to Be Alone*. New York: Picador USA, 2014.

Matt, Susan J. *Keeping Up with the Joneses: Envy in American Consumer Society, 1890–1930*. Philadelphia: University of Pennsylvania Press, 2013.

May, Elaine Tyler. *Homeward Bound: American Families in the Cold War Era*. New York: Basic Books, 1999.

McCarthy, Mary. *The Group*. San Diego: Harcourt Brace, 2001. First published 1963.

Milkman, Ruth. *On Gender, Labor, and Inequality*. Champaign-Urbana: University of Illinois Press, 2016.

Mordden, Ethan. *The Guest List: How Manhattan Defined American Sophistication, from the Algonquin Round Table to Truman Capote's Ball*. New York: St. Martin's Press, 2010.

Morley, Christopher. *Kitty Foyle*. New York: Grosset & Dunlap, 1939.

Murdock, Catherine Gilbert. *Domesticating Drink: Women, Men, and Alcohol in America, 1870–1940*. Baltimore: Johns Hopkins University Press, 2002.

Myers, Eric. *Uncle Mame: The Life of Patrick Dennis*. Cambridge, MA: Da Capo Press, 2002.

Neuhaus, Jessamyn. *Manly Meals and Mom's Home Cooking: Cookbooks and Gender in Modern America*. Baltimore: Johns Hopkins University Press, 2012.

Onion, Rebecca. "Lock Up Your Wives." *Aeon* (September 2014).

Owens, Mitchell. "Living Large: The Brash, Bodacious Hotels of Dorothy Draper." *Journal of Decorative and Propaganda Arts* 25 (2005): 254–287.

Parrish, Michael E. *Anxious Decades: America in Prosperity and Depression 1920–1941*. New York: W. W. Norton, 1994.

Peiss, Kathy Lee. *Hope in a Jar: The Making of America's Beauty Culture*. New York: Henry Holt, 2007.

Peril, Lynn. *Swimming in the Steno Pool: A Retro Guide to Making It in the Office*. New York: W. W. Norton, 2011.

Petry, Ann. *The Street*. Boston: Houghton Mifflin, 1991. First published 1946.

Recken, Stephen. "Fitting-In: The Redefenition of Success in the 1930s." *Journal of Popular Culture* 27 (Winter 1993): 205–222.

Rombauer, Irma S. *The Joy of Cooking: A Compilation of Reliable Recipes with a Casual Culinary Chat*. New York: Scribner, 1998. First published 1936 by Bobbs-Merrill.

Samuel, Lawrence R. *Shrink: A Cultural History of Psychoanalysis in America*. Lincoln: University of Nebraska Press, 2013.

Saval, Nikil. *Cubed: A Secret History of the Workplace*. New York: Doubleday, 2014.

Schaap, Rosie. *Drinking with Men: A Memoir*. New York: Riverhead Books, 2014.

Schwartz, Hillel. *Never Satisfied: A Cultural History of Diets, Fantasies, and Fat*. New York: Anchor Books, 1990.

Seebohm, Caroline. *The Man Who Was Vogue: The Life and Times of Condé Nast*. New York: Viking Press, 1982.

Shapiro, Laura. *Something from the Oven: Reinventing Dinner in 1950s America*. New York: Penguin Books, 2005.

Shetterly, Margot Lee. *Hidden Figures: The Untold Story of the African American Women Who Helped Win the Space Race*. New York: William Morrow, 2016.

Shulman, Robin. *Eat the City: A Tale of the Fishers, Trappers, Hunters, Foragers, Slaughterers, Butchers, Farmers, Poultry Minders, Sugar Refiners, Cane Cutters, Beekeepers, Winemakers, and Brewers Who Built New York*. New York: Crown, 2012.

Simonds, Wendy. *Women and Self-Help Culture: Reading between the Lines*. New Brunswick, NJ: Rutgers University Press, 1992.

Staggs, Sam. *Inventing Elsa Maxwell: How an Irrepressible Nobody Conquered High Society, Hollywood, the Press, and the World*. New York: St. Martin's Press, 2012.

Stannard, Una. *Mrs. Man*. San Francisco, CA: Germain Books, 1977.

Starker, Steven. *Oracle at the Supermarket: The American Preoccupation with Self-Help Books*. New Brunswick, NJ: Transaction, 2007.

Tapert, Annette. *The Power of Glamour: The Women Who Defined the Magic of Stardom*. New York: Crown, 1998.

Traister, Rebecca. *All the Single Ladies: Unmarried Women and the Rise of an Independent Nation*. New York: Simon & Schuster, 2016.

Varney, Carleton. *The Draper Touch: The High Life & High Style of Dorothy Draper*. New York: Shannongrove Press, 1988.

Walker, Nancy A. *Women's Magazines, 1940–1960: Gender Roles and the Popular Press*. Boston: Bedford/St. Martin's, 1998.

Ware, Susan. *Holding Their Own: American Women in the 1930s*. Boston: Twayne, 1982.

Watts, Steven. *Self-Help Messiah: Dale Carnegie and Success in Modern America*. New York: Other Press, 2013.

Wharton, Edith. *French Ways and Their Meaning*. New York: D. Appleton, 1919.

Whitaker, Alma Fullford. *Bacchus Behave! The Lost Art of Polite Drinking*. New York: Frederick A. Stokes, 1933.

Whitfield, Stephen J. *The Culture of the Cold War*. Baltimore: Johns Hopkins University Press, 1996.

Whitt, Jan. *Women in American Journalism: A New History*. Champaign-Urbana: University of Illinois Press, 2008.

Whyte, William Hollingsworth. *The WPA Guide to New York City: The Federal Writers' Project Guide to 1930s New York*. New York: New Press, 1996. First published 1939.

Wilson, Kristina. *Livable Modernism: Interior Decorating and Design during the Great Depression*. New Haven, CT: Yale University Press and Yale University Art Gallery, 2004.

Wilson, Margery. *Make Up Your Mind*. New York: J. B. Lippincott, 1940.

———. *The Woman You Want to Be: Margery Wilson's Complete Book of Charm*. New York: J. B. Lippincott, 1942. First published 1928.

Witalec, Janet, ed. *The Harlem Renaissance: A Gale Critical Companion*. Vol. II. Detroit: Gale, 2003.

CREDITS

INDEX